A GUIDE TO CRUISING NORTHERN AUSTRALIA

Anchorages
Cairns to Darwin,

Leslie P. Richards

Fifth Edition

Niblock
PUBLISHING

A Guide to Cruising Northern Australia: Anchorages Cairns to Darwin

Published 2008 by Niblock Publishing
POB 912, Nightcliff, 0814 NT, Australia

info@niblockpublishing.com.au

www.niblockpublishing.com.au

Copyright © Leslie P. Richards 2008

Except as permitted under the *Australian Copyright Act 1968* (for example, any fair dealing for the purposes of study, research, criticism or review), no part of this book may be reproduced, stored in a retrieval system, communicated or transmitted in any form or by any means without prior written permission. All inquiries should be made to the publisher at the address above.

Cover designed by Sarah Fletcher

Cover photograph by Sunsail Yacht Charters.

Printed in Australia by Griffin Press

National Library of Australia Cataloguing-in-Publication entry:

Author: Richards, Leslie P.
Title: A guide to cruising Northern Australia: anchorages Cairns to Darwin / Leslie P. Richards.
Edition: 5th ed.
ISBN: 9780980390438 (pbk.)
Subjects: Sailing—Queensland.
Sailing—Northern Territory.
Boats and boating—Queensland.
Boats and boating—Northern Territory.
Dewey Number: 797.1099429

DISCLAIMER

All information contained in this book is correct at the time of writing. However, owing to changes beyond the control of the author, no responsibility is accepted or implied for errors or omissions or for any damage that may be sustained. The information contained in this book is a guide only, and all maps are MUD MAPS (a rough sketch), NOT to scale, and are to be used only in this manner.

All anchorages shown are for keelboats with a draft of 1.5 metres. Multi-hulls will be able to anchor in closer. Larger draft vessels will need to anchor further out where depth allows.

All tides shown are a guide only to assist with tidal calculations and are taken from the Australian National Tide Tables (ANTT).

All coordinates shown are CHART COORDINATES ONLY to facilitate chart location and are NOT to be used as waypoints.

All depths are in metres and all distances are in nautical miles unless otherwise stated. Please note these pages are not waterproof.

The author would be pleased to receive any information regarding errors, omissions, updates or new anchorages. Please forward to Leslie P. Richards, C/o PO Box 912, Nightcliff, NT, 0814, Australia. Information on new anchorages and updates will be acknowledged in all future editions.

CONTENTS

Introduction	1
List of charts	4
Rescue Groups' radios	6
Helpful reading	6

Section 1: Queensland east coast, Cairns to Bamaga (Cape York) — 7

Cairns	8
Yorkeys Knob	11
Port Douglas	13
Low Isles	15
Daintree River	16
Cape Kimberley	18
Snapper Island	18
Anchorages in Alexander Bay	20
Bailey Creek	20
Myall Creek	21
Cape Tribulation	21
Bloomfield River	23
Cedar Bay	25
Hope Isles	26
Cairns Reef	28
Annan River	29
Cooktown	31
Lark Reef	33
Cape Bedford	35
Conical Rock	37

McIvor River		38
Forrester Reef		40
Cape Flattery		41
Lookout Point		43
Lookout Point Creek		44
Starcke River		46
Rocky Isles		47
South Direction Island		49
Lizard Island		51
Eagle Island		53
Nymph Island		54
The Turtle Group		55
Pethebridge Islets		57
Dead Dog Inlet		59
Rocky Creek		61
Howick Islands		63
Cole Island Group, Sinclair Island		67
Ingram Island		69
Noble Island		70
Barrow Island	*NEW*	71
Ninian Bay		72
Pipon Islets		74
King Island		76
Bathurst Bay and Flinders Group		78
Blackwood Island	*NEW*	81
Maclean Island	*NEW*	82
Unnamed Island	*NEW*	83
Henning Point, Stanley Island	*NEW*	84
Stokes Bay		85
Princess Charlotte Bay	*NEW*	87
Hedge Reef		89

v

Burkitt Island		90
Pelican Island		91
Hannah Island		92
Wilkie Island		93
Fife Island		94
Noddy Reef		95
Morris Island		96
Night Island		98
Lloyd Bay Anchorages		99
Portland Roads		101
Temple Bay		103
Beesley Island		105
Forbes Island		106
Gore Island	*NEW*	108
Cape Grenville		109
Shelburne Bay		111
Macarthur Island	*NEW*	112
Hannibal Islets		113
Bushy Islet	*Updated*	114
Escape River		115
Albany Passage		117
Pioneer Bay		119
Shallow Bay		121
Mount Aldophus Island		122
Cape York		123
Possession Island (Roonga Creek)		125
Possession Island (outside)		126
Bamaga (Seisia)		127
Passage notes		129

Section 2: The Gulf of Carpentaria　　　　　**130**

Passage notes　　　　　　　　　　　　　　132
Muttee Bay　　　　　　　　　　　　　　　134
Unnamed bay south of Crab Island　　　　　136
Vrilya Point　　　　　　　　　　　　　　　137
Cotterell River　　　　　　　　*NEW*　　　138
Doughboy River　　　　　　　　*NEW*　　　139
Macdonald River　　　　　　　　　　　　　141
Jackson River　　　　　　　　　　　　　　142
Skadon River　　　　　　　　　*NEW*　　　143
Cullen Point　　　　　　　　　　　　　　　144
Port Musgrave　　　　　　　　　　　　　　144
Pennefather River　　　　　　　　　　　　146
Duyfkin Point Anchorage　　　　　　　　　147
Duyfkin Point　　　　　　　　　　　　　　148
Albatross Bay　　　　　　　　　　　　　　148
Weipa　　　　　　　　　　　　　　　　　　150
Boyd Point　　　　　　　　　　　　　　　152
False Para Head　　　　　　　　　　　　　153
Archer River　　　　　　　　　　　　　　　154
Cape Keerweer　　　　　　　　　　　　　　156
Kendall River　　　　　　　　　　　　　　157
Edward River　　　　　　　　　　　　　　158
Chapman River　　　　　　　　　　　　　　159
Mitchell River　　　　　　　　　　　　　　160
Nassau River　　　　　　　　　　　　　　162
Staaten River　　　　　　　　　　　　　　163
Gilbert River　　　　　　　　　　　　　　164
Point Burrows　　　　　　　　　　　　　　165

vii

Karumba		166
Albert River		168
Sweers Island		170
Point Parker		172
Mornington Island	*Updated*	174
Tully Inlet		176
Calvert River		177
Robinson River		179
Vanderlin Island		181
Observation Island		183
North Island		183
West Island and Bing Bong		185
Limmen Bight River		188
Maria Island		190
Roper River entrance		192
Unnamed Bay east of Tasman Point		194
Dalumba Bay		196
Scott Point		198
Port Langdon		200
North West Bay		202
Bartalumba Bay		203
Milner Bay		205
Bickerton Island (North Bay)		207
Bustard Island	*NEW*	209
Hawknest Island	*NEW*	211
Nicole Island	*NEW*	212
Myaoola Bay		214
Point Arrowsmith	*NEW*	215
Trial Bay		216
Caledon Bay		218
Port Bradshaw		220

Cape Arnhem		222
Gove Harbour		224

Section 3: Gove to Darwin — **227**

Passage notes		228
Elizabeth Bay		230
Bosanquet Island	*NEW*	231
Raragala Island	*NEW*	232
Wigram Island		233
Truant Island		235
Two Island Bay		236
Trafalgar Bay		238
Jensen Bay		239
Gedge Point, Temple Bay		241
Hammer Point		242
Hopeful Bay		243
Guluwuru Island		244
Guruliya Bay		245
Alger Island		246
Cadell Straits		247
Refuge Bay, Elcho Island		249
Elcho Island, unnamed bay east of Warronga Point		250
Howard Island	*NEW*	251
Cape Stewart		252
Blyth River		254
Liverpool River		256
Haul Around Island		258
Cuthbert Point	*NEW*	260
Guion Point		261

King River		262
North Goulburn Island, Mullet Bay		263
White Point	*NEW*	265
Malay Bay		267
Valentia Island		269
Oxley Island		271
Somerville Bay		272
Palm Bay		273
Raffles Bay		274
Port Bremer		276
Port Essington		278
Smiths Point (Port Essington)		280
Black Point (Port Essington)		280
Berkeley Bay (Port Essington)		282
Barrow Bay (Port Essington)		283
Mangrove Point (Port Essington)		284
Victoria Ruins (Port Essington)		285
Knocker Bay (Port Essington)		286
Curlew Bay (Port Essington)		287
Kennedy Bay (Port Essington)		288
Coral Bay (Port Essington)		289
Gunners Quoin (Port Essington)		291
Trepang Bay		292
Blue Mud Bay		294
Popham Bay		295
Alcora Bay		297
Adam Bay and Adelaide River		299
Port of Darwin		301

Useful information   **304**

Toilet maintenance	304
Salt water bathing	304
Storing eggs	304
Recipes	305
Royal Flying Doctor Service	307
Cyclone anchoring	309
Useful rhymes	312

> **CAUTION**
> **CROCODILES ARE PROLIFIC THROUGHOUT THE ENTIRE AREA**
> **CAIRNS TO DARWIN**

INTRODUCTION

My yacht is a Hartley Queenslander with a 22-hp diesel motor. After lying over in Port Douglas for the cyclone season, I left in April when the monsoon trough started to break up. I will give the approximate timetable I used along with a list of charts and some other useful information further on.

At no time do I give courses and navigation details, except where it is necessary for safety, as navigation is the responsibility of the individual vessels. All maps are MUD MAPS (rough sketches) and they are to be used as a guide only. It does not hurt to take the time to check the area in the dinghy first, before final entry. I have only shown the anchorages that I have used.

I cannot stress enough the necessity for constant vigilance at all times, as vast areas have not been surveyed or have only been partially surveyed.

Crocodiles are prolific. They have no fear of humans, as they are protected and have not been shot at for over twenty years. However, if some common sense rules are applied they are not a problem. **DO NOT** set up any sort of a routine. **DO NOT** feed them or throw scraps over the side. **DO NOT** clean fish on board and throw the frames over the side; take them well away from the boat to dispose of them. Remember that they are wild animals. **DO NOT** leave a dinghy hanging out the back, especially at night. In particular a rubber duck. Either tie it alongside or lift it out of the water. The crocodiles seem to have a love affair with outboard motors and rubber ducks in particular. More than one boat owner has woken up to find the tender and outboard under water.

A torch shone around at night will show a number of red dots. These are not landing lights for UFOs, but are the eyes of crocodiles watching. They will watch for some time before doing anything. They have also been known to attack dinghies. I also know of more than one instance where one has tried to come over the stern. There is a false belief that crocodiles cannot run or jump. Believe this and you will be dinner. They can do both very well and can run at 26 km per hour – can you? When in the dinghy I always go armed, but have never had to use a firearm. They are territorial so retreat if necessary. I have seen crocodiles 20 miles out at sea on coral cays, islands, and travelling with the tide. **As a general rule of thumb, if there are mangroves, there are crocodiles. Just because you cannot see them does not mean that they are not there.**

When you get sick of eating seafood, there is an abundance of wild game around, but be careful, as if you get hurt help is a long way off.

A well maintained vessel, forward planning, up-to-date charts and tide tables, constant position fixing (at least hourly), and constant care and vigilance are absolutely necessary.

The timetable that I use is to leave Port Douglas in April and arrive in Darwin no later than mid November. When returning east, it is best in October when the wind changes.

Supplies along the east coast can be arranged through the supply ships that service the fishing fleet. Give them your shopping list when they are returning south to Cairns, and it will then come up on their next trip. It is necessary to make arrangements with the supermarket of your choice before leaving Cairns. This includes giving them your credit card details.

Fuel and water can be obtained from the supply ships if it is necessary, as there are no longer any fuel barges stationed along the east coast. Do not take these services for granted; make the necessary arrangements with the skipper first. I myself prefer services of Sea Swift in Cairns. The ship can be contacted on VHF Ch 16 and 14. Register your credit card with them before leaving Cairns.

I have included the Royal Flying Doctor details, including their clinics and how to contact them.

One final note, if you suffer from any breathing problems and intend travelling into the Gulf of Carpentaria, make sure that you have plenty of medication, as the smoke from the fires lit by the Aboriginals can be very thick. I have had times where I have had to use radar in daylight to see where I am going one mile offshore. This holds from Bamaga to Darwin.

Unless Thursday and Horn Islands are a necessary stop, I stay well away from there. This is a special quarantine area, and the restrictions make it not worthwhile.

LIST OF CHARTS

Queensland east coast, Cairns to Darwin

AUS 830:	Russell Island – Low Islets
AUS 831:	Low Isles – Cape Flattery
AUS 832:	Cape Flattery – Barrow Point
AUS 833:	Barrow Point – Claremont Isles
AUS 834:	Claremont Isles – Cape Weymouth
AUS 835:	Cape Weymouth – Cairncross Islets
AUS 839:	Cairncross Islets – Arden Islet
AUS 292:	Adolphus Channel & Prince of Wales Channel
AUS 294:	Endeavour Straits

If not going down through the Gulf of Carpentaria
AUS 410:   Booby Island – Cape Wessel

Gulf of Carpentaria

AUS 301:	Booby Island – Archer River
AUS 302:	Archer River – Nassau River
AUS 303:	Nassau River – Wellesley Islands
AUS 304:	Wellesley Islands – Vanderlin Island
AUS 305:	Vanderlin Island – Cape Grey
AUS 14:	Groote Eylandt
AUS 306:	Cape Grey – Cape Wessel
AUS 15:	Plans of the Northern Territory

Gove to Darwin

AUS 715:	Cape Arnhem – Cape Wessel
AUS 716:	Gugari Rip – Caddel Strait
AUS 442:	Cape Wessel – Cape Don
AUS 308:	Goulburn Islands – Melville Island
AUS 18:	Port Essington
AUS 720:	Port Essington – Cape Hotham
AUS 20:	Clarence Strait
AUS 26:	Approaches to Darwin

Ports of entry

Cairns, Thursday Island, Weipa, Groote Eylandt Gove, Darwin

RESCUE GROUPS' RADIOS

Cairns Coast Guard	VMR 409
Cairns Marine Radio	VMR 444
Port Douglas Coast Guard	VMR 410
Cooktown Coast Guard	VMR 416
Portland Roads Coast Guard	VMR 433
Thursday Is Coast Guard	VMR 422
Bamaga Coast Guard	VMR 424
Weipa Air Sea Rescue	VMR 430
Mornington Is. A.S.R	VMR 609

HELPFUL READING

Sailing Directions (Enroute) Pub 175.

Current list of admiralty lights (not necessary, but helpful).

Australian National Tide Tables (ANTT)

Queensland Tide Tables (not necessary, but helpful)

SECTION 1

Queensland east coast,

Cairns to Bamaga (Cape York)

CAUTION
Crocodiles are prolific throughout the entire area from Cairns to Bamaga.

CAIRNS

CHART	AUS 830
LIGHTS	Channel marked with lit red and green piles. Red/white/green laser light on the roof of the Pier Market Place (green roof).
TIDES	Cairns (Standard Port) ANTT
RESCUE	Cairns Coast Guard VMR 409
	Cairns Marine Radio Club VMR 444

Full facilities are available in Cairns, with most being located in Portsmith. I found chandlery a bit difficult. Paint is best from Norship in Portsmith. They have the best price and range. It is also worthwhile to ask about haul-out, as they have a large travel-lift. Shopping for stores is best at Smithfield, where there is a large Coles, K-Mart and Woolworths (see Yorkey's Knob for details). Bi-Lo in Cairns Central is very good. Haul-out is available at the Cairns Cruising Yacht Squadron in Smiths Creek and slip at Coconut Slipway.

Whitworths Discount Marine has now opened a store at the corner of Hartley and Brown streets, Bungalow. Phone (07) 4035 2655. Taylor Marine is located at the Cruising Yacht Squadron in Portsmith.

At the end of the shipping channel, a red board with a black stripe will be seen. Treat this as a green; it flashes yellow at night. Anchorage can be taken anywhere to the north or south of the piles. Stay clear of the ship-turning basin marked by yellow buoys. Make sure that you have plenty of chain out and the anchor is well dug in, as the bottom is poor holding sandy clay and the tide race on spring tides can reach 4–5 knots.

Cairns is the last Port of Entry until Thursday Island. Boats leaving Cairns should not exit the shipping channel until between the 5th and 6th green pile outbound, at which time there is enough water to clear the shallows.

Cairns Trinity Inlet

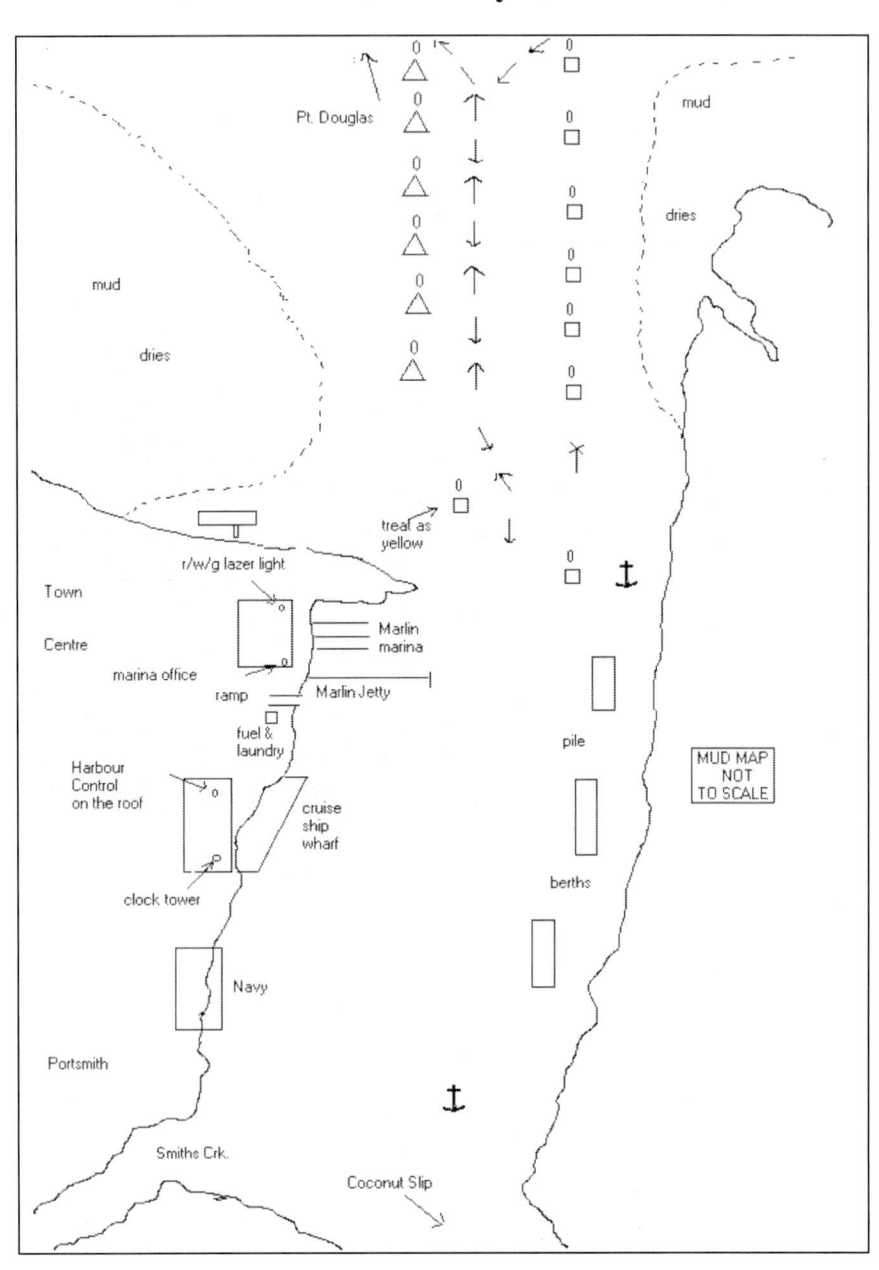

YORKEYS KNOB

CHART AUS 830
LIGHTS Port and starboard beacons approximately 0.5 miles to the north. Back leads on the western end of the rock wall.
TIDES Cairns (Standard Port) ANTT

Entry is between a set of port and starboard beacons. After clearing these, pick up a set of back leads on the western end of the rock wall. Entry is recommended on a rising tide, as the channel is both narrow and shallow. There is a 200-berth marina called Half Moon Bay Marina, call on VHF 16 or telephone 4055 57711 between 0800 and 1700, 7 days a week. The club is friendly and has good meals. There is a free bus to Smithfield Shopping Centre running Monday to Saturday. There is a Sunbus to Cairns, at the end of the street, which runs hourly (bus ID). There are no haul-out or careening facilities. It is a top-class marina.

Yorkeys Knob

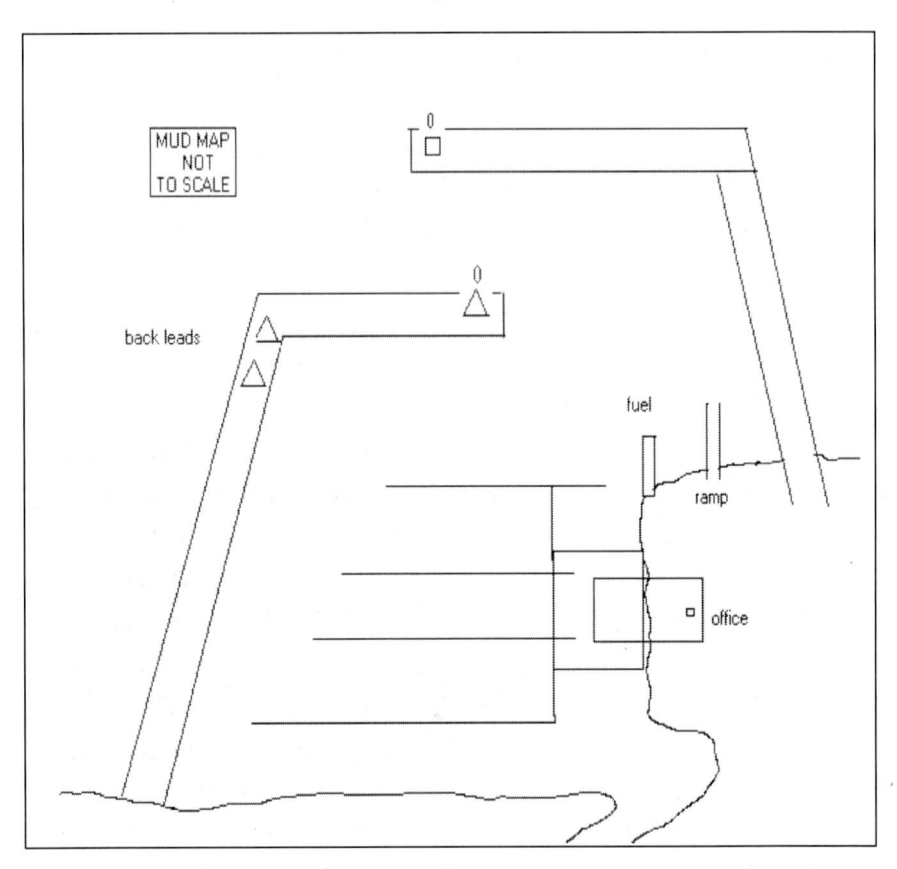

PORT DOUGLAS

CHART AUS 830
LIGHTS Island Point Lighthouse displays a red and white sector light (see chart for sectors). Light flashes 4 times every 20 seconds, visible 12 miles and red for 8 miles. Red and green buoys and beacons lit in the entry and in the harbour.
TIDES Port Douglas (Standard Port) ANTT

After clearing Egmont Reef, this is found 5 miles south of Island Point. There, is a red beacon on the outer end of Egmont Reef. When coming from Cairns keep this well to port. Once past Egmont Reef, steer towards Island Point, where the first of the two red and green buoys will be seen. Proceed up the channel, keeping red to red. DO NOT take any notice of the old back leads. To anchor, carry on past the small yacht club to the end of the piles; go around the next bend and anchor. Fuel is at Marina Mirage and is cheaper than Cairns or Yorkeys Knob. The old slipway has been rebuilt and is now operating, though rather expensive.

Port Douglas

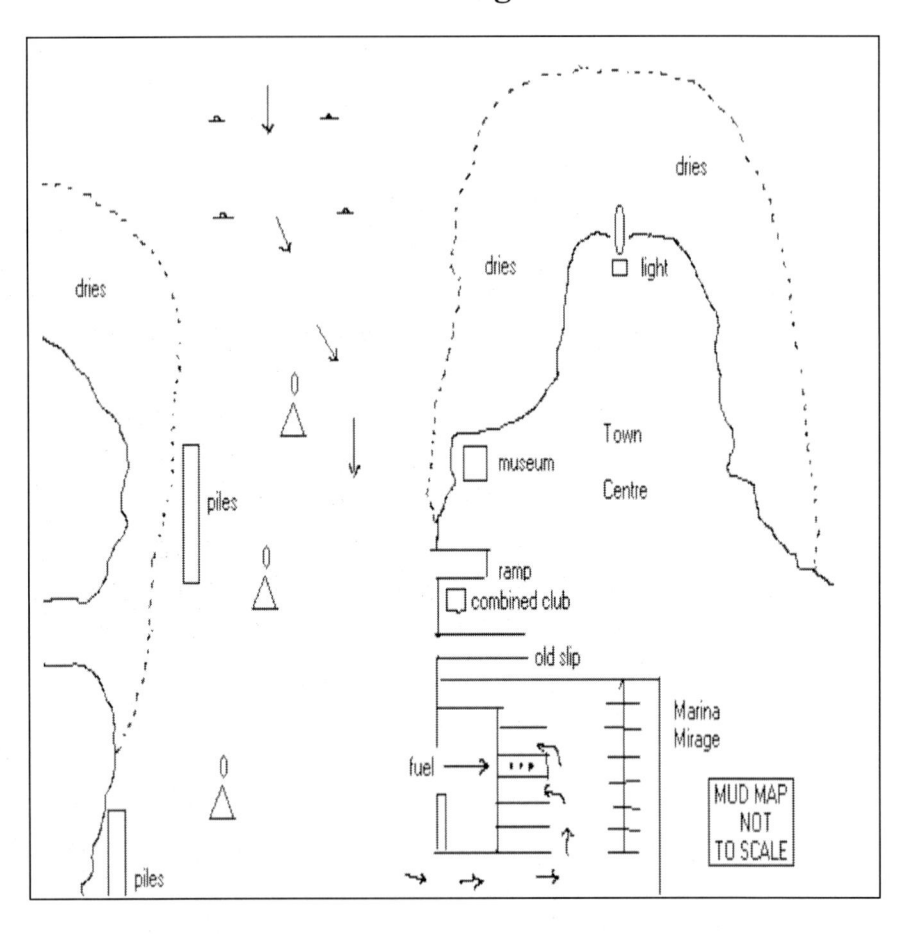

LOW ISLES

CHARTS   AUS 830, 831
LIGHTS   Lighthouse flashes 12 seconds, visible 25 miles.
TIDES   Cairns (Low Isles) ANTT

Low Isles is 7 miles northeast from Port Douglas. Tourist boats visit daily. Anchorage is over white sand, in 3–5 metres clear of the tourist pontoon and moorings. It is secure in east to southeast winds. A swell invades on winds from the east. Do not anchor inside the white buoys out from the lighthouse. There is no northerly anchorage. The closest is Cape Kimberley or Port Douglas. Be aware of the reef extending out from the eastern side of the lagoon. The National Parks has placed four free public moorings here.

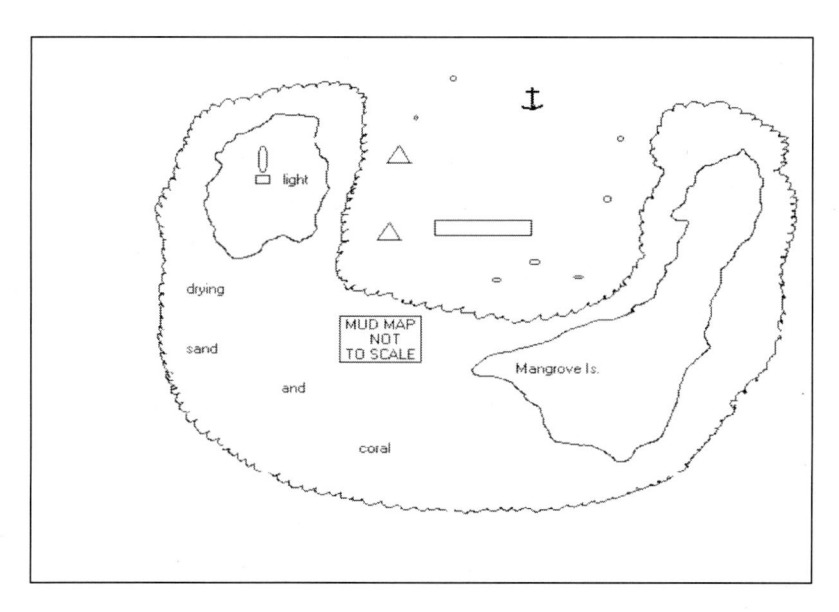

DAINTREE RIVER

CHART AUS 831
LIGHTS Lit back leads on the south channel.
TIDES Cairns (Low Isles) ANTT

As with nearly all the creeks and rivers north of Port Douglas, the Daintree has a barred entrance. Entry is recommended on a rising tide with 0.5 plus your draft. There are 2 channels across the entrance bar. Which one is used is up to individual choice, however the south channel has a set of leads over the bar. Once across the bar, turn to starboard and follow close in along the mangroves. Whichever channel is used, a forward lookout is recommended. After entering, vessels can proceed up to the vehicle ferry about 6 miles upstream. I did not go past the ferry, but was told there was deep water for a few miles upstream. Although there are steering marks along the bank, stay to the outside of the curves. Visual navigation and an eye on the sounder should be maintained. There are a few houses along the bank. At one time, the river carried a lot of traffic, but nowadays only the occasional yacht and tourist boats from Daintree ply its waters.

Daintree River

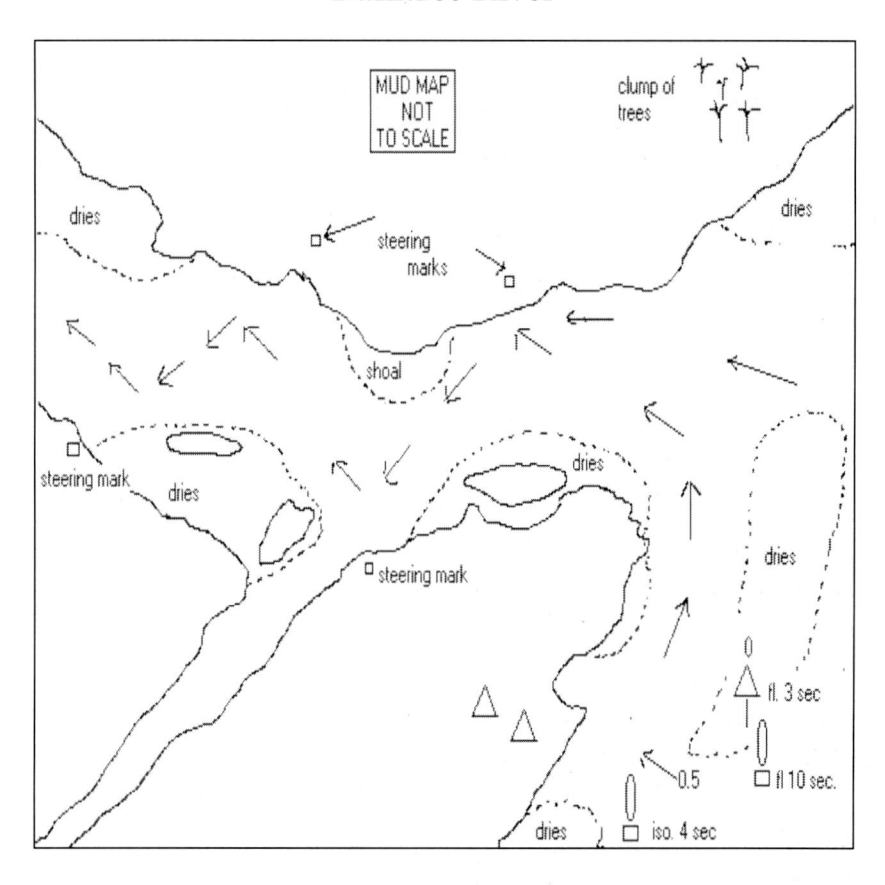

CAPE KIMBERLEY

CHART   AUS 831
LIGHTS   Nil
TIDES   Cairns (Low Isles) ANTT

Cape Kimberley is on the mainland north of the Daintree River. It is a reasonably secure anchorage in northerly winds. Anchor in 3 metres to the west of the cape. Entry from the north is between Snapper Island and Cape Kimberley, through Penguin Channel, where depths vary from 16–25 metres. The chart shows patches of reef, but I have not seen any. However, I have shown reef throughout the bay as a precaution.

SNAPPER ISLAND

Snapper Island lies to the east of Cape Kimberley and is another northerly anchorage. It is not recommended except in light winds. The only reasonably secure spot is hard in against the northwest corner. From here, a dinghy can be landed on the beach on the western side of the island. There is a free National Park mooring here.

Cape Kimberley and Snapper Island

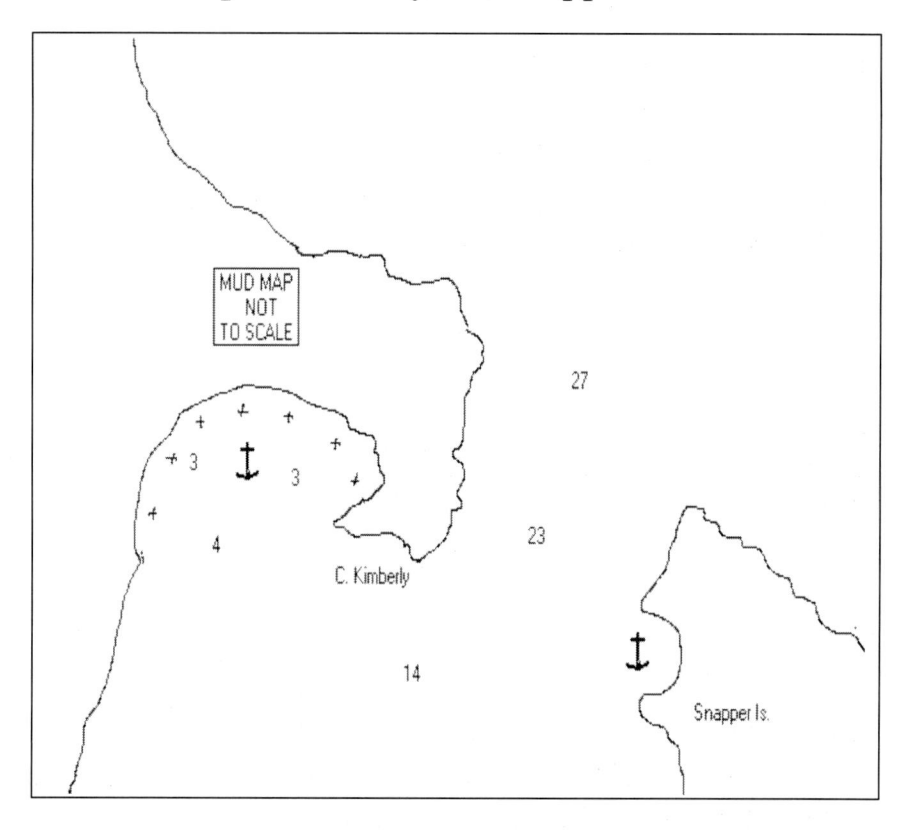

ANCHORAGES IN ALEXANDER BAY

CHART   AUS 831
LIGHTS   Nil
TIDES   Cairns (Bailey Creek) ANTT

The creeks in this area are all either barred or drying. All can be entered on a rising tide with ship's draft plus at least 0.6 and a bit for safety. Once inside, all have deep water. I have only shown Bailey Creek, as it is the only one with a difficult entrance.

BAILEY CREEK

After rounding Cape Kimberley, continue around to the southwest corner of the bay staying out in deep water until the entrance is identified. There is a house on the southern bank. Once the entrance is located, line up the northern headland on the tree line. Hold this course until just past the southern headland, then turn and head for the house. Hold this course until the centre of the creek, then turn and straight in. The best anchorage I found was towards the end, where the creek divides in 2–3 metres.

The next two creeks are either side of Table Mountain. On old charts, they are named Noahs and Coopers in that order coming from the south. On the new metric charts, they are not named, but are readily accessible on a rising tide plus 0.5. Entry is straight in over the bar and deep water will be found inside.

MYALL CREEK

Myall Creek is located south of Cape Tribulation, and is the best anchorage in the area. Entry is over a reef. There is a small resort on the southern headland, which makes the creek easy to find. Entry is at high tide with ship's draft plus 0.6. Once inside there is deep water. There are no mangroves or mossies. A cement jetty is found inside and is used by tourist boats. The locals are very friendly and make you feel welcome.

There is a creek immediately under the southern side of Cape Tribulation. I have not used it, but have been told that there is deep water inside. It is not shown on the chart and is a bit hard to locate.

CAPE TRIBULATION

On the northern side of the cape, tucked back in the corner is a pretty anchorage in calm conditions. Trawlers working the area anchor here during the day. There are a number of moorings here for tourist boats. Take care, as they use them as fore and aft moorings and there is no room in the area nearby. Anchor in 2 metres outside the moorings.

Alexander Bay

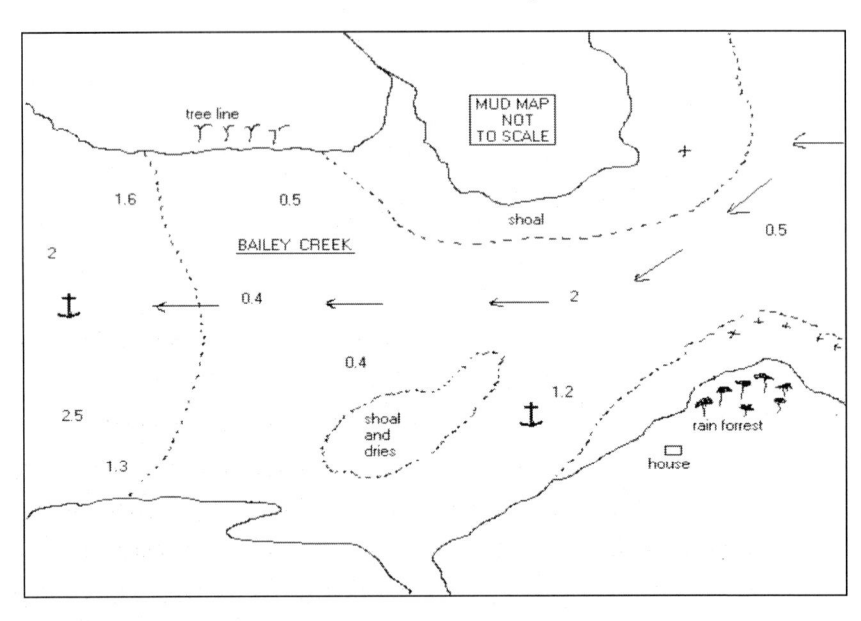

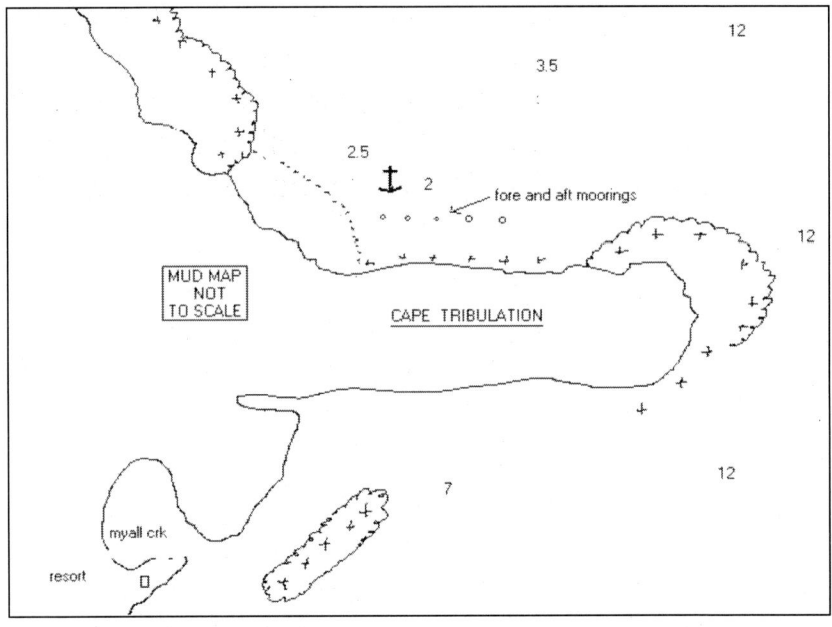

BLOOMFIELD RIVER

CHART   AUS 831
LIGHTS   Nil
TIDES   Cairns (Cooktown) ANTT
RESCUE   Outpost of Cairns Coast Guard VMR 409

There are no navigation aids, but the locals mark the channel. When approaching, be aware of Lake Reef approximately 1 mile to the east of the entrance. This carries 0.8 metres and is hard to find in calm conditions. The entrance bar has 0.3 at low tide, so entry is only possible at high tide. A forward lookout is necessary. Once inside, anchorage can be found anywhere from the log wharf and ramp, along to the pretty BBQ area and campsite on the northern bank. Anchor in 3–5 metres. Anchorage is possible for a further 4 miles, but is of no benefit, as many rocks will be found. A general store and restaurant is at the small township of Ayton. Nine miles upstream is the Wugul Wugul Mission, with stores, fuel, post office, Commonwealth Bank and hot bread all available.

Bloomfield River

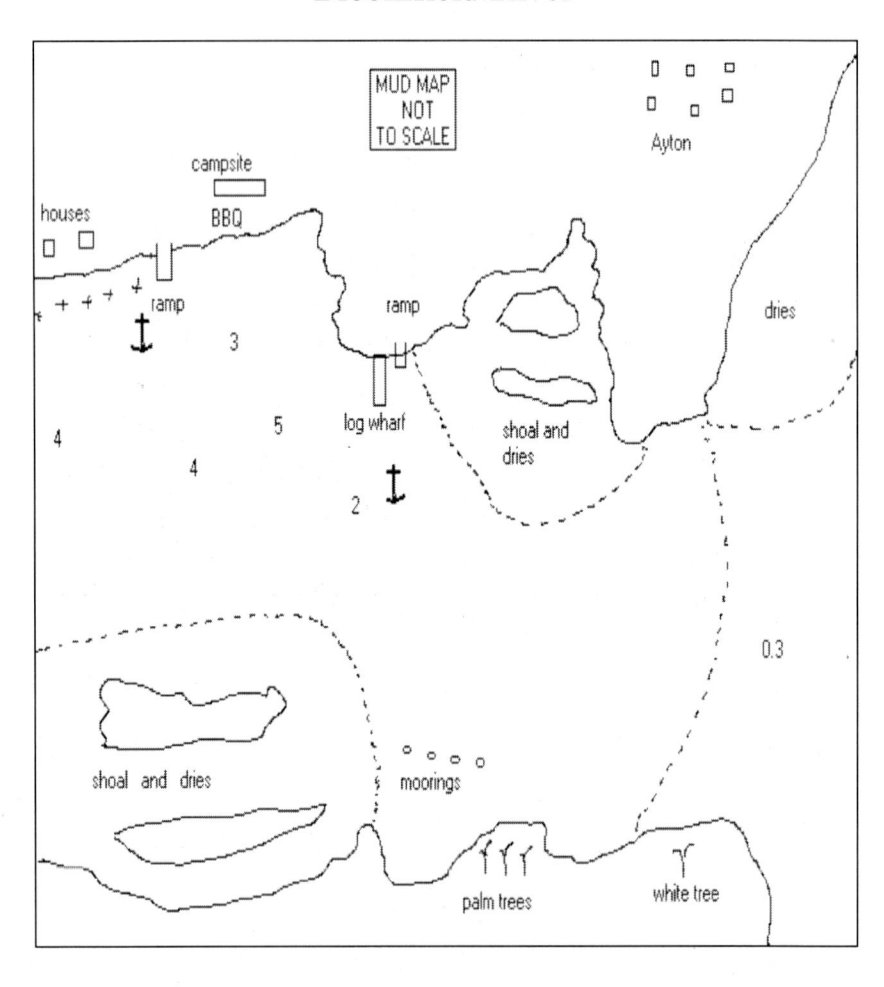

CEDAR BAY

CHART AUS 831
LIGHTS Nil
TIDES Port Douglas (East Hope Is) ANTT

Cedar Bay is located to the north of Rattlesnake Point. The entrance is 5 miles north of the Bloomfield River. Anchor over a sandy bottom in 2 metres. Holding is good, can be uncomfortable in developed winds, but is all right in up to moderate strength. High rainforest-covered ranges surround the bay. The highest is Mt Finlay. There are no offshore dangers except the reef area 2.4 miles north of the Bloomfield River and extending out 1 mile from Bauer Inlet.

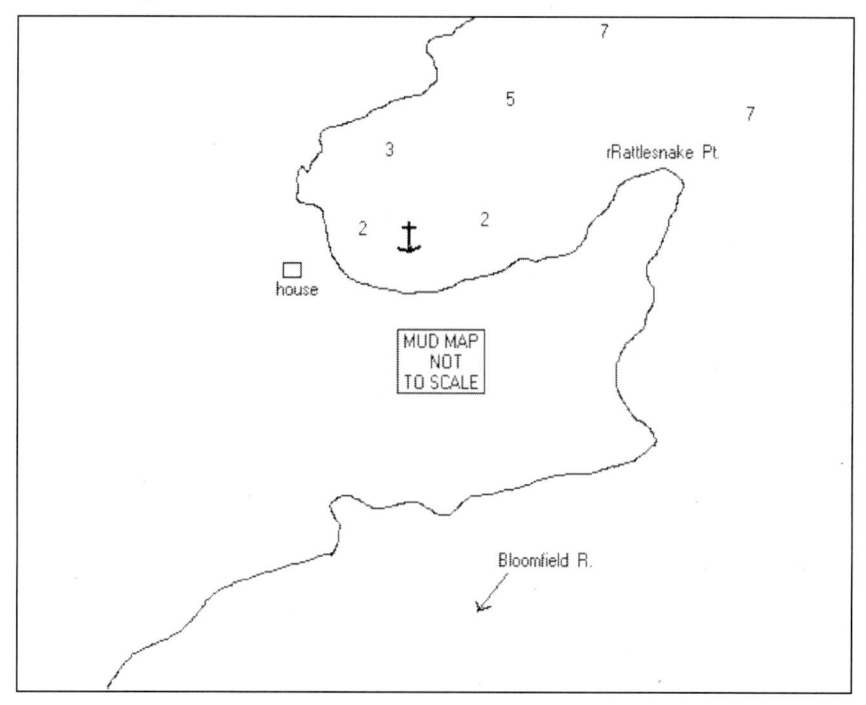

25

HOPE ISLES

CHART	AUS 831
LIGHTS	Gibbons Reef flashes 3 every 15 seconds, visible 15 miles.
TIDES	Port Douglas (East Hope Island) ANTT
CAUTION	Be certain that the anchor is dug in well and plenty of scope is out to prevent dragging in the night. This could have disastrous results, owing to the scattered coral heads and rocks in the nearby area.

Hope Isles are 21 miles south of Cooktown. They consist of two coral cays on two separate reefs. The channel between the two is deep, with an average depth of 10 metres. The eastern island has a well-protected anchorage in winds from the south and east along its western shore, with the southern end of the island on your beam, in a depth of 5–7 metres. There is access to a beautiful sandy beach with National Park facilities. There is a calm weather anchorage on the western side of the western island at the northern end of the reef. There are two free National Park moorings here.

Hope Isles

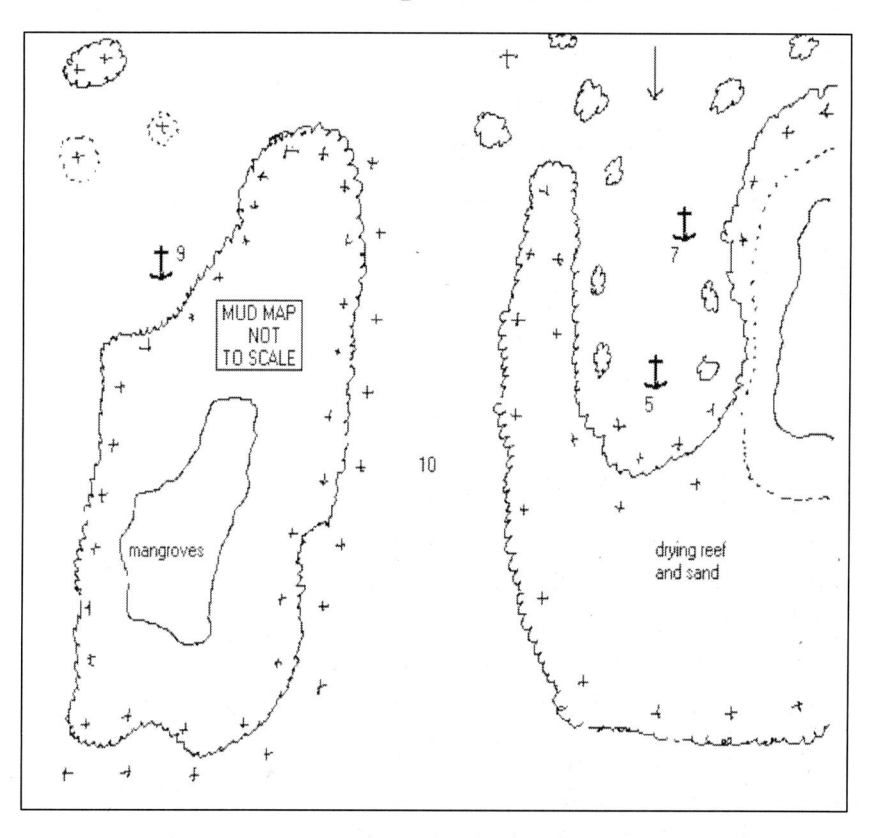

CAIRNS REEF

CHART   AUS 831
LIGHTS   Nil
TIDES   Port Douglas (East Hope Island) ANTT

Entry to Cairns Reef is between Bee Reef and the western side of Cairns Reef. When 0.6 miles past the northern end of Cairns Reef it is safe to turn in, but be sure to clear the underwater reef first. There is deep water between the two reefs. I found no dangers in this area. Anchor in 5 metres over coral rubble at the southern end. Do not go far past the 5-metre mark, or you could be in trouble. Do not attempt passage through the break in the eastern arm. The fishing is good with a lure trolled behind the dinghy. Protection is good in winds from the east through south to west.

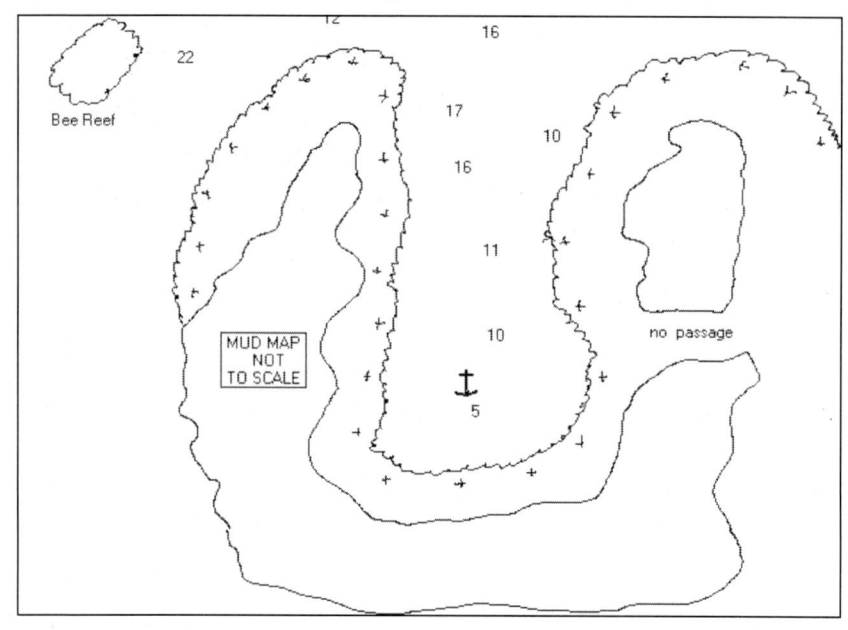

ANNAN RIVER

CHART   AUS 831
LIGHTS   Archer Point shows a G/W/R sector light (see chart for sectors) flashing every 20 seconds, visible white 18 miles, red and green 14 miles. Cardinal marks on Cowlishaw and Dawson Reefs.
TIDES   Cairns (Cooktown) ANTT

The entrance to the Annan River is about 14.5 miles north of Hope Isles. Give Grave Point a 1-mile clearance. This will also clear Draper Patch. Hold this course until 1 mile past Grave Point. At this time, the river mouth should be seen. Draper Patch dries 0.3, so be careful. The bar at the mouth has a depth of 0.5 metres, so this plus ship's draft is needed to enter on a rising tide. Entry to the river is the easiest on the coast. Simply hold the conspicuous pyramid-shaped hill over the centre of the mouth. The river is shallow, but anchorage can be found in mud immediately inside the south headland where depth allows. Entry is not recommended in rough conditions unless necessary.

Annan River

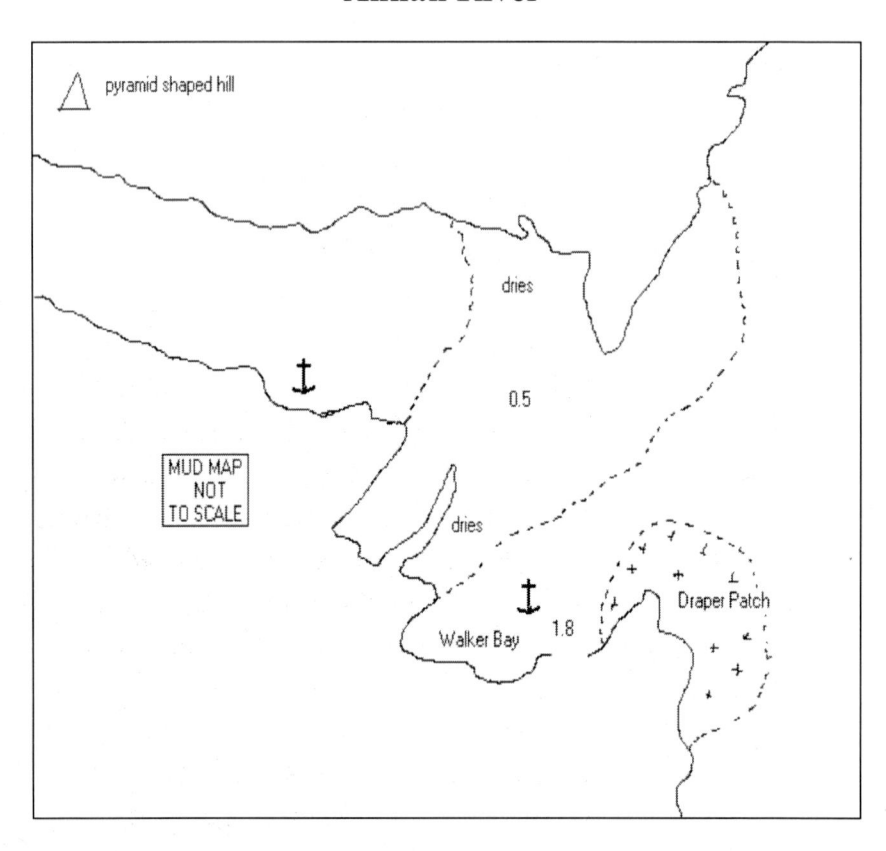

COOKTOWN

CHART   AUS 831
LIGHTS   Grassy Hill lighthouse flashes 2 every 6 seconds, visible 8 miles.
TIDES   Cairns (Cooktown) ANTT

Cooktown is over 70 miles from Port Douglas and 400 miles south of Thursday Island. This is the last place along the east coast for supplies, except for the supply ships. The entry as shown on the chart is now incorrect, as in early 1997, an all-tide entry channel was dredged. There are now three sets of red and green leads. The Fairway buoy has also gone. This now makes Cooktown an easy entry. After clearing Blackbird Patches, which carries 1.8 metres and extends out 1.5 miles from the shore, steer for Grassy Point, where the entry channel will be easily found. At no time should the large lit back leads be used, as they no longer line up. Once clear of the channel, two yellow buoys will be seen. These are the turning basin for tourist ships. Anchorage space is seriously limited. It gets crowded at times, however those prepared to set a stern anchor, will find space upstream against the mangroves, where the risk of collision can be avoided. The mossies are friendly here. Dinghy landing can be anywhere along the shoreline. Cooktown has all basic facilities, but nothing is reasonably priced.

Cooktown

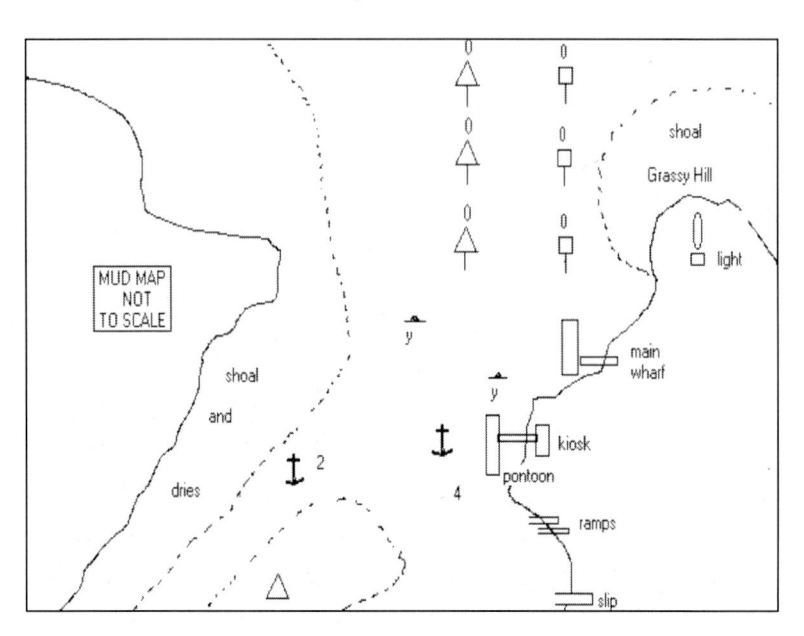

LARK REEF

15°17.60′S – 145°33.80′E

CHART	AUS 831
LIGHTS	Nil
TIDES	Cairns (Cape Bedford) ANTT

Lark Reef lies 11 miles east of South Cape Bedford. Entry is to the south of Swinger and Pullen Reefs. There is a wide break in the reef, giving access to the lagoon, where depths of 6–13 metres will be found. Although passage is possible straight in over the reef coming from Cape Bedford, it is not recommended. The lagoon is similar to Hope Isles to the south, except there is no island and the seas invade when the reef is covered, but it remains reasonably comfortable. Anchorage is deep, but secure. The bottom shoals towards the west, and there is a 0.5-knot current in the area. The fishing is tops and it is possible to catch a crayfish or two.

Lark Reef

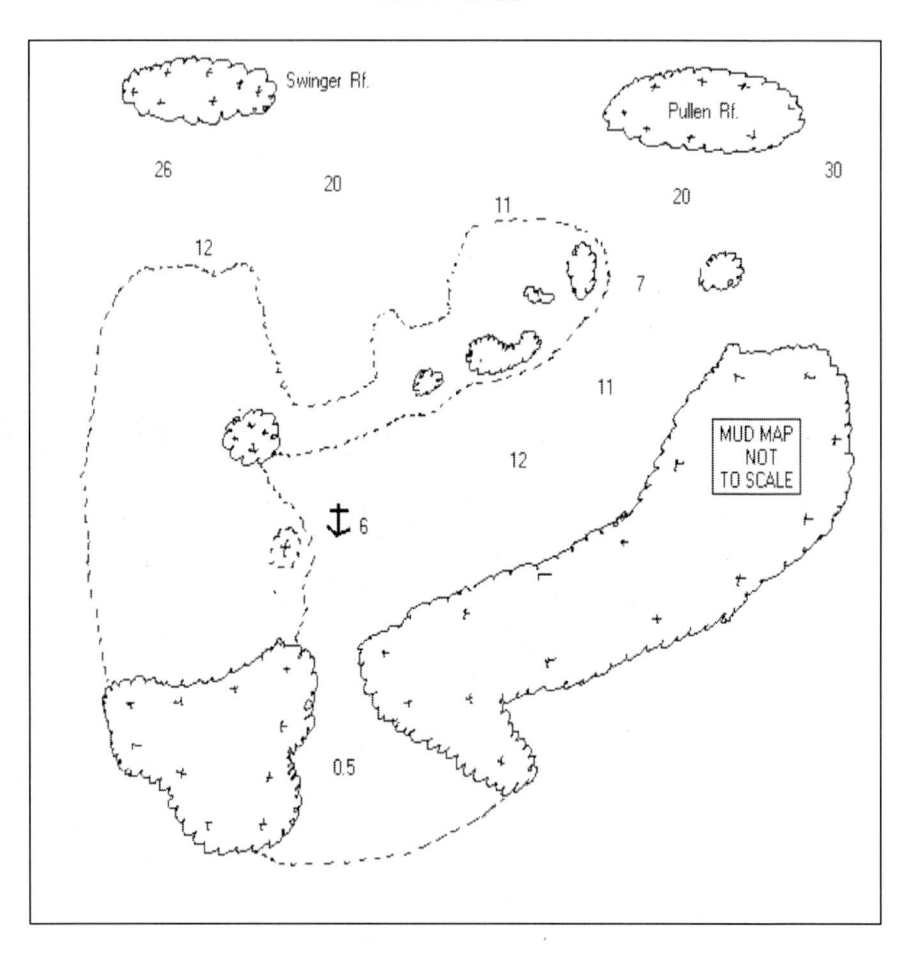

CAPE BEDFORD

CHART   AUS 831
LIGHTS Nil
TIDES   Cairns (Cape Bedford) ANTT

Cape Bedford can be seen from about 25 miles away coming from the south. The cape's highest peak is 260 metres, while the others are around 100 metres. They are first sighted as three islands, which quickly join to become Cape Bedford. It is a good anchorage, but can be uncomfortable in a blow. Because of the shoaling bottom, vessels must stay well out. Anchorage is in 2–3 metres over sand, but mud may be found in closer. There are no dangers around Cape Bedford, but suggest that vessels stay about 1 mile offshore until the cape is rounded. The best anchorage is out from the western side of the cape, which cannot be held close in without neap tides or shallow draft.

Cape Bedford

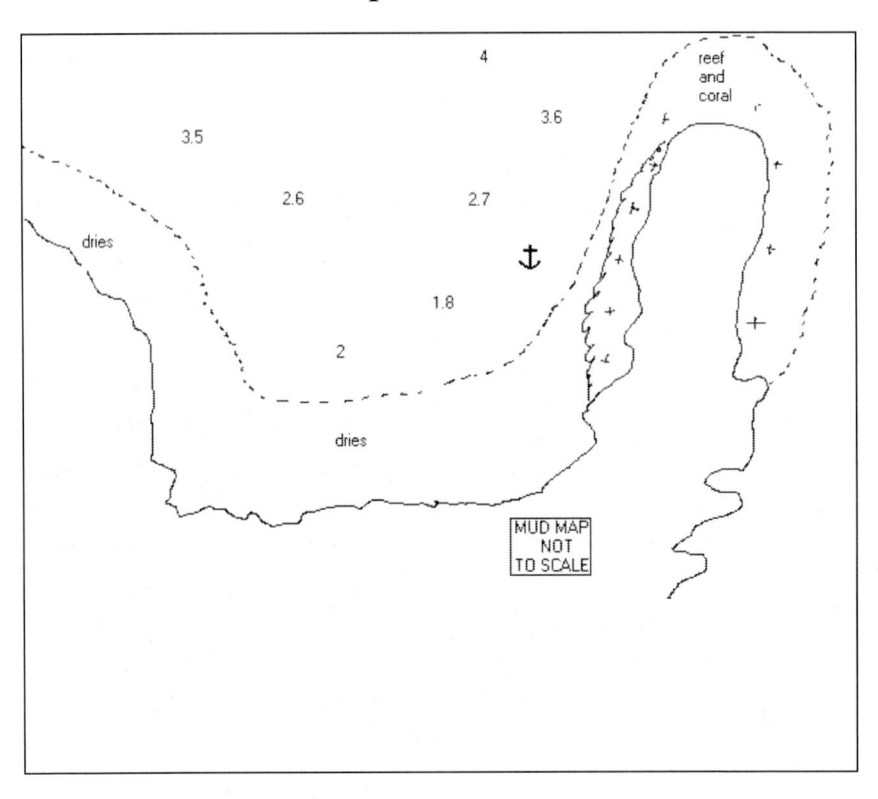

CONICAL ROCK

CHART AUS 831
LIGHTS Three Isles flashes 3 every 15 seconds, visible 10 miles.
TIDES Cairns (Cape Bedford) ANTT

Conical Rock is found 5 miles to the north of Cape Bedford. There is a large sand-spit to the west, where a secure anchorage is found in 3 metres over sand. The chart shows a reef, but this is incorrect. The anchorage is secure and surprisingly comfortable in winds up to 20 knots. From here, it is a short run west to the McIvor River.

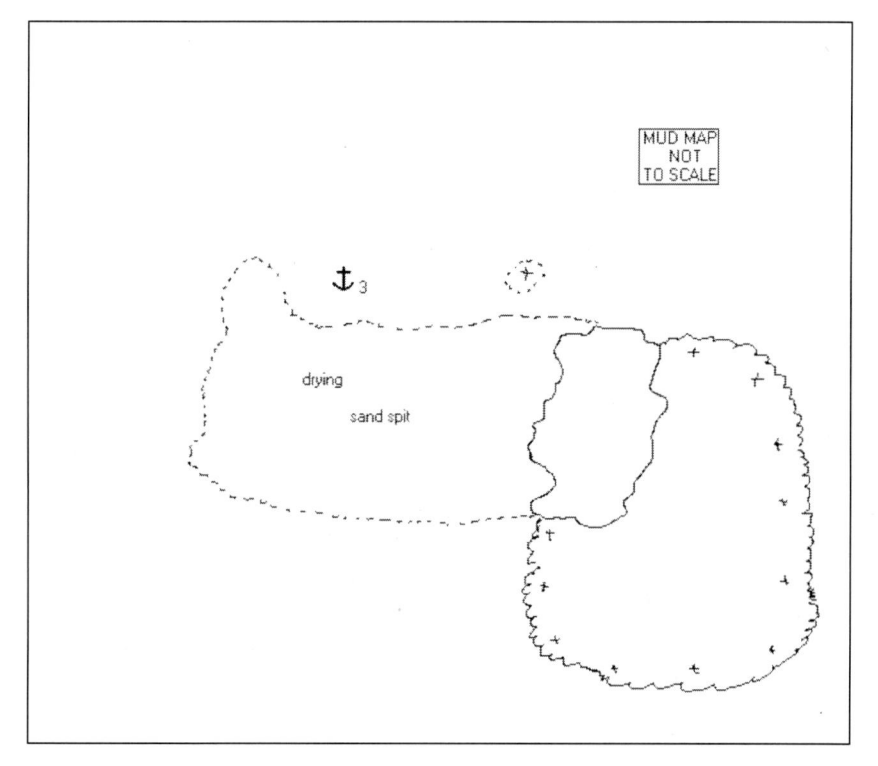

MUD MAP NOT TO SCALE

drying sand spit

McIVOR RIVER

CHART   AUS 831
LIGHTS   Three Isles flashes 3 every 15 seconds, visible 10 miles.
TIDES   Cairns (Cape Bedford) ANTT

The McIvor River is on the mainland, 4.5 miles due west of Conical Rock. There is a drying sandbar across its entrance, so a high tide is needed to enter. The entrance channel has a dogleg through the sandbanks, but once inside deep water will be found. The river is navigable for around 2 miles with care. There is a waterhole inside the entrance on the northern bank behind the coconut tree and amongst the ti-trees. There are nipa palms here, which is as far south as they are found. To enter, take a bearing of 270° T from Conical Rock to the northern headland. Once inside the sandbanks, turn to port to a bearing of 200° T on the mangroves. This clears the sandbar in front of the mouth. Once around this, entry is straight in. These directions may change with wet season floods, so check first in the dinghy. Entry is advised in suitably calm conditions only.

McIvor River

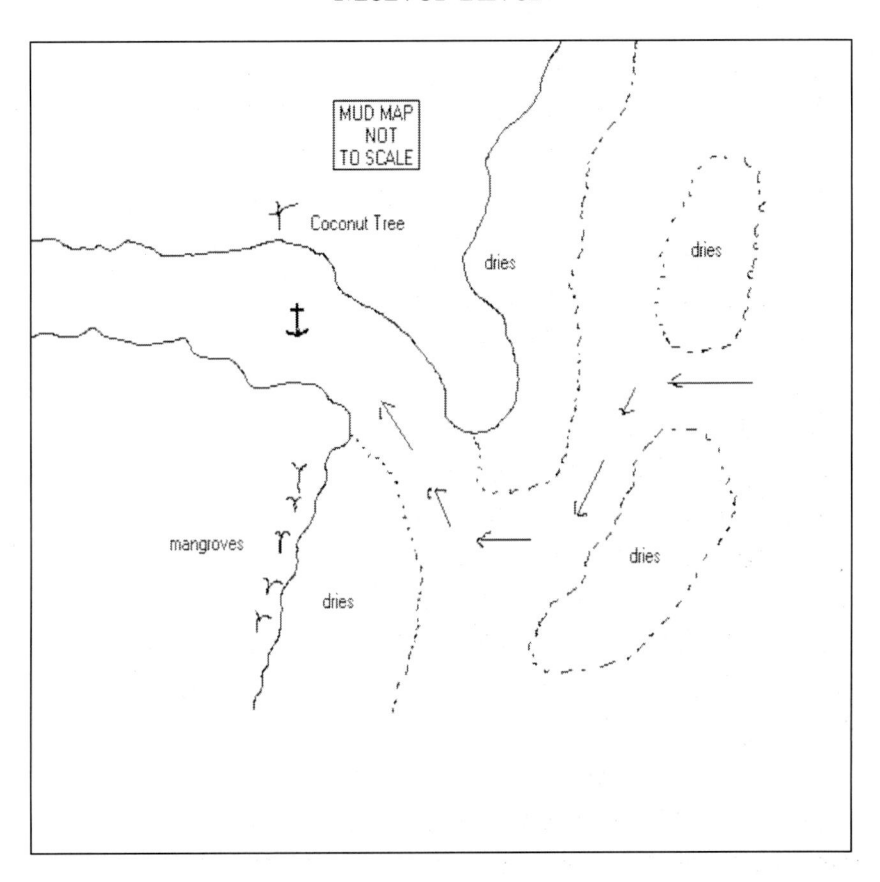

FORRESTER REEF

CHART   AUS 832
LIGHTS   Three Isles flashes 3 every 15 seconds, visible 10 miles.
TIDES: Cairns (low wooded isles) ANTT

Forrester Reef is about 10 miles northeast of Cape Bedford, providing reasonable shelter in light to moderate conditions. Anchorage is off the northern side of the reef in deep water. However, it may be possible to anchor over the reef; I did not try. The good fishing makes up for the deep anchorage. There is very little tide run here, about 0.5 of a knot.

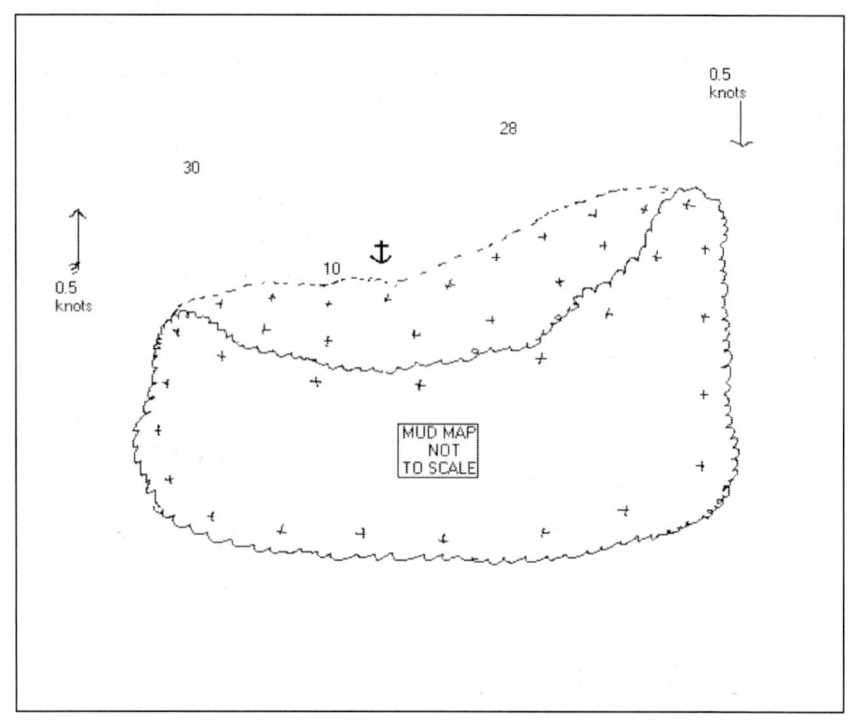

CAPE FLATTERY

CHART AUS 832
LIGHTS The loading wharf on the southern side of the cape carries 3 lights that flash the letter 'U' in Morse every 10.5 seconds, visible 8 miles.
TIDES Leggatti Island (Cape Flattery) ANTT

A sandy shoal extends some distance north from the cape, however, there is generally enough water for moderate draft vessels. The best anchorage is in the first of the two bays in sandy mud. Seagrass will be encountered further in. A small swell does invade, but this depends on the wind and tide conditions; it is still reasonably comfortable. This is a secure anchorage in a southerly blow. The second bay is also accessible, but I found it not as secure. There is a Japanese company carrying out sand mining here. There is an airstrip and STD telephone available, but **only in an emergency**. The Flying Doctor has a clinic here once a month. There is water behind the coconut trees in amongst the ti-trees. There is an old triangle lead on the beach; if you come to this you have gone too far. This water is OK for washing and bathing, but I would not drink it, as there are a number of soak holes further along the beach, towards the house, with sandy bottoms and the water is quite good. If you are into walking, there is a cairn on top of the highest point in front of the anchorage. Everyone who gets to the top places a rock on it.

The wharf complex is now only used to moor the tugs and unload the supply barges. There are wild pigs, and a large crocodile visits occasionally.

Cape Flattery

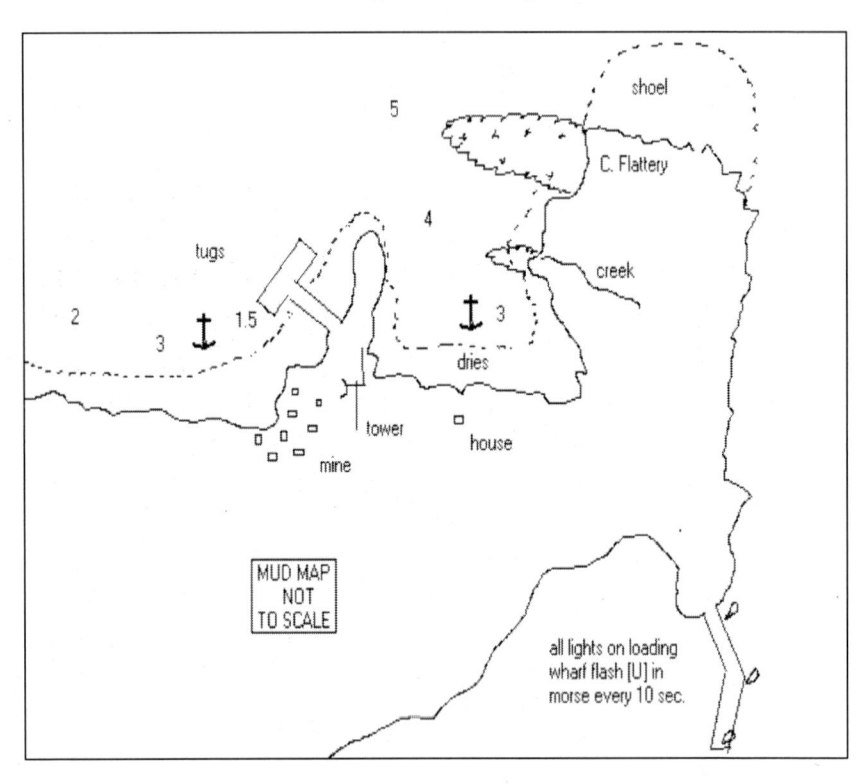

Mud map not to scale

all lights on loading wharf flash [U] in morse every 10 sec.

LOOKOUT POINT

CHART AUS 832
LIGHTS Decapolis Reef flashes 2 every 6 seconds, visible 9 miles.
TIDES Leggatti Island (Cape Flattery) ANTT

Lookout Point is 9.5 miles northwest of Cape Flattery. When approaching Decapolis Reef, beware of Four-Foot Rock lying to the west and the rocky area to the south. After rounding Lookout Point, you will suddenly come from 6 metres down to 2 metres. This depth holds right to the anchorage, which is in 2.5 metres over sand. The best place was found 2.4 miles to the west. Anywhere along the coast west from the point is all right. Anchor well out, as close in is shoal and drying sand.

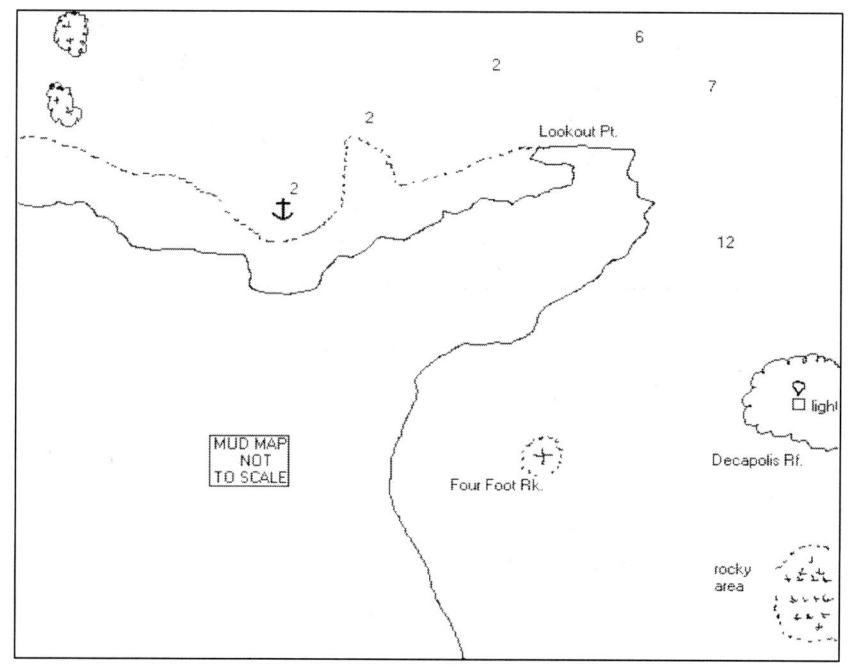

LOOKOUT POINT CREEK

14°50′S – 145°08′E

CHART   AUS 832
LIGHTS   East Pethebridge Islet flashes 2 every 10 seconds, visible 10 miles.
TIDES   Leggatti Is (East Pethebridge Islet) ANTT

This creek is not shown on the chart, so I have shown the coordinates. After clearing the anchorage at Lookout Point, make sure to clear the two drying patches to the northwest. The depth is 3.5 metres between these and the drying rocks one mile to the northwest. Make sure not to go too far, as there are two patches of drying reef and rocks out from the creek entrance. Anchor in 2 metres out from the pyramid-shaped sand-hill, about one mile offshore from the entrance. A 2.5-metre tide is needed to enter. Approach slowly and line up the gap in the mangroves with Mt Kookaburra. Hold this until the mangroves blot out the mountain, then turn hard to port and move towards the eastern side of the entrance. Then head towards the clump of tall mangroves. Keep to the eastern side of the entrance and follow the bank. I only went as far as the eastern side of the large island at the base of the big sand-hill on the east bank. It is advised to check in the dinghy first, as the channel may change with the floods.

Lookout Point Creek

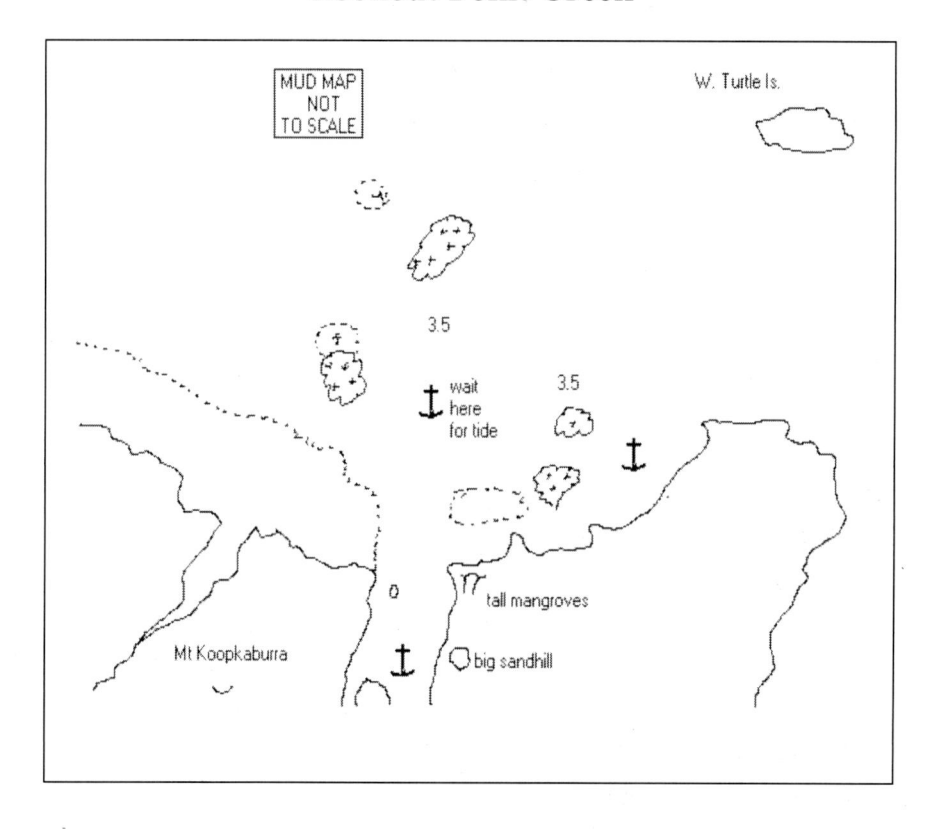

STARCKE RIVER

CHART AUS 832
LIGHTS East Pethebridge Islet flashes 2 every 10 seconds, visible 10 miles.
TIDES Leggatti Is (East Pethebridge Islet) ANTT

The Starcke River is blocked by a drying sandbank, which extends seawards for one mile and extends into the river mouth. To enter, line up the top of Round Hill with the middle of the entrance and enter **only** at or near the top of the tide. There are the remains of a wreck on the starboard bank. From here, there is a deep-water channel up to the disused landing on the east bank. Anchorage can be found in 2.3 metres. Before entering, check in the dinghy, as floods may change the channel.

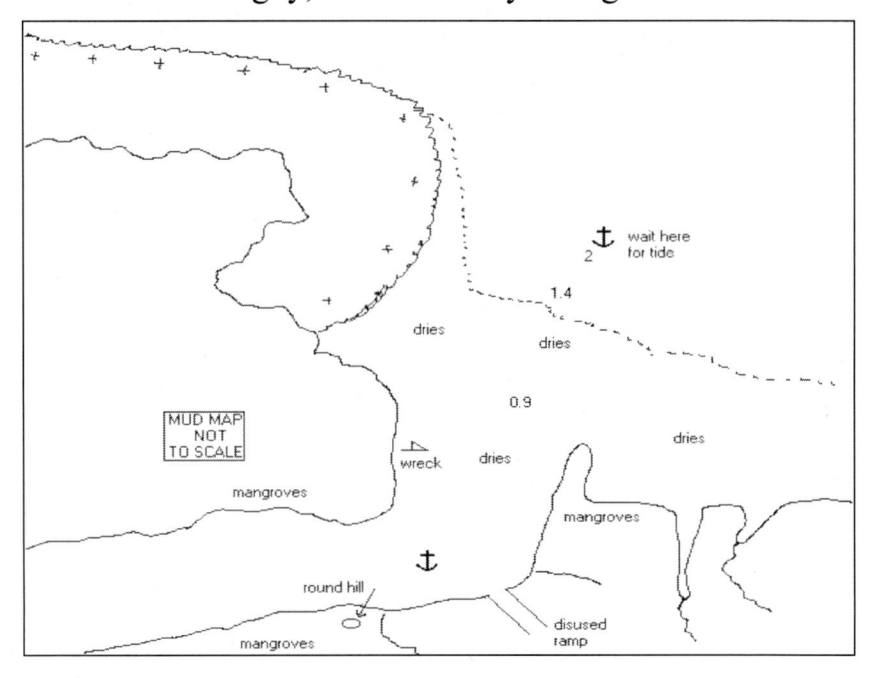

ROCKY ISLES

CHART   AUS 832
LIGHTS   Nil
TIDES   Leggatti Island (Cape Flattery) ANTT

Rocky Isles are continental islands on top of an extensive reef area. The best anchorage is in the half moon shaped area, out from the fringing reef on the northern side. Anchor in 5 metres over sand. The reef out from the northeast corner extends to the north for some distance. The reef on the northwest side does also, but not as far. Be aware of the scattered coral heads to the north. The southwest island is bare rock, while the southeast island is scrub covered. There is no passage between the two. The anchorage was found to be clear of coral heads, but be very careful getting there. The anchorage is also secure in a blow.

Rocky Isles

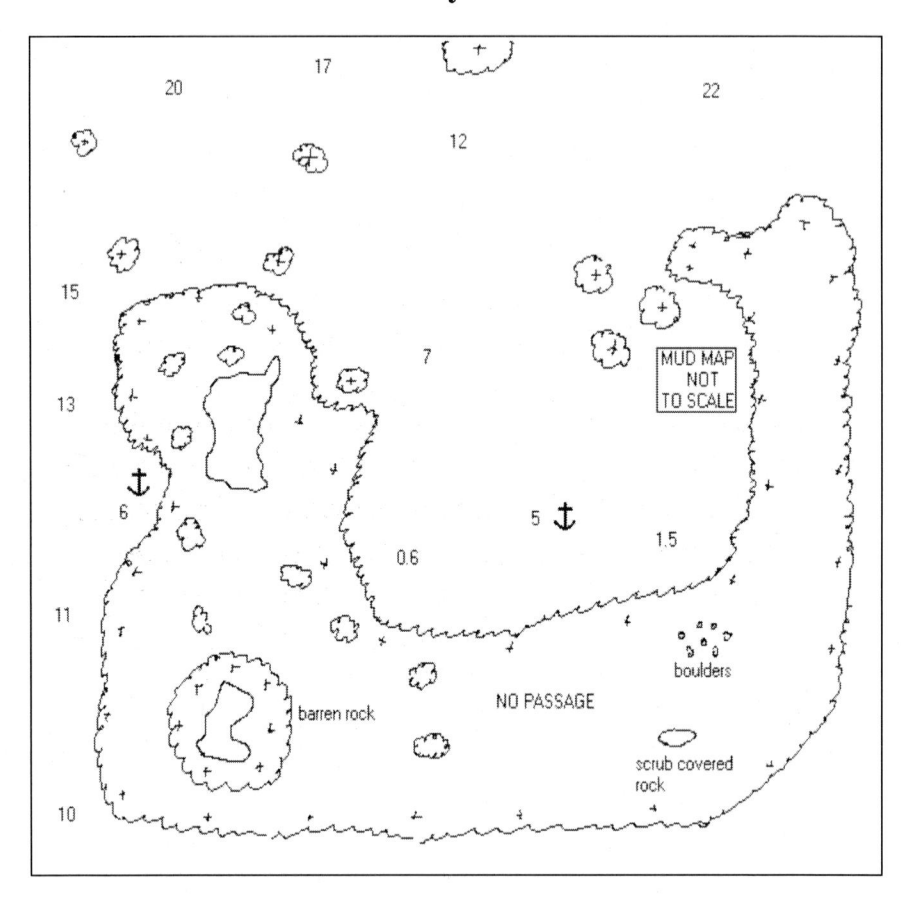

SOUTH DIRECTION ISLAND

CHART AUS 832
LIGHTS Nil
TIDES Leggatti Is (North Direction Islet) ANTT

South Direction Island lies about 3 miles northeast of Rocky Isles. It consists of a high mountain peak that is visible for some distance. There is no place to land, and it is a light weather anchorage only. A swell invades at high tide, which makes it a bit uncomfortable.
Anchorage is in 9 metres over sand in a lagoon in the reef off the northeast side. A forward lookout is strongly recommended, as there are many scattered coral heads. Approach the anchorage on or near the top of the tide, with the sun behind or overhead. The entry I used was found it to be all right, although not very deep, 3 metres.

South Direction Island

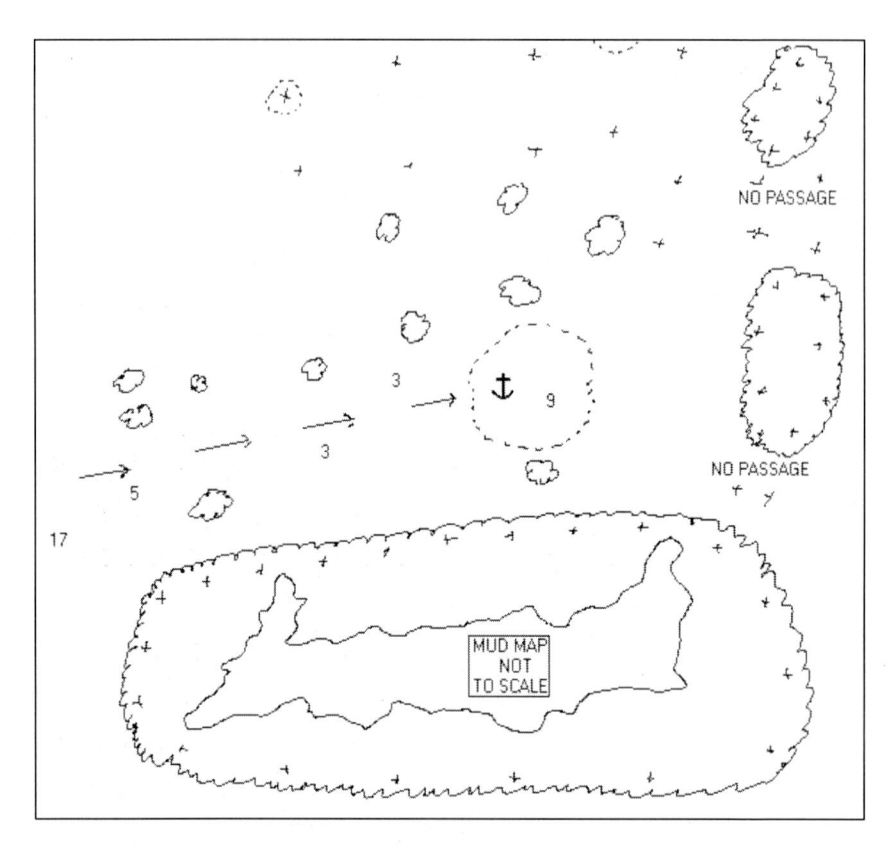

LIZARD ISLAND

CHART	AUS 832
LIGHTS	Palfrey Island flashes 4 every 12 seconds, visible 10 miles.
TIDES	Leggatti Island (Lizard Island) ANTT

Lizard Island is surrounded by numerous coral reefs, particularly off the southern and eastern shores. There is a Marine Research Station situated at the southwest corner. They conduct tours. The resort facilities are off limits to cruising yachts, except at the Marlin Bar. The bore water is no longer drinkable. If it is needed, it costs 5 cents a litre at water sports. There is a track to Cook's Lookout. The ruins of Mrs Watson's house are in from the southern end of the beach.

WATSONS BAY is good holding in sand in 2–5 metres, and the bottom is clearly visible. Strong bullets will be experienced in heavy Trade Winds. To the north, **NORTH WEST BAY** is in deep water in the apex of the surrounding reef or over the edge in suitably light weather. This is a top spot for diving and snorkelling. To the south is **THE LAGOON**, which gives shelter in northerly winds. This is secure in moderate southerlies. Although the lagoon and the entrance have deep water, do not attempt to enter in strong winds, as the entrance breaks right across and is hard to define.

Lizard Island

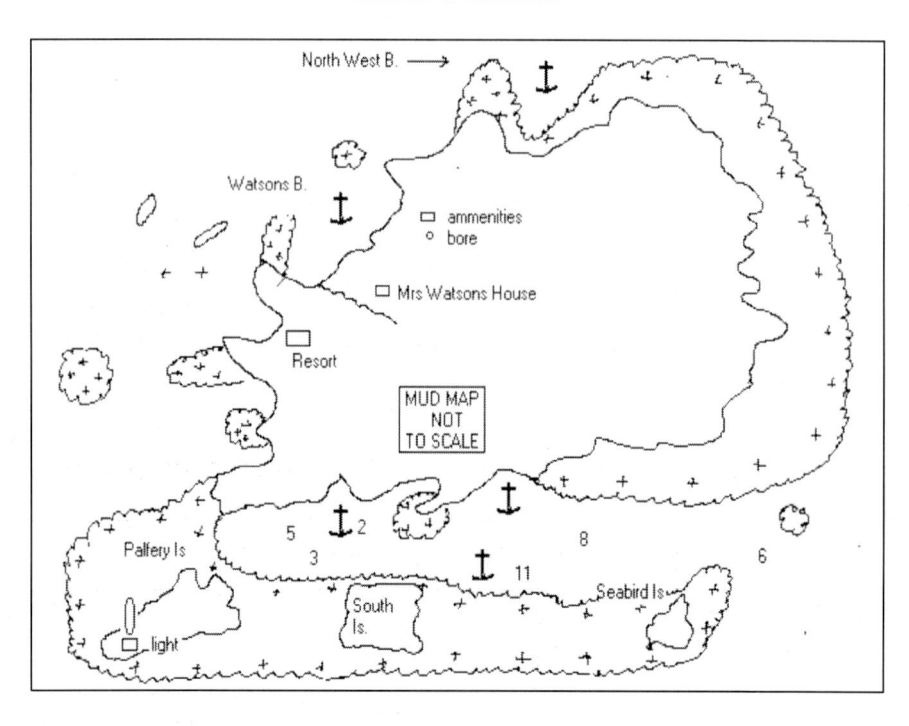

EAGLE ISLAND

CHART AUS 832
LIGHTS Nil
TIDES Leggatti Island (Lizard Island) ANTT

Eagle Island sits on the northern end of Eyrie Reef. It is a barren cay with enormous bird life. Sea eagles are common. The rock ledge on the southern side of the cay is remarkably straight. Anchorage is anywhere along the western side of the reef, in around 7 metres over sand. The anchorage is fair in strong winds, but is good in light to moderate conditions. There is a tidal sand beach on the northern side, and drying sand patches on the southern end of the reef.

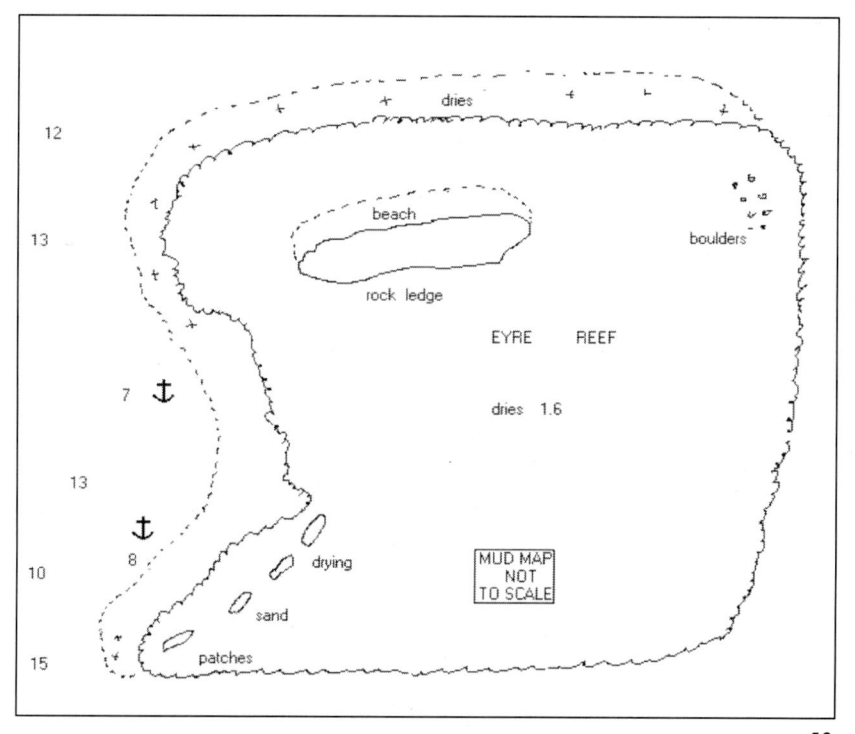

NYMPH ISLAND

CHART AUS 832
LIGHTS Nil
TIDES Leggatti Is (East Pethebridge Islet) ANTT

Nymph Island lies about 7 miles west-northwest of Eagle Islet, and is square, being as long as it is wide. There is a shallow lagoon in the southern half of the reef that may be suitable for multi-hulls only. There are some tall trees at the northeast corner; the rest is dry scrub. A ledge that is barely awash at high tide surrounds the island. There are also some coral patches out from the northwest corner. There are coral and sand patches around the island, especially along the northern side. Anchorage is off the northwest corner in 5–6 metres, but take care to avoid the scattered coral heads. Anchorage is reasonable in light to moderate conditions.

THE TURTLE GROUP

CHART   AUS 832
LIGHTS   Pethebridge Islet flashes 2 every 10 seconds, visible 10 miles.
TIDES   Leggatti Is. (East Pethebridge Islet) ANTT

The Turtle Group lies 4 miles south of Nymph Island and is a group of coral reefs. Of these, six have sparse scrub, and some have tidal sand cays. When coming from Nymph Island, make sure to clear Gunga Shoals. Anchorage is in varying depths of 7–9 metres. The most comfortable anchorage I found was in 6 metres at the southern end of the group. Anchorage is comfortable and secure in strong winds. The Turtle Group dries on average 9 metres, making it easily visible. When coming from Cape Flattery, the Turtles are 6 miles north of Lookout Point. The safest passage is around the outside of the Western Islands, then turn to come down into the anchorage. Give the islands a wide clearance to avoid off laying reefs. Passage between the Western Islands is possible on high tide, but is not recommended as they have extensive reef areas between them. Anchorage here is comfortable in winds 10–15 knots. Beware of the reef that extends out from the islands at the anchorage. The water is clear, so they can easily be seen.

Turtle Island Group

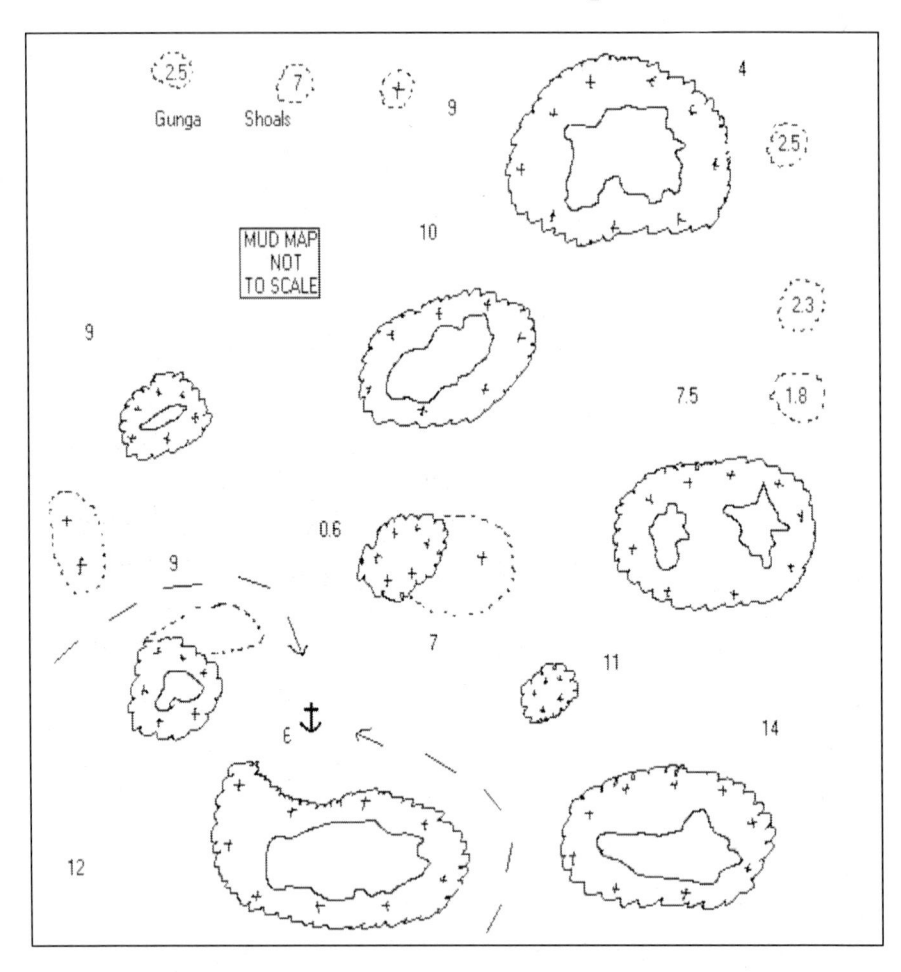

PETHEBRIDGE ISLETS

14°43.90′S – 145°05.90′E

CHART AUS 832
LIGHTS East Pethebridge flashes 2 every 8 seconds, visible 10 miles.
TIDES Leggatti Is (East Pethebridge Islet) ANTT

The Pethebridge group of islets is on the mainland side of the shipping channel, and 10 miles north of Lookout Point. The light is located on East Pethebridge, however the best anchorage is on the northern side of the western islet in 4 metres over sand. It is a calm weather anchorage, but is tenable to 10 knots. The Turtle Islands are best in developed winds. The passage between the two islets is deep, with 8 metres; however favour the western side, as there is a sand-spit running southwest from the eastern islet. Give the western islet a wide berth, as there are reef areas out from it. Once clear of the reef, anchor behind the islet and the reef.

Pethebridge Islets

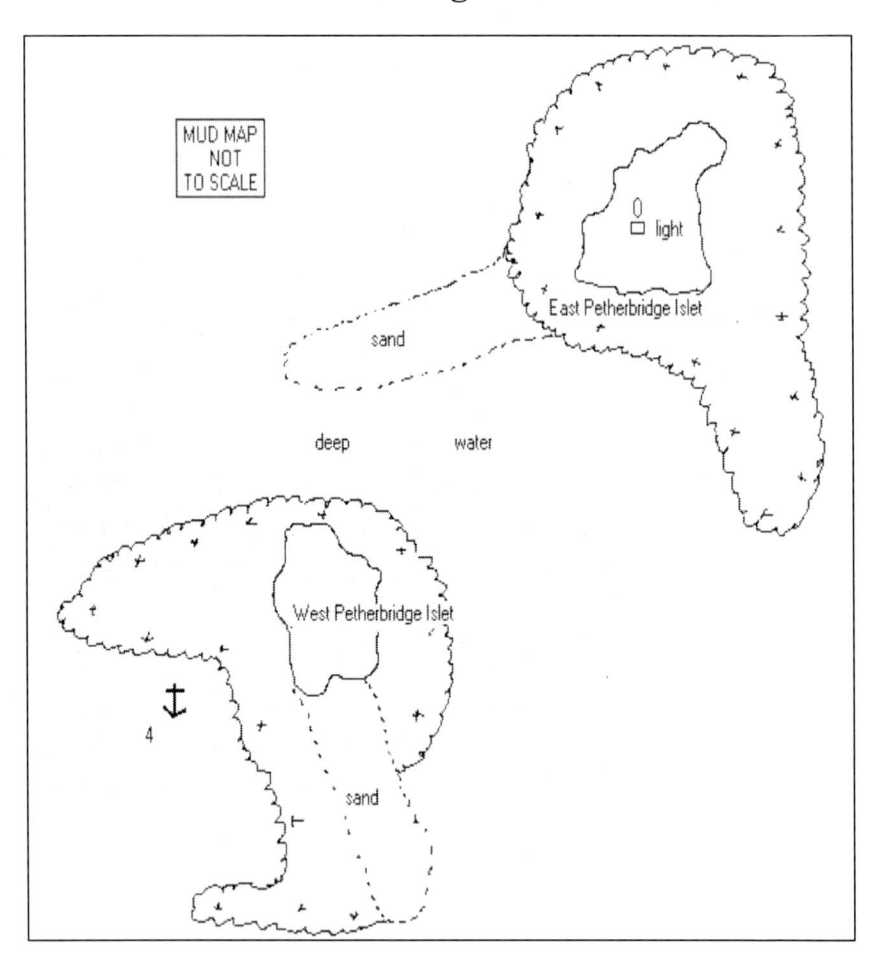

DEAD DOG INLET

14°36.6′S – 144°52.4′E

CHART   AUS 832
LIGHTS   Nil
TIDES   Leggatti Island (Carter Reef) ANTT

Dead Dog Inlet is found to the west of Murdock Point and is blocked by drying sand and shallows, which extend out for 1.4 miles until a depth of 2 metres is found. Entry is at or near the top of the tide, and is direct into the centre of the tall mangroves. Before making entry, a drying 1-metre sandbar will be seen extending out from both headlands, with a 1-metre deep channel in the centre at low tide. Once inside, anchor where depth allows, but take care to stay in deep water, as both sides of the inlet are tidal flats. While waiting for the tide to enter, anchorage can be found northwest of Murdock Island in suitably light conditions, but take care, as there are a lot of rocks and reefs around here.

Dead Dog Inlet

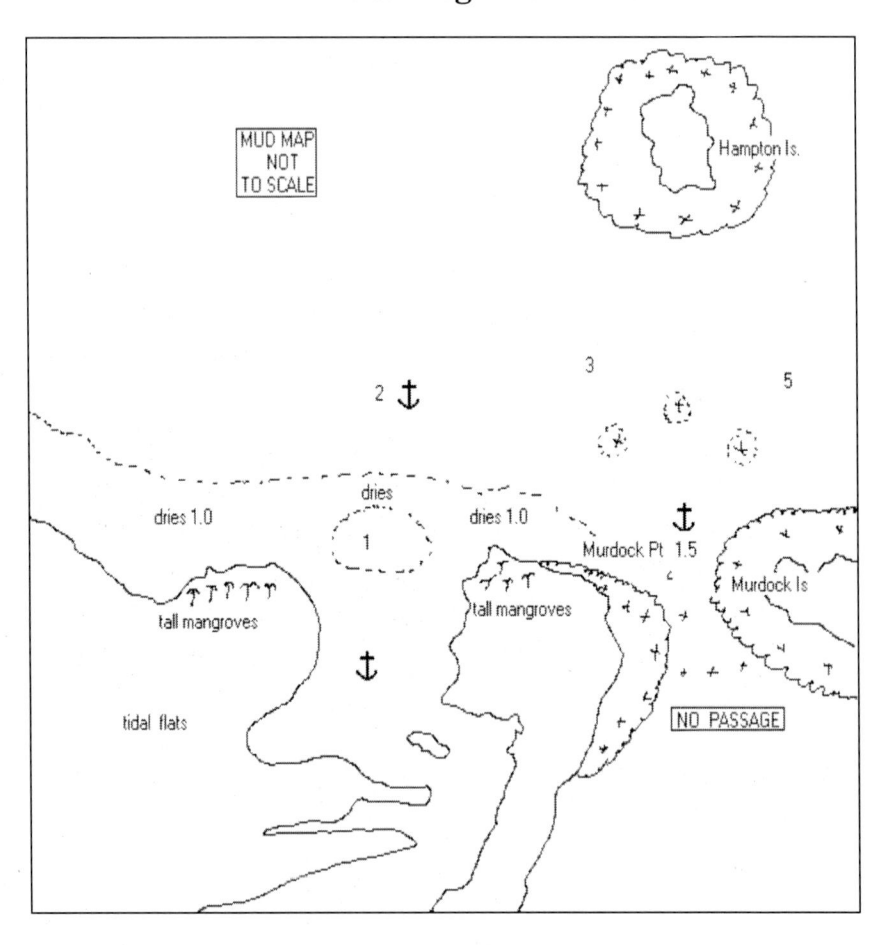

ROCKY CREEK

14°36′S – 144°47.8′E

CHART   AUS 832
LIGHTS   Nil
TIDES   Leggatti Island (Normanby River) ANTT

Rocky Creek is located 3 miles to the south of Red Point. A sandbar extending out for 0.6 miles dries 1 metre. Shallows extend out a further 1.5 miles. Anchor in 2.5 metres while waiting for the tide to enter, or time your run across from Hampton Island. A tide of ship's draft plus 1 metre, plus a bit for safety to enter. Once inside, I anchored in 2 metres inside the mouth. Then after a check in the dinghy, I moved up to the old campsite further upstream. From the old campsite, up the depth, shallows to 0.9 until a rock ledge where 0.4 will be found.

Rocky Creek

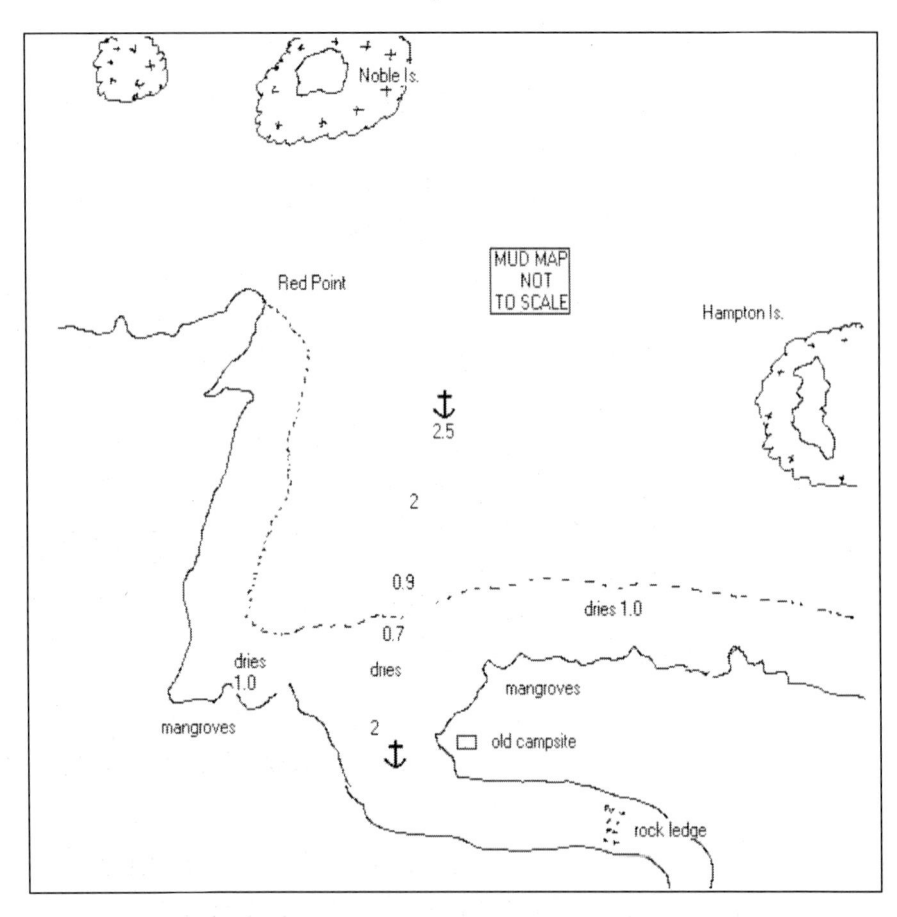

HOWICK ISLANDS

CHART   AUS 832
LIGHTS   **Coquet Island** flashes 5 seconds, visible 10 miles.
Miles Reef flashes 2 every 8 seconds, visible 10 miles.
Howick Island white/green sector flashing 3 every 12 seconds (see chart for sectors), visible white 9 miles, green 7 miles.
Megeera Reef white/green/red sector light flashing every 2.5 seconds, visible white 9 miles, red and green 7 miles (see chart for sectors).
Watson Island flashes 4 every 16 seconds, visible 9 miles.
TIDES   Leggatti Island (Munro Reef) ANTT

The Howick Islands are a natural stopover after leaving Lizard Island.

COQUET ISLAND has an anchorage on the northern side out from the landing for the light maintenance crews. Anchorage can also be found in the lagoon at the eastern end. (Shallow draft vessels only.)

HOWICK ISLAND is 33 miles from Lizard Island. It has a large mangrove forest. Anchorage is in mud in 8 metres out from the northwest corner. The water is murky, hiding many coral heads, so take care. In well-developed winds, a beam swell runs along the shore, and conditions can become uncomfortable.

NEWTON ISLAND is 2 miles west of Howick Island and lies on the northern side of the shipping channel. Anchorage is found on the northern side of the reef in 2 metres over sand and coral.

WATSON ISLAND is a mangrove island with sandy cays at the northern and southern ends of the surrounding reef, but are not connected to the island. They could be visited in suitable light conditions. Anchorage is in 10 metres off the northwest tip of the island. This is definitely a light weather anchorage only. I noticed a few scattered boulders near the light, which exposed at low tide. This is where Mrs Watson died after escaping from Lizard Island in a bêche-de-mer cooking tub.

Coquet Island

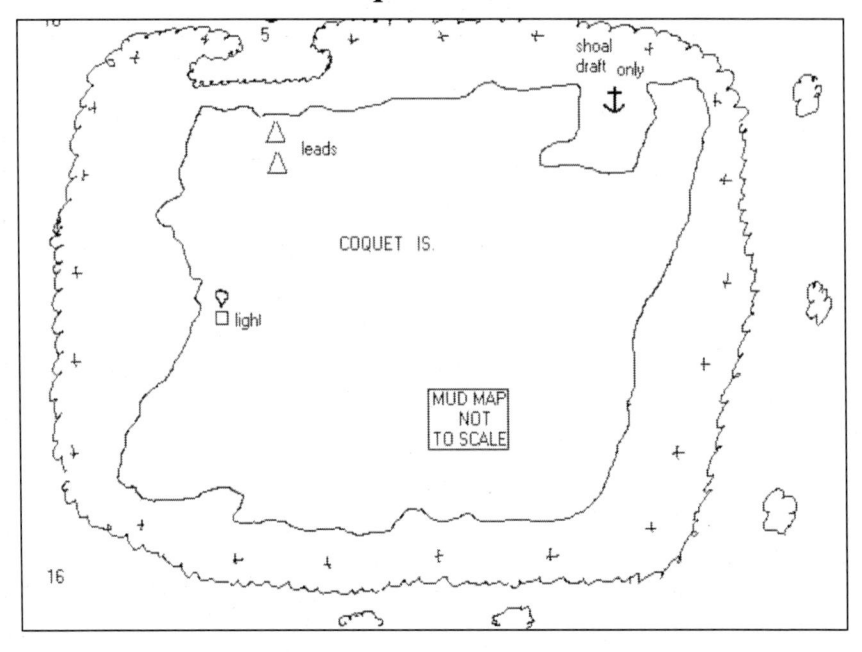

Howick Island

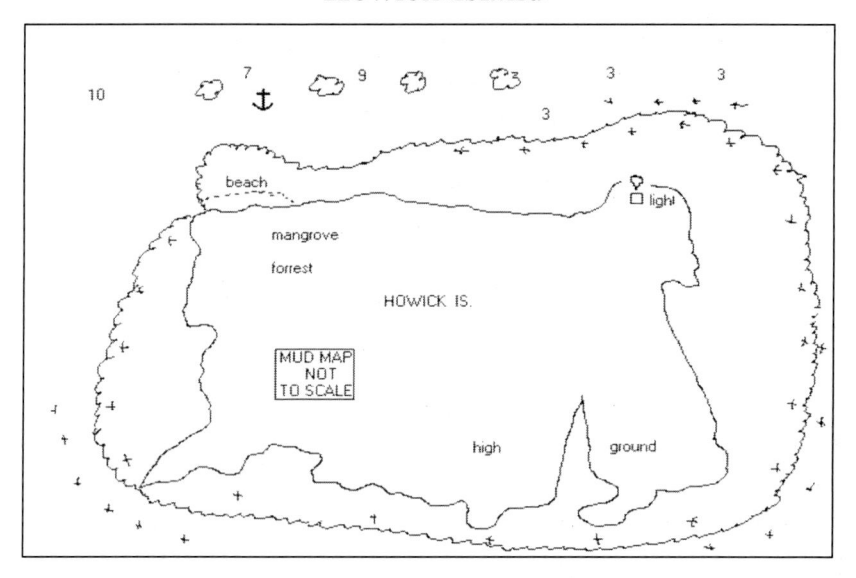

Newton Island

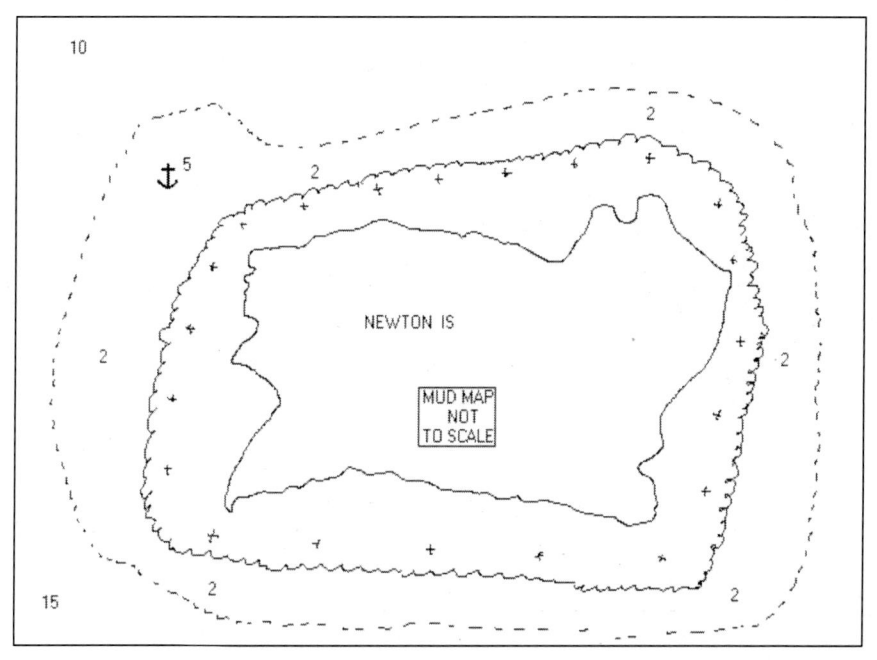

Watson Island

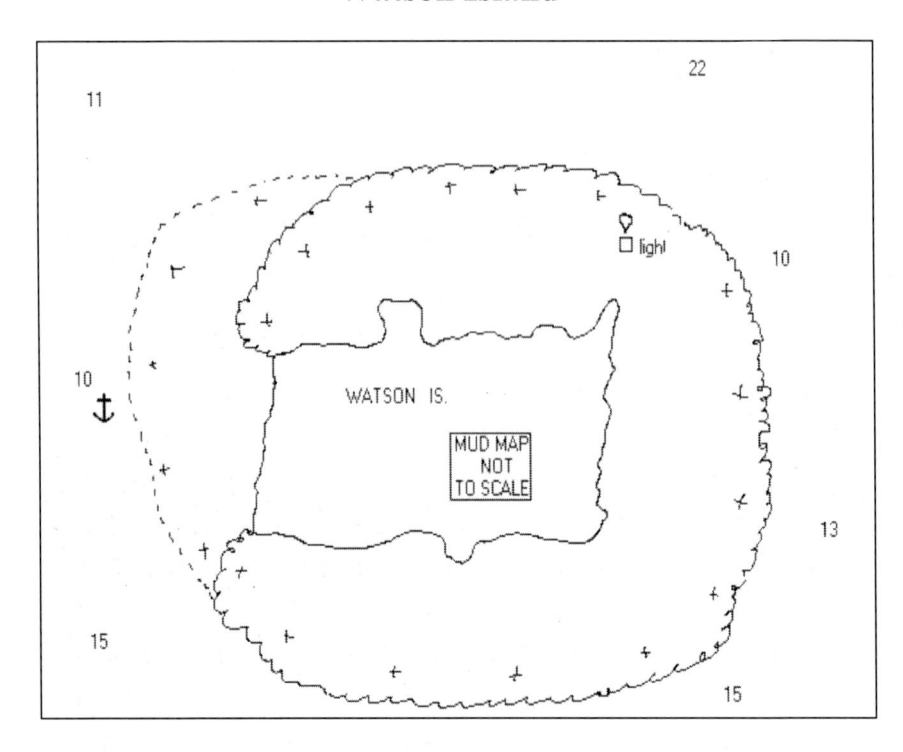

COLE ISLAND GROUP

SINCLAIR ISLAND

14°33.00'S – 144°54.00'E

CHART   AUS 832
LIGHTS   Miles Reef flashes 2 every 8 seconds, visible 10 miles.
TIDES   Cairns (Howick Island) ANTT

Anchorage here is on the northern side of Sinclair Island in 4 metres over sandy mud. It is reasonably comfortable in winds to 10 knots, and reasonably tenable to 15 knots. The channel between Hampton and Sinclair islands has deep water, except in the centre, where 3 metres will be encountered. There is deep water between Sinclair Island and Miles Reef. When entering from the south, go past Sinclair Island, then come in from the north, as there is a sand-spit extending out from the western side of the island, and there is reef out from the northeast corner, both for some distance. There is no passage between Sinclair and Morris islands.

Sinclair Island

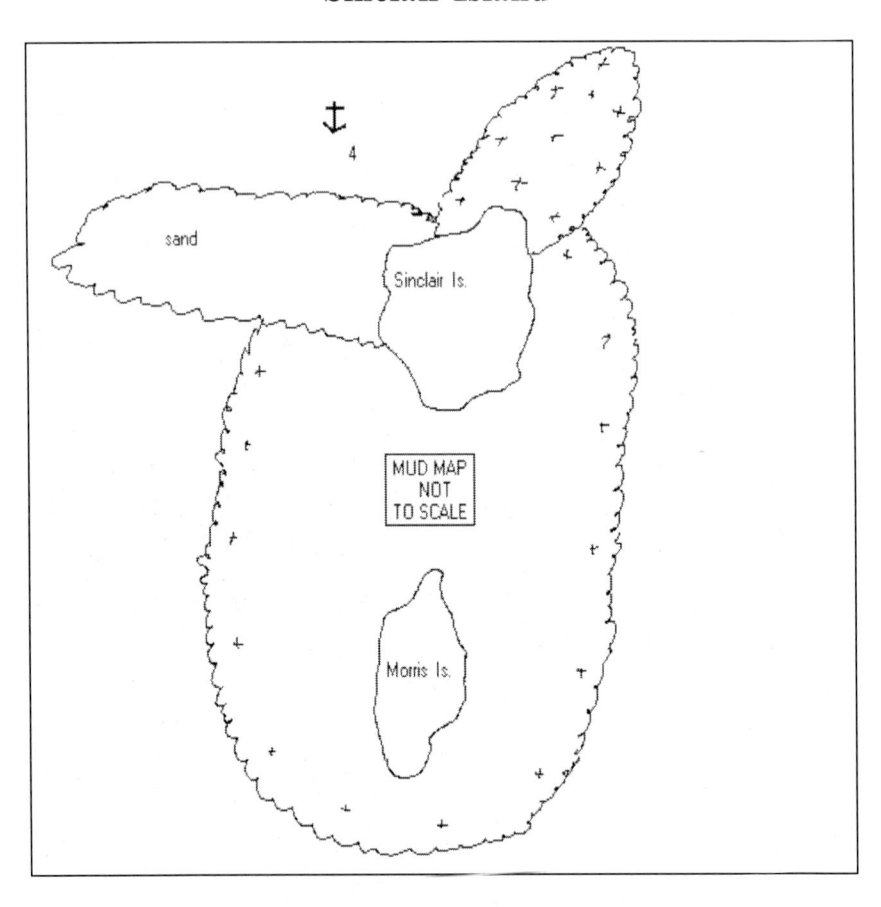

INGRAM ISLAND

CHART AUS 832
LIGHTS Watson Island flashes 4 every 16 seconds, visible 9 miles.
TIDES Leggatti Island (Munro Reef) ANTT

Ingram Island is to the north of Watson Island and shares the same reef as the Beanley Islet group, but lies on the northern end. There is a wrap around beach on the northern side of the island, which gives good shelter, even in strong winds. The bay has scattered coral heads throughout, so care is needed to enter. I have ridden out 35 knots here in complete comfort. My waypoint for the best anchorage is 14°25.10′S and 144°52.47′E. When coming in to the anchorage, it is recommended that a wide berth be given. Come in from the north to avoid the hidden dangers.

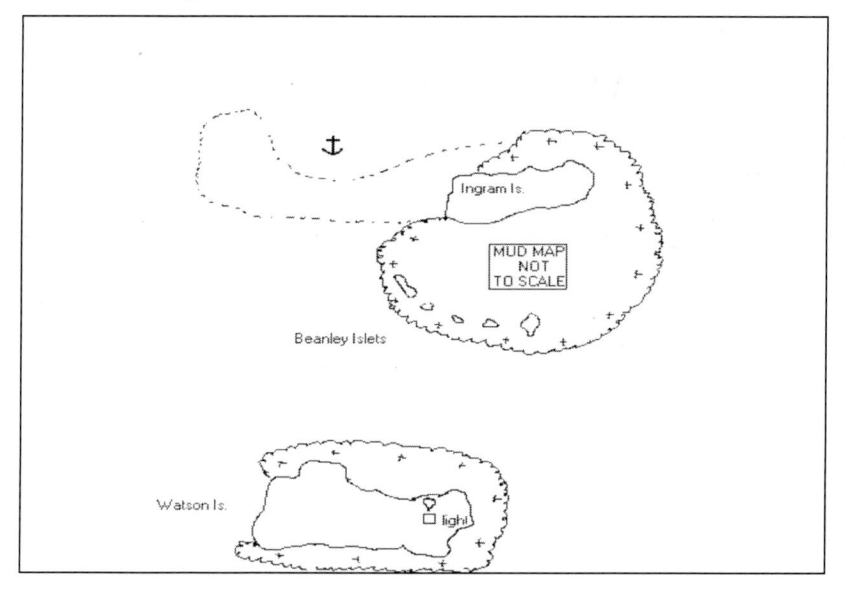

NOBLE ISLAND

CHART AUS 832
LIGHTS Nil
TIDES Leggatti Island (Munro Reef) ANTT

Noble Island is a calm weather anchorage only, and is found 2.4 miles north of Red Point. Anchorage is in 3 metres out from the western shore. Take care to clear the numerous reefs around the island. It is a dull sort of island, but does give the opportunity to stretch your legs. There was a gold and copper mine here once, but it was not productive. Now there is only rusting machinery.

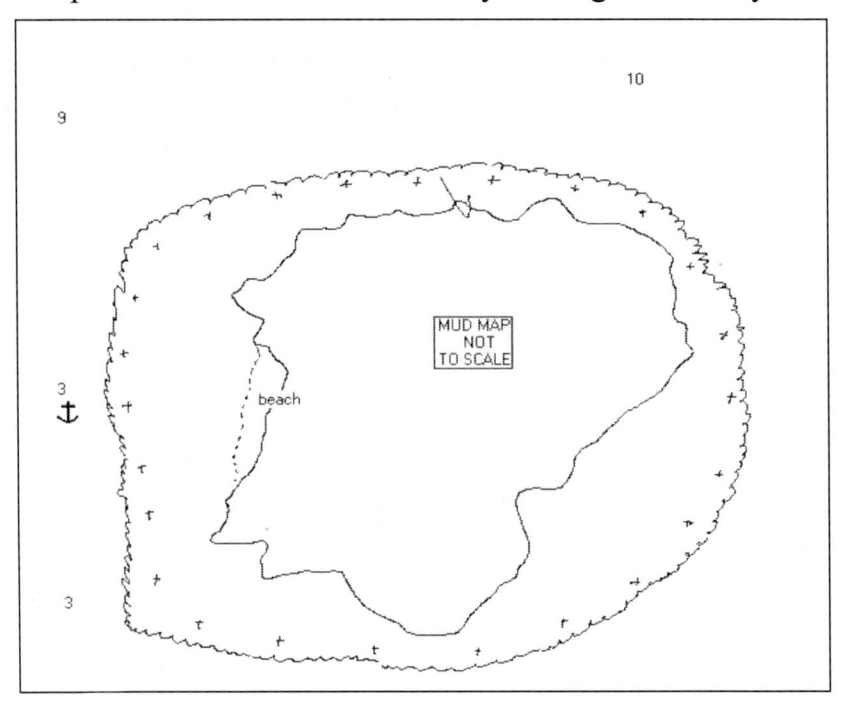

MUD MAP NOT TO SCALE

BARROW ISLAND – (New)

CHART AUS 832
LIGHTS Barrow Island flashes 5 seconds red/white
Green sector light (see chart for sectors).
Red and white visible 10 miles, green 7 miles.
TIDES Leggatti Island (Munro Reef) ANTT

This is quite a secure anchorage. When entering come in from the northern side, but stay out wide, as there is extensive reef around the island. Anchor off the northwest corner in 3 metres out from the drying sandbank. When leaving, return the same way as you entered until deep water is found.

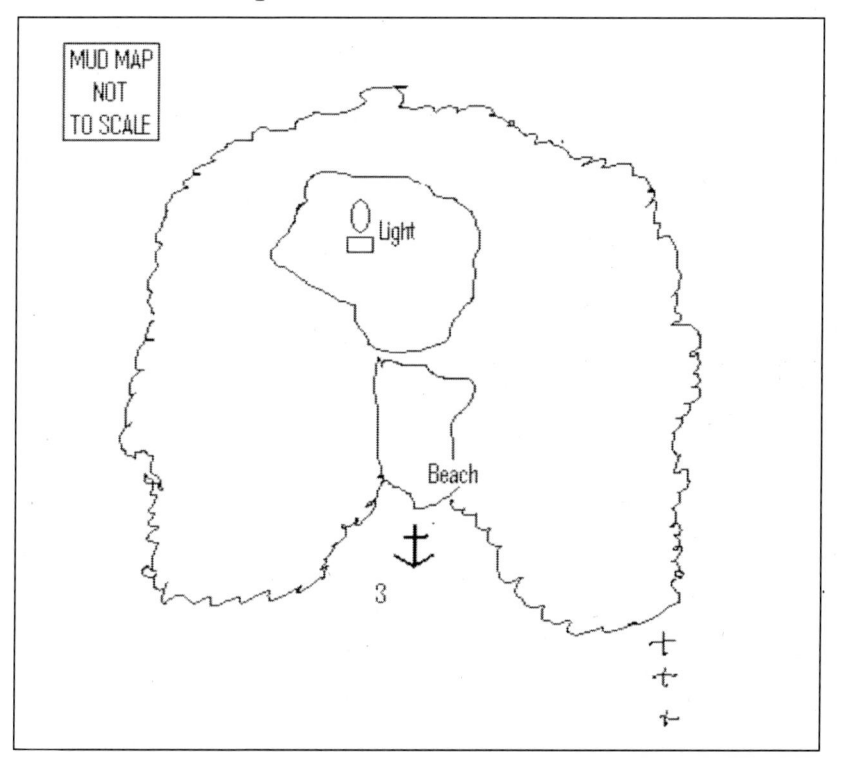

NINIAN BAY

CHART   AUS 832
LIGHTS   Barrow Island shows a red/white/green sector light (see chart for sectors) flashing every 5 seconds. The red and white sectors are visible for 10 miles, and the green sector is visible for 7 miles.
TIDES   Leggatti Island (Munro Reef) ANTT

Ninian Bay is some 22 miles northwest of the Howick Islands and is to the west of Barrow Island. It provides a tolerable anchorage. The best I have found to be at waypoint 14°21.40′E – 144°36.76′S. I rode out 37 knots in comfort and safety. Anchor in two metres over sandy mud and seagrass; this dictates anchor security. An admiralty anchor may be necessary. Beware of the shallows to the west and north of Barrow Island. This is the recommended entry, as the passage to the south of Barrow Island was found to only have 2 metres.

Ninian Bay

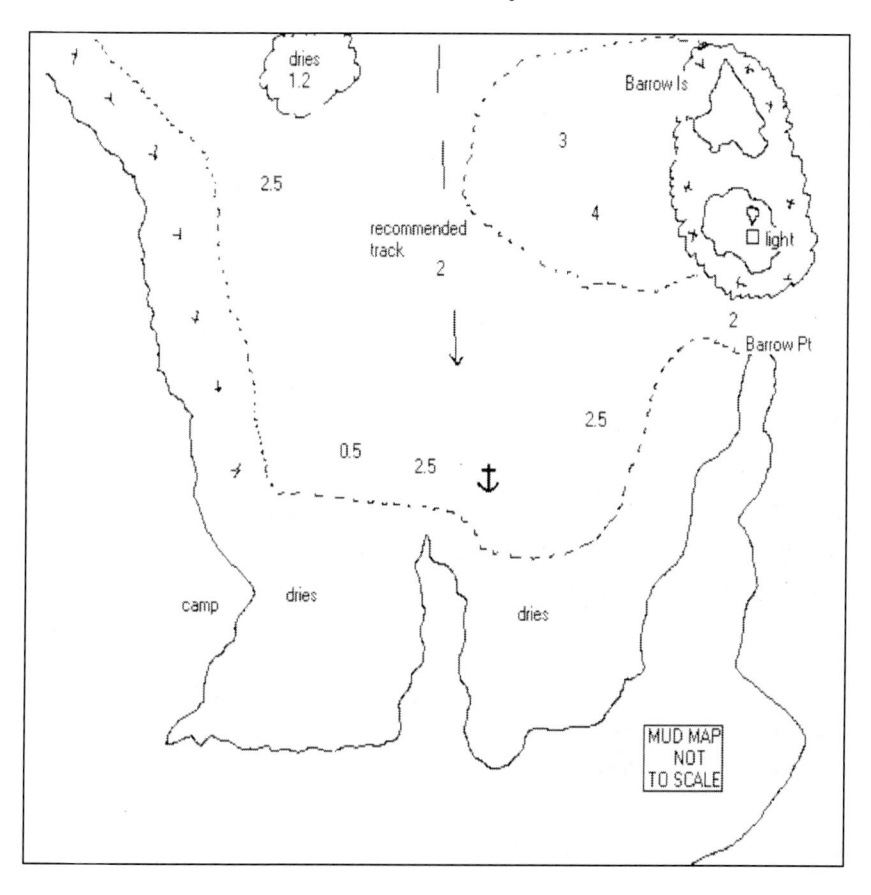

PIPON ISLETS

CHART AUS 833
LIGHTS Pipon Island red/white sector light (see chart for sectors) flashes 3 every 15 seconds, visible white 10 miles, red 7 miles.
TIDES Cairns (Pipon Island) ANTT

The Pipon Islets lie to the north of Cape Melville. There are six islets in the group with the light being situated on the small southwest islet. Anchorage is behind the big islet in 4–8 metres out from the fringing reef off the northwest corner, where you are sheltered behind the mangroves. Although I did not see any sign of crocodiles, it is a good bet that there would be one here. This is only a calm weather anchorage; it is reasonably comfortable in winds up to around 10 knots.

Pipon Islets

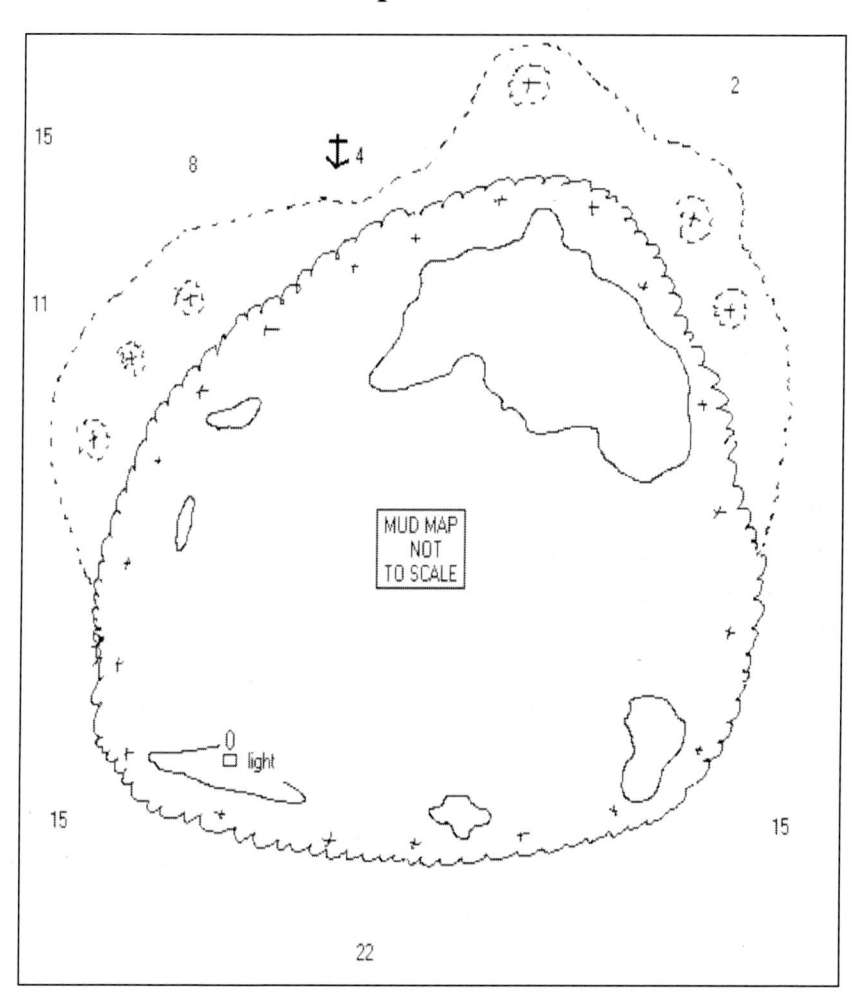

KING ISLAND

CHART   AUS 833
LIGHTS   King Island flashes 2 every 6 seconds, visible 10 miles.
TIDES   Cairns (Pipon Island) ANTT

King Island is found to the west of the Pipon Islets and northeast of Flinders Island. Anchorage is along the western side, out from the reef edge in 5 metres towards the light. The best way is to go around the northern end of the island to avoid the shallow patches at the southern end and Atkinson Reef. The shelter here is better than the Pipon Islets to the east. The fishing is good, however I did see what looked like old crocodile tracks, and although I saw neither fresh tracks nor the crocodile, take care. I was secure and comfortable here in 15 knots of southeast winds, and should expect that it would remain the same in winds up to 20–25 knots. Swell from the shipping channel can be a bit of a problem, but it only lasts a short time.

King Island

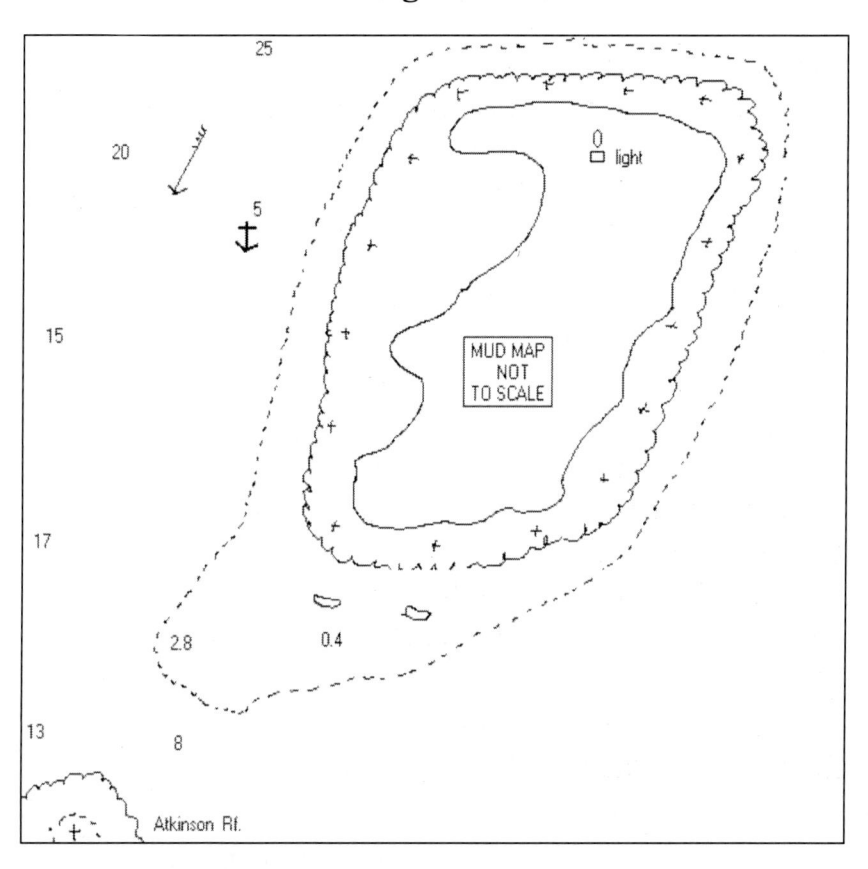

BATHURST BAY and FLINDERS GROUP

CHARTS AUS 833/280
LIGHTS **Pipon Island** has a white/red sector light (see chart for sectors) flashing 3 times every 15 seconds, visible white 10 miles, red 7 miles.
King Island flashes twice every 6 seconds, visible for 7 miles.
TIDES Leggatti Is. (Pipon Island) (Flinders Island) ANTT
CAUTION There is a 2-metre crocodile in the Flinders Island Creek, which is on the Owen Channel side of the island.

Bathurst Bay is 17 miles north of Ninian Bay and lies to the west of Cape Melville. From Ninian Bay, it is recommended that a distance of 1.5 miles offshore to clear coastal shoals, and a maximum of 3.25 miles to clear offshore reefs, be held. After rounding Cape Melville, course can be taken to the south of Boulder Rock in 6 metres, however a course around the outside is recommended. Once in the bay, stay well out to clear the shoal area to the west of the cape. Anchorage can be taken anywhere along the length of the bay in 2.5 metres over sand and mud. Seagrass can be a bit of a problem. Dugongs are often seen in this area. They are protected animals. Cape Melville is not a real good anchorage, as 15–20 knots outside will create 30–40 knots behind the cape. The Owen Channel at Flinders Island is by far the better of the two.

FLINDERS ISLAND is 15 miles west of Cape Melville and provides good shelter between Cape Melville and Princess Charlotte Bay. Ashore at Flinders Island, behind the mangroves well above high tide mark, is a boulder with the name of the ship that surveyed the area chiselled into it with the old convict sign above it. This is the Datum mark of H.M.S. *Dart*. The well is no longer useable. Supply ships service the area every 3–4 days. Ashore at the bottom of the cliffs, there is a cleared circular area with four graves of white men. There was once a flourishing trading post here, and a British garrison was stationed here in the 1800s.

CROCODILE ALERT

On three consecutive days, 27/5/04 to 31/5/04, four crocodiles were sighted on the sandspit in the Owen Channel. One was 4 metres (13 feet), one 3 metres (10 feet) and two 1.5 metres (5 feet). A fifth, sighted on the beach at the National Park facility, was 4 metres (13 feet).

Flinders Island

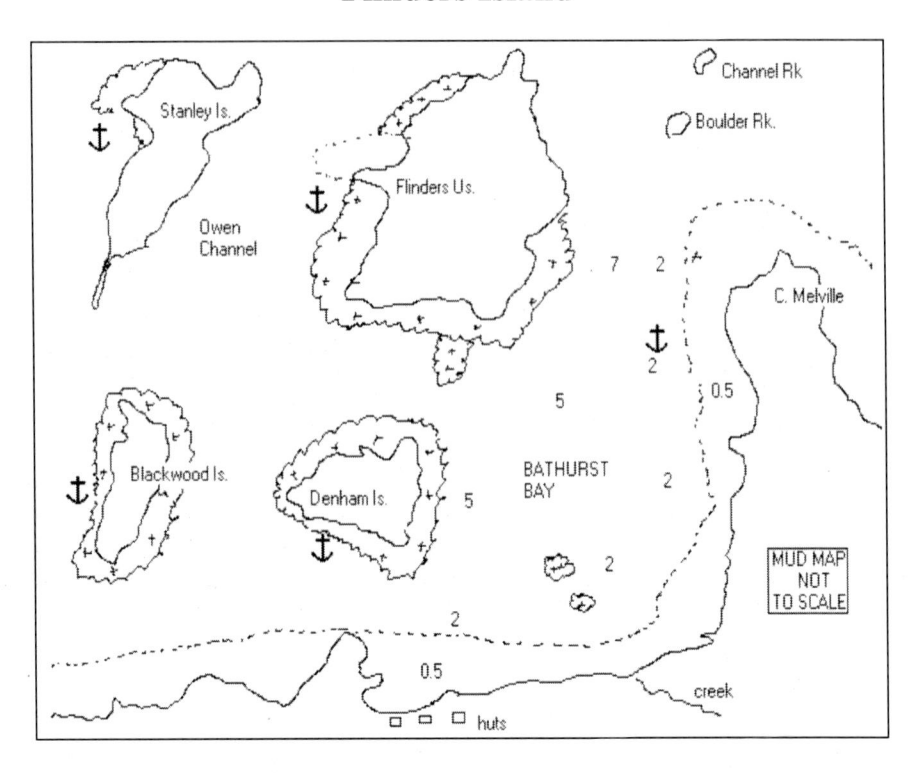

BLACKWOOD ISLAND – (New)
(FLINDERS GROUP)

CHART   AUS 833
LIGHTS   Nil
TIDES   Leggatti Island (Flinders Island) ANTT

A secure anchorage away from the bullets of Flinders Island. Anchor out from the fringing reef in 5 metres. Protected from most winds except west and northwest. There is very little swell, but no beach.

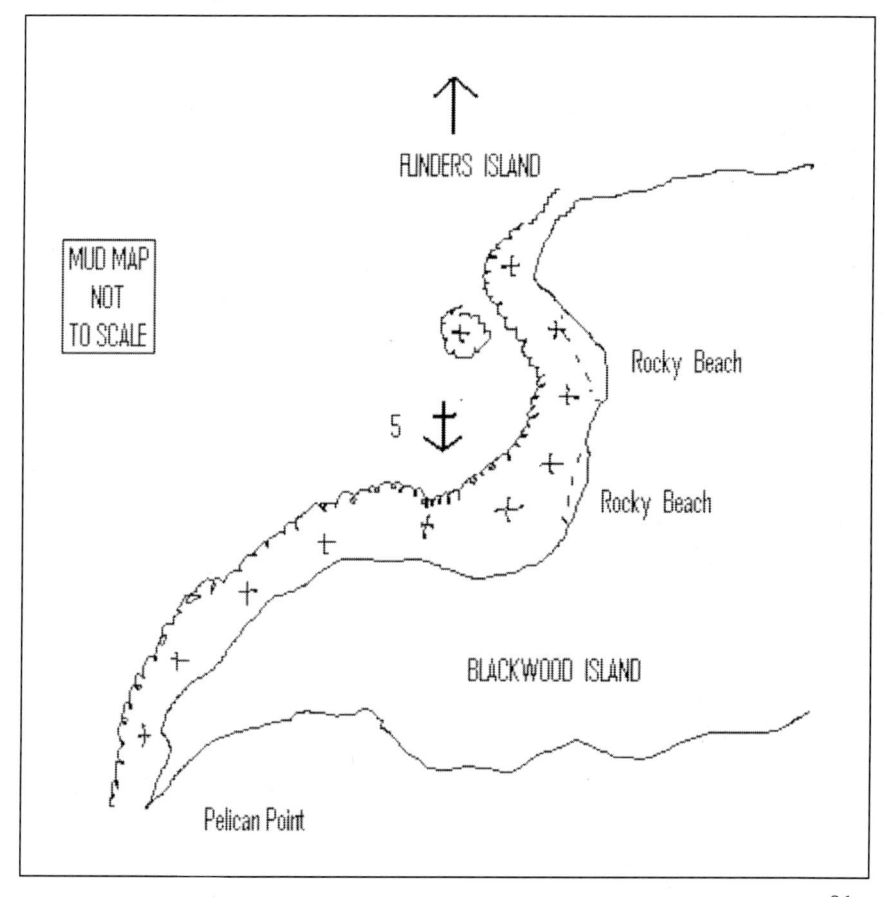

MACLEAN ISLAND – (New)
(FLINDERS GROUP)

CHART   AUS 833
LIGHTS   Nil
TIDES   Leggatti Island (Flinders Island) ANTT

This anchorage is only suitable in winds up to 10 knots. Anchor in 8 metres out from the fringing reef. It may also be possible to anchor in a clear area over the reef. The large sand spit dries, giving access to a large area to explore.

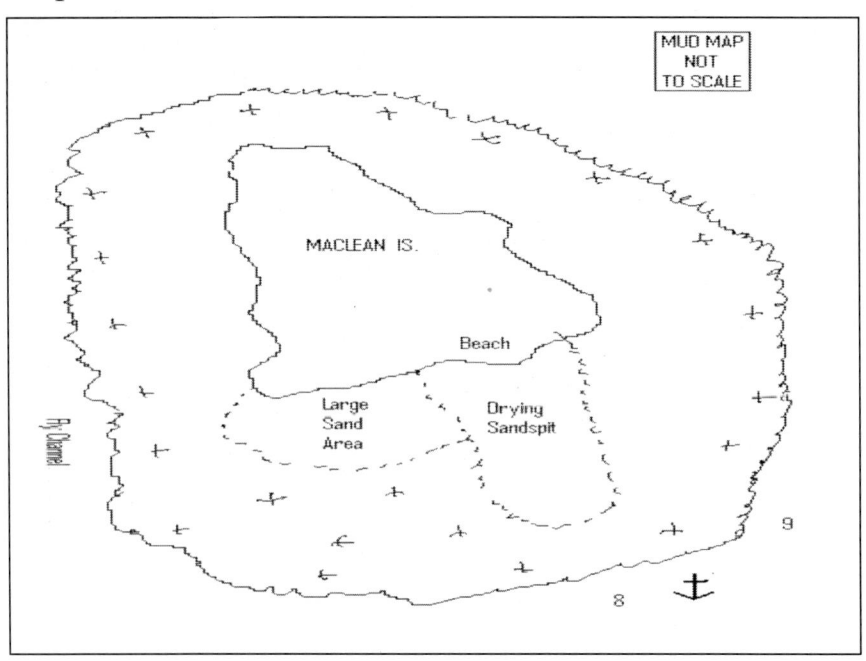

UNNAMED ISLAND – (New)

West of MACLEAN ISLAND

(FLINDERS GROUP)

This island is found west of Maclean Island. On the western side, a drying sand spit joins to two beaches. Anchor out from the reef face in 6 metres. It is a calm weather anchorage, up to 10 knots. If intending to try to anchor over the reef, be aware of the drying rock off the southwest corner.

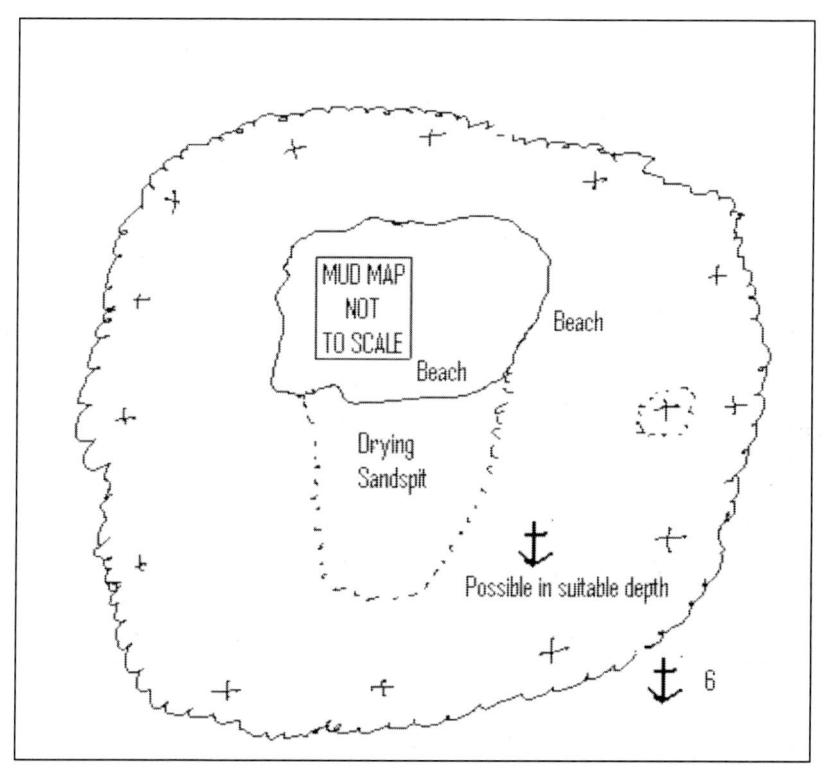

HENNING POINT, STANLEY ISLAND
(New)

CHARTS   AUS 833, 280
LIGHTS   Nil
TIDES   Leggatti Island (Flinders Island) ANTT

This anchorage is at the southern end of Stanley Island. It is secure in 10–15 knots. When coming from the Owen Channel, give Henning Point a clearance of at least 0.25 miles to clear the reef area. Anchor in 5 metres between the two beaches. There are two balancing rocks just north of the first beach. I anchor just past them.

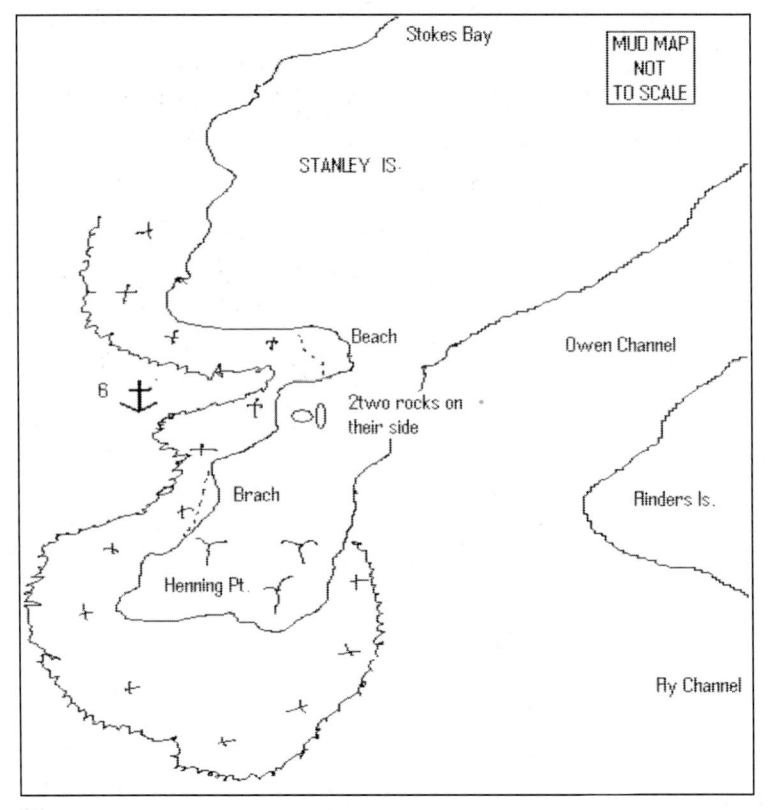

STOKES BAY

CHART AUS 833
LIGHTS Nil
TIDES Leggatti Island (Flinders Island) ANTT

Stokes Bay is the large bay on the western side of Stanley Island and is part of the Flinders Group. This is a more comfortable and secure anchorage than the Owen Channel on the eastern side. Although the bay has considerable reef areas, and it is necessary to anchor well out, it is still well sheltered. I spent three weeks here, with strong wind warnings, in complete safety and comfort. Those interested in walking will find plenty to do. On the steep hills to the northern end of the bay, there is a well about half way up. Right on the top is a flat area where a radar emplacement was located in World War 2. The reef can be crossed by dinghy safely, giving access to the shelly beach. In suitably calm conditions, there is a nice sandy beach on the northern side of the island, where anchorage can be found out from the fringing reef. You need to pick your tide to cross the reef, but the effort is worthwhile.

Stokes Bay

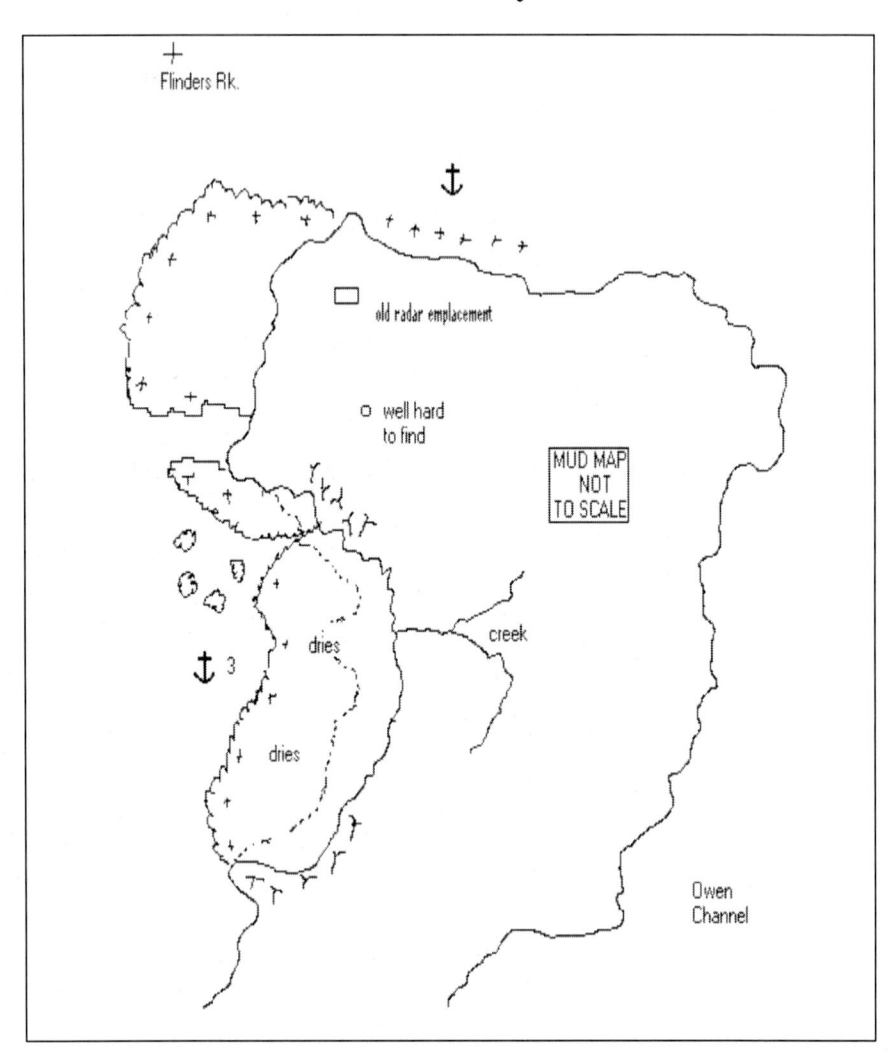

PRINCESS CHARLOTTE BAY

CHART   AUS 830
LIGHTS Nil
TIDES   Leggatti Island (Flinders Island) ANTT

Princess Charlotte Bay is a vast area to the west of Bathurst Head. The waters are murky and not very deep. The rivers are navigable, but are barred by drying mud. Ship's draft plus a bit is required to enter. The rivers have deep water, but hold nothing much of interest except to offer a secure place to anchor or to go crabbing. The Kennedy River is the easiest one to enter.

The waypoints to enter are:

1	14°26.950'S	143°59.160'E
2	14°27.470'S	143°58.850'E
3	14°27.800'S	143°58.500'E
4	14°28.570'S	143°57.860'E
5	14°28.820'S	143°57.700'E
6	14°29.157'S	143°57.325'E

Kennedy River

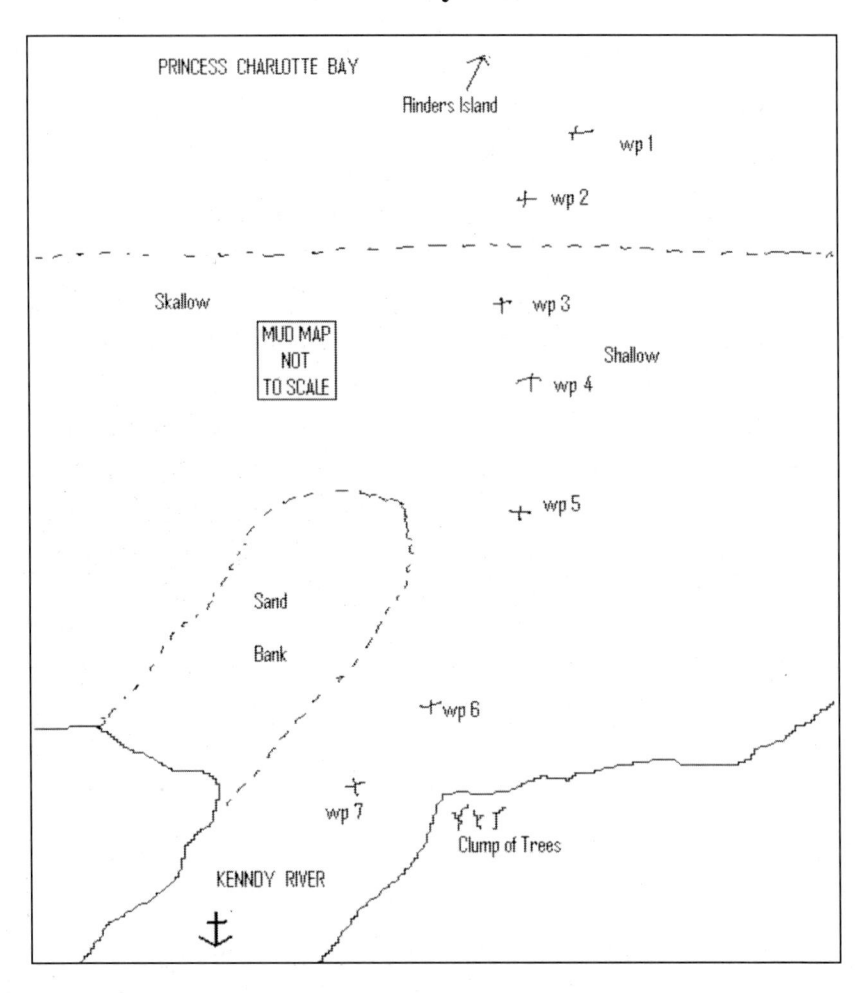

HEDGE REEF

CHART AUS 833
LIGHTS Nil
TIDES Leggatti Island (Pelican Island) ANTT

Hedge Reef is about 24 miles northwest of Flinders Island. It is a secure anchorage over shoaling sand with isolated coral heads. I anchored in 5 metres to the south of Kestrel Reef. Anchorage is good in developed winds from the east and southeast. When coming from the south, favour Iris Reef; there are many uncharted coral heads. There is a large sand cay along the northern side of the reef with good landing. At high tide, a small sea crosses the reef, but the anchorage stays calm. The water is murky, so a forward lookout and slow speed is recommended. A delightful anchorage.

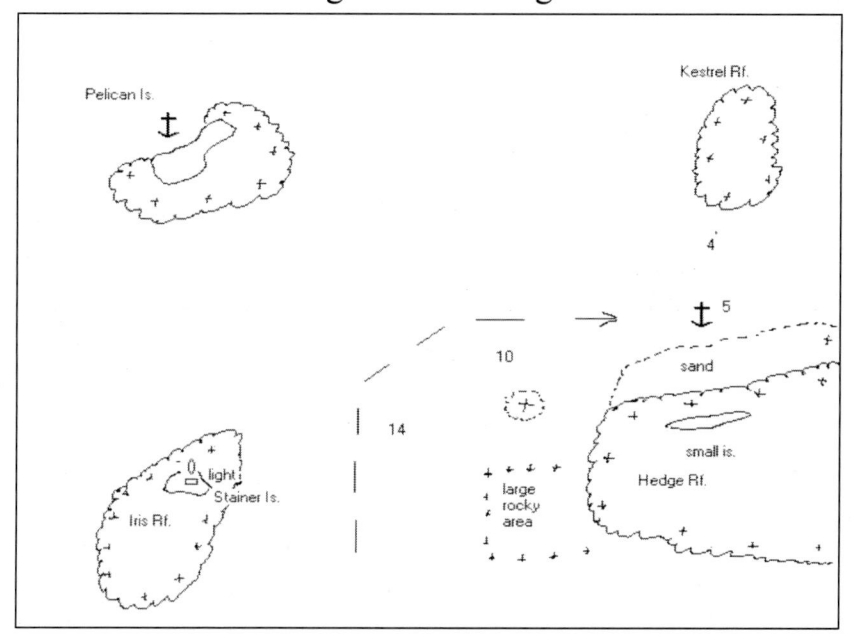

BURKITT ISLAND

CHART   AUS 833
LIGHTS Nil
TIDES   Leggatti Island (Pelican Island) ANTT

Burkitt Island is a mangrove island. The mangroves cover practically the entire reef. There is a sandy cay along the north and northwest sides. The only anchorage is off the northwest corner in 10 metres. It is definitely a calm weather anchorage, as it is extremely uncomfortable in any developed wind strength.

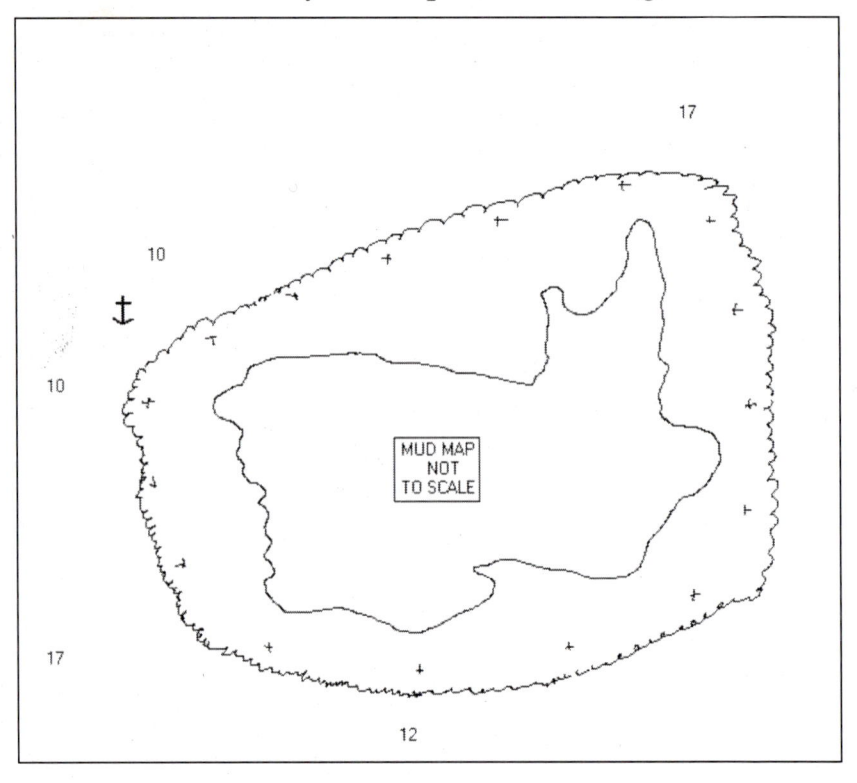

PELICAN ISLAND

CHART AUS 833
LIGHTS Stainer Island flashes green/white/red 4 every 10 seconds, visible green 10 miles, white 14 miles, red 11 miles.
TIDES Leggatti Island (Pelican Island) ANTT

Pelican Island is to the northeast of Hedge Reef. It is a small island on a large surrounding reef. The anchorage is on the western side of the island out from the sandy beach in 8 metres over sand. It is quite comfortable in winds to 10 knots. A nice spot to spend a few days.

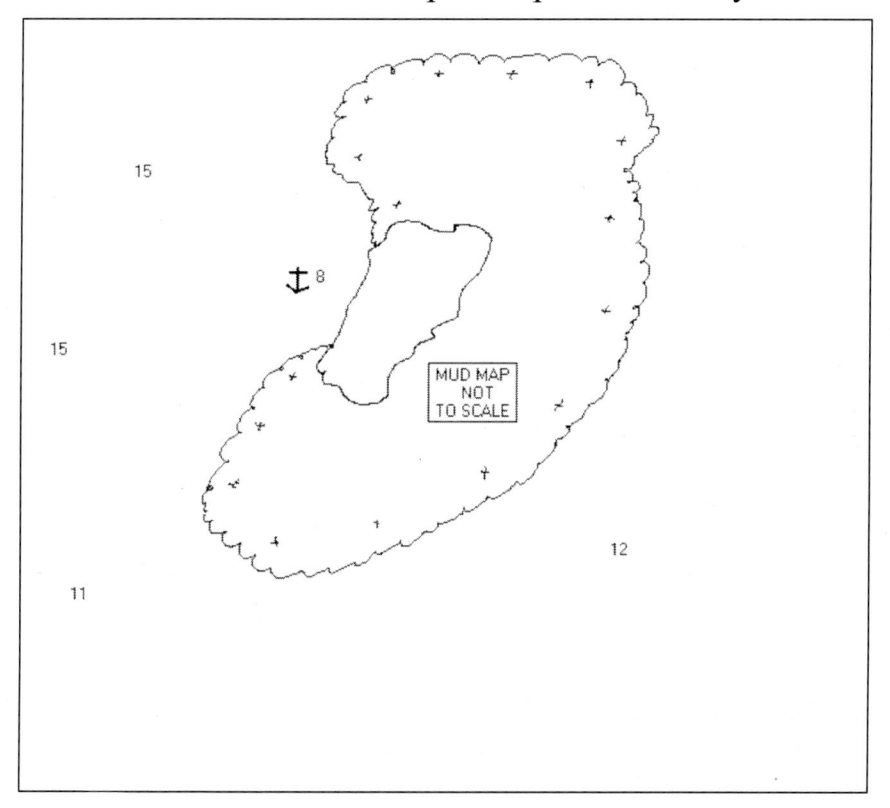

HANNAH ISLAND

CHARTS AUS 833, 834
LIGHTS Hannah Island flashes 3 every 15 seconds, visible 10 miles.
TIDES Leggatti Island (Pelican Island) ANTT

Hannah Island is one of many cays found close to the mainland. It is covered in mangroves. The only safe anchorage is in 8 metres out from the light. There is a small beach here. During the prawn season, trawlers will be seen anchored here during the day. Hannah Island is not comfortable in winds over around 15 knots. There is extensive reef surrounding the island, so stay out in deep water until able to come straight in to the light. The reef face rises steeply, rather suddenly, so take care.

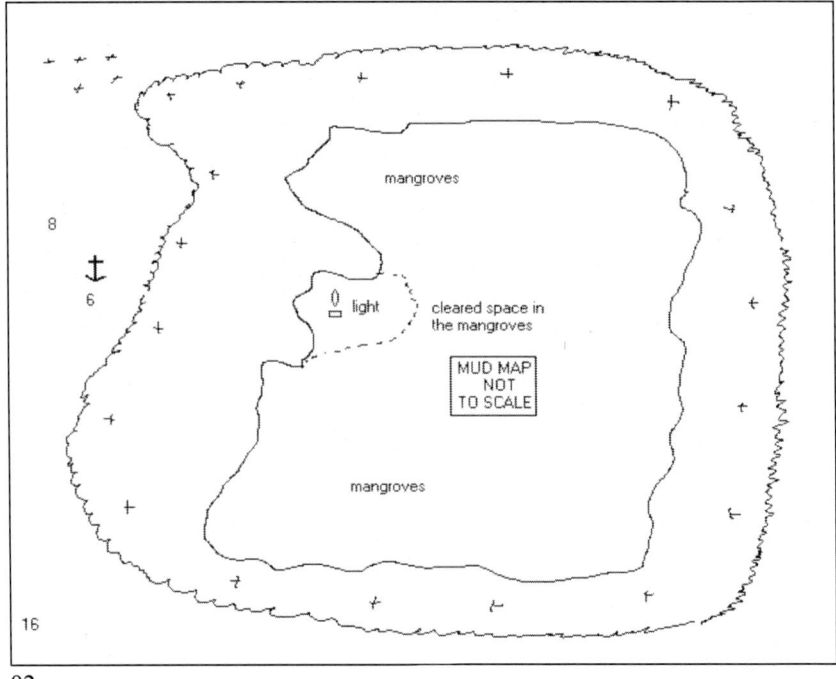

WILKIE ISLAND

CHART   AUS 834
LIGHTS Nil
TIDES   Leggatti Island (Fife Island) ANTT

Wilkie Island lies on the western side of the shipping channel. It is 5.75 miles off the mainland. It is another mangrove islet and is a dull speck in the ocean. Anchor in 7 metres out from the sandy beach at the northwest corner in good holding mud. This is another calm weather anchorage. You roll or the sandflies let you know that your presence is most welcome.

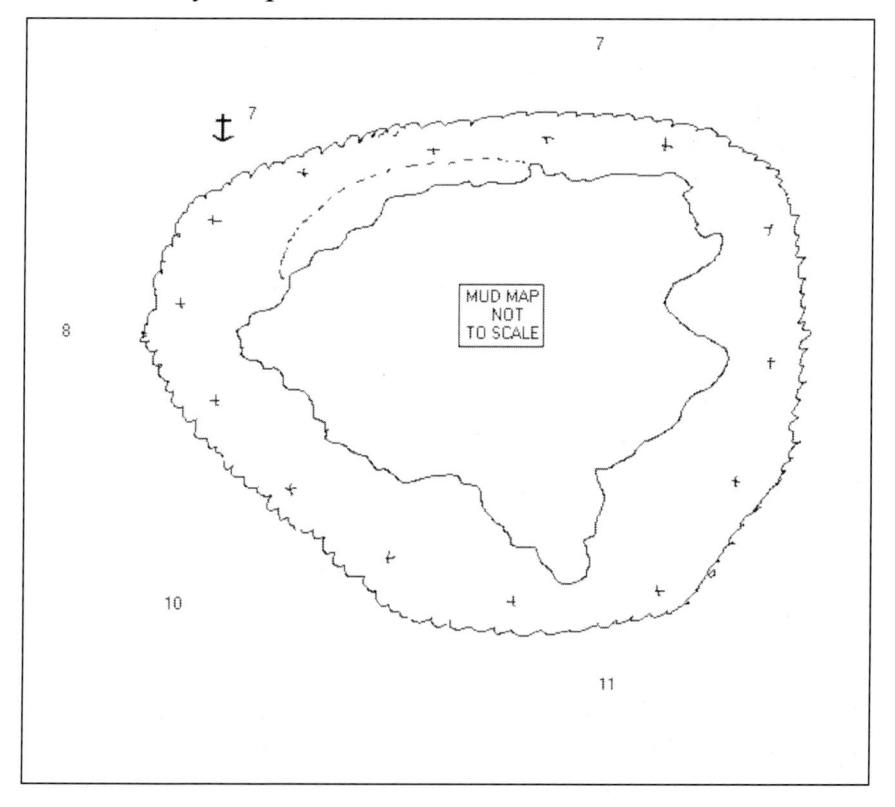

MUD MAP NOT TO SCALE

FIFE ISLAND

CHART AUS 833
LIGHTS Fife Island flashes 2 every 5 seconds, visible 10 miles.
TIDES Leggatti Island (Fife Island) ANTT

This is a well-sheltered anchorage. The island is surrounded by beaches and protected by off-lying sand cays and reef. Anchor on the northern side in 10 metres over sand. Trawlers anchor here during the day. The anchorage is comfortable in winds around 15 knots. The sea covers the reef at high tide, but does not cause any problems.

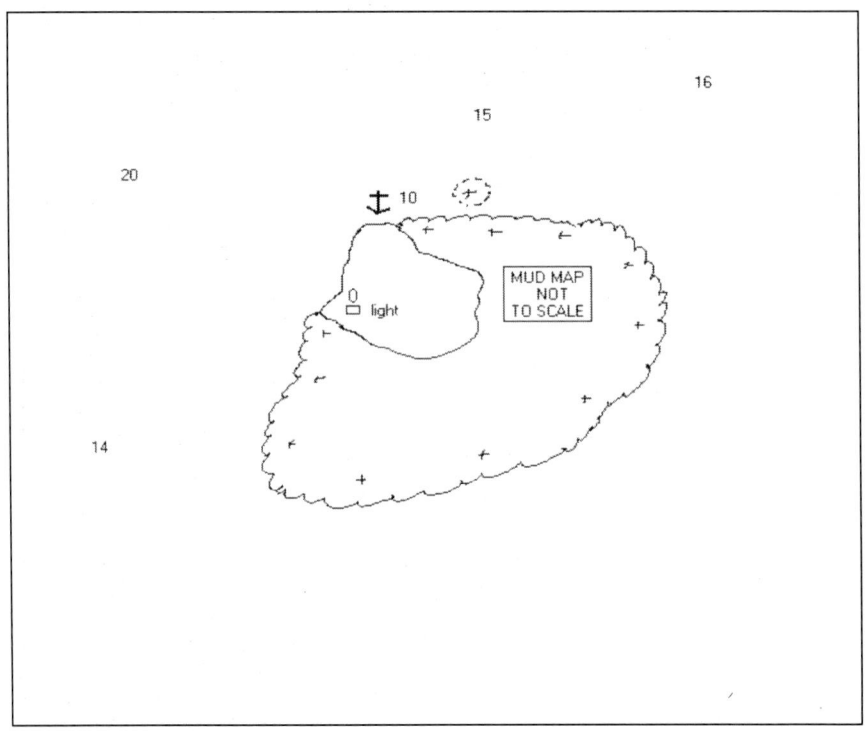

MUD MAP NOT TO SCALE

NODDY REEF

CHART   AUS 834
LIGHTS   Fife Island flashes 2.5 seconds, visible 10 miles.
TIDES   Leggatti Island (Fife Island) ANTT

Noddy Reef lies northeast of Wilkie Island. Anchorage is over sand and coral in 6 metres, about midway along its western side. Numerous coral heads require careful navigation. The anchorage is surprisingly comfortable in most winds. Approaching from the south, there is a good navigation mark off the southern end, in the shape of a very large boulder, which really stands out at low tide. I anchored in the reasonably clear area southeast of Fife Island. A forward lookout is recommended.

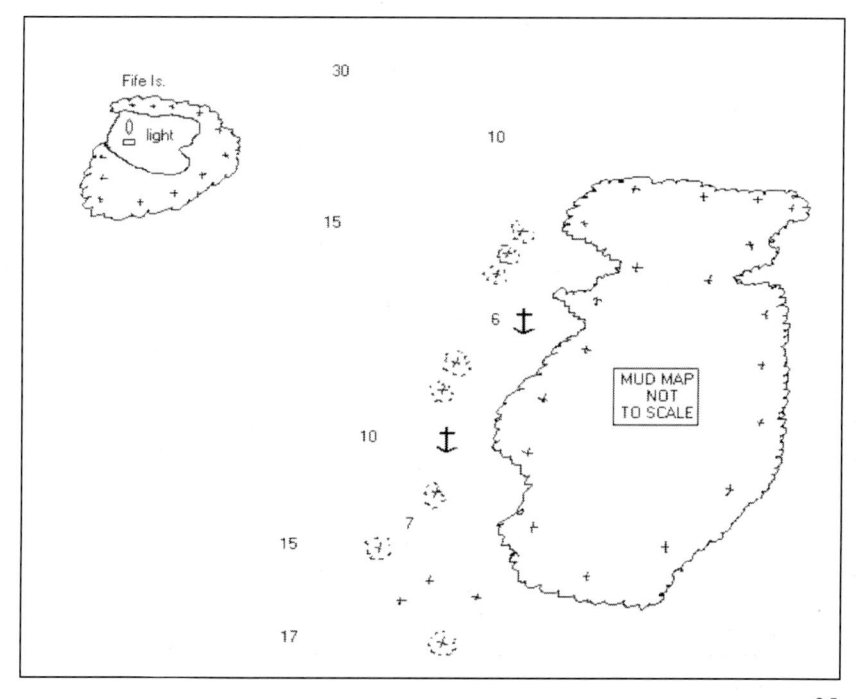

MORRIS ISLAND

CHART   AUS 834
LIGHTS Heath Reef flashes white/red sector light (see chart for sectors) flashes 3 times every 15 seconds, visible for white 11 miles, red for 8 miles.
TIDES   Leggatti Island (Morris Island) ANTT

Morris Island is found approximately 11 miles north of Fife Island. Anchorage is in 3 metres over sand, out from the break in the reef off the northern side. A nice beach here provides good dinghy landing. Located at the southern end is a lone coconut tree with a diver's grave nearby. The holding is excellent and developed winds from the east or south can be ridden out in safety. The southern side of the island yields interesting beachcombing. There is a vast area of sand to explore on low tide, which extends all the way out to the outer edge of the reef.

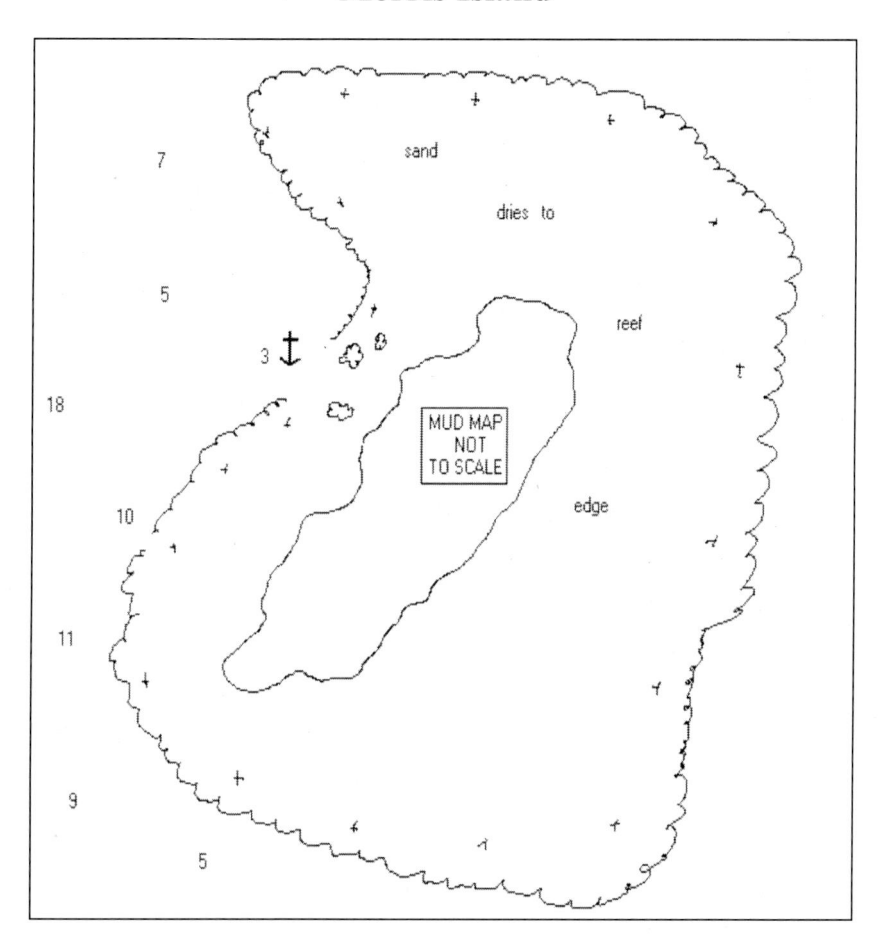

Morris Island

NIGHT ISLAND

CHART AUS 834
LIGHTS Nil
TIDES Leggatti Island (Night Island) ANTT

Night Island is the logical stopover before Portland Roads or the Lockhart River. Anchorage can be found off the beach at the northwest corner of the island. Anchor in 9–10 metres over good holding mud. Night Island is 4 miles out from the mainland and is home to thousands of noisy Torres Strait pigeons.

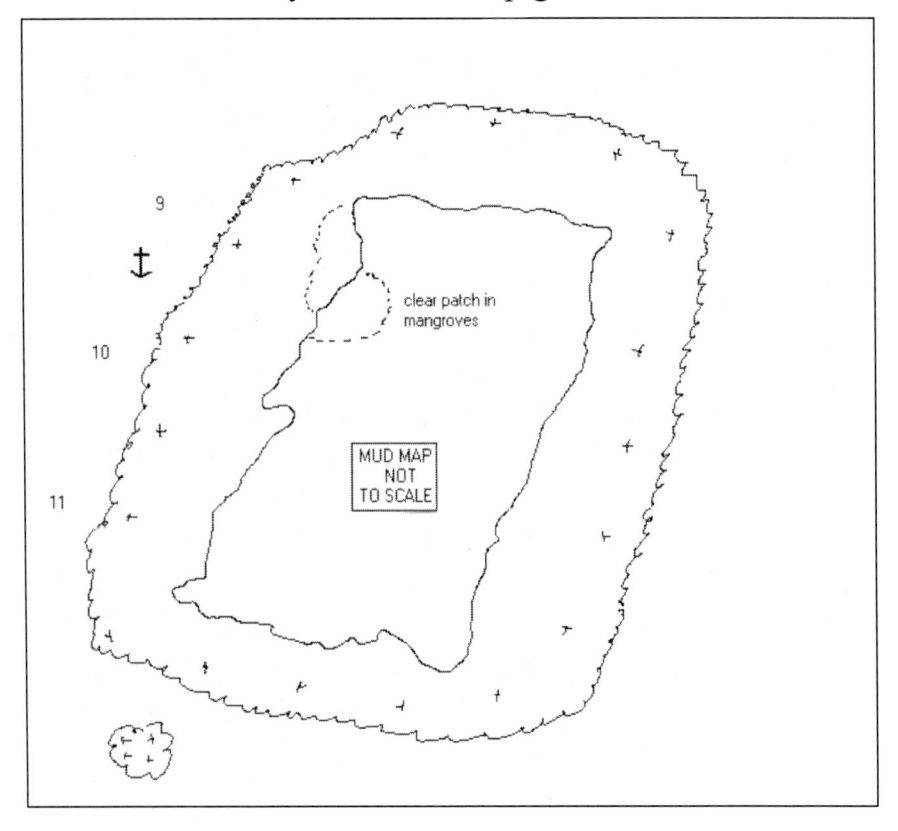

LLOYD BAY ANCHORAGES

CHART AUS 834
LIGHTS Qintell Beach Barge landing flashes isolated 2 seconds and quick yellow.
TIDES Leggatti Is (Restoration Island) ANTT

There are six anchorages in the area of Lloyd Bay. The first is out from **ORCHID POINT**; holding is good over sandy mud in 2 metres. Next is the **LOCKHART RIVER**, which is readily accessible and can be navigated for some distance. It is a maze of other creeks and rivers. Anchorage is in mud in the middle of the river, away from the friendly sandfly population. Drying mud banks, which can only be crossed at high tide, block the three mouths of the river. Once inside, anchor where depths allow. There are two places to anchor while waiting for the tide. The first is out from **ALMOND POINT** in 2–3 metres. The second is in the indentation to the west of the river, again in 2–3 metres of mud. Northwest of the Lockhart River is the **CLAUDIE RIVER**; the entrance dries 0.9 metres. There is a sandbar, so a high tide is necessary to enter. Once inside, anchor in midstream in 3 metres or where depth allows. Along the northern bank there are numerous huts belonging to the Lockhart River Mission people. To the north of the barge landing is **LLOYD ISLAND**. Anchorage can be found on the western side in 2 metres. Do not go too far north, as there is an area of 0.8 between the island and the mainland.

Just to the north of Cape Griffith is **ALBATROSS BAY**, where a reasonable anchorage can be found in 3 metres. It is a calm weather anchorage only, and is a bit prone to swell from the shipping channel.

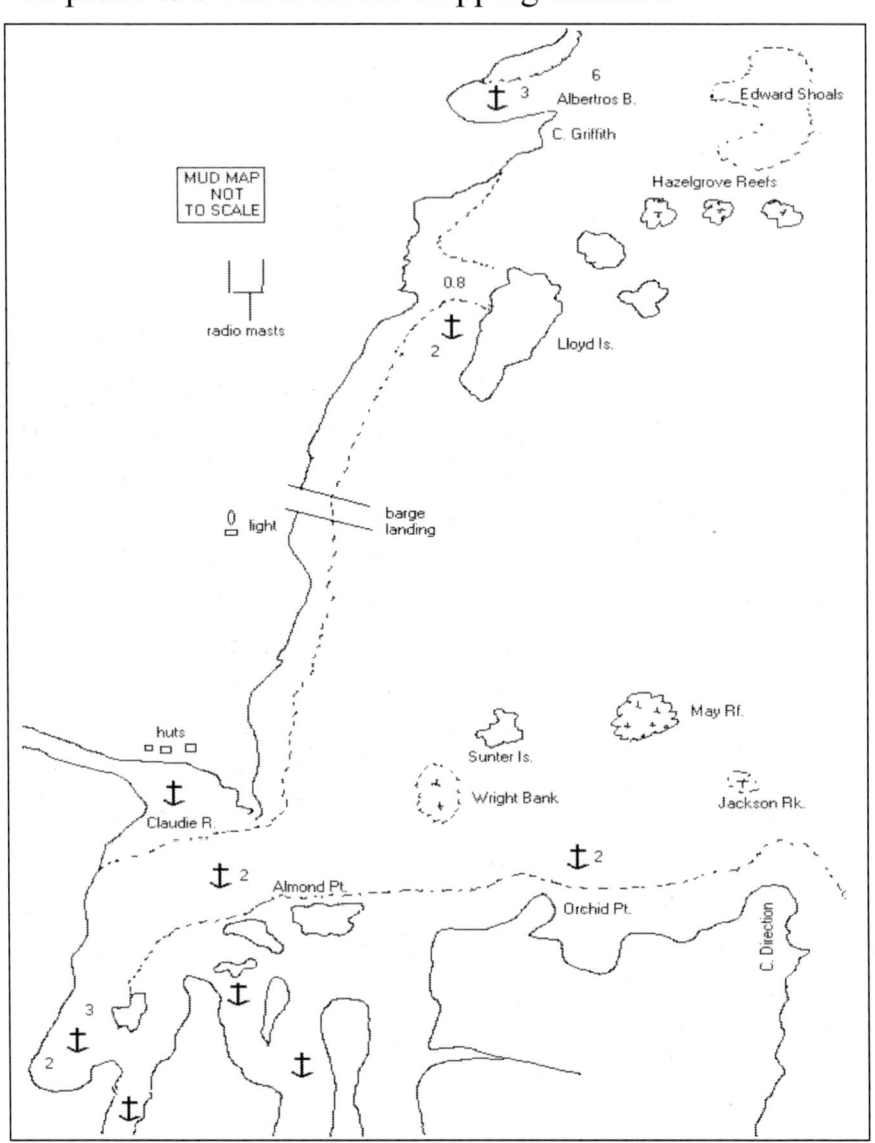

PORTLAND ROADS

CHARTS	AUS 834, 835
LIGHTS	Restoration Rock flashes 2 every 8 seconds, visible 8 miles
TIDES	Leggatti Island (Portland Roads) ANTT
RESCUE	Coast Guard VMR 433

From the south, a track between Restoration Rock and Restoration Island is safe in 20 metres. **Do not** attempt passage between Restoration Island and Cape Weymouth. Course is then to the north of Rocky Island in 10 metres, then into Portland Roads. Anchor wherever possible in 2–3 metres. There are a few moorings in the area. They are private. The holding is good in mud. During developed southeast winds, the bay is invaded by a swell, and can get very uncomfortable. A stern anchor set to have the bow into the swell does make life a bit more bearable. Seagrass may be encountered and an admiralty anchor will give a more secure holding. Water is available from the tank near the public telephones. These have recently been updated and now take telephone cards. Supply ships service the area and arrangements can be made for supplies with them.

Portland Roads

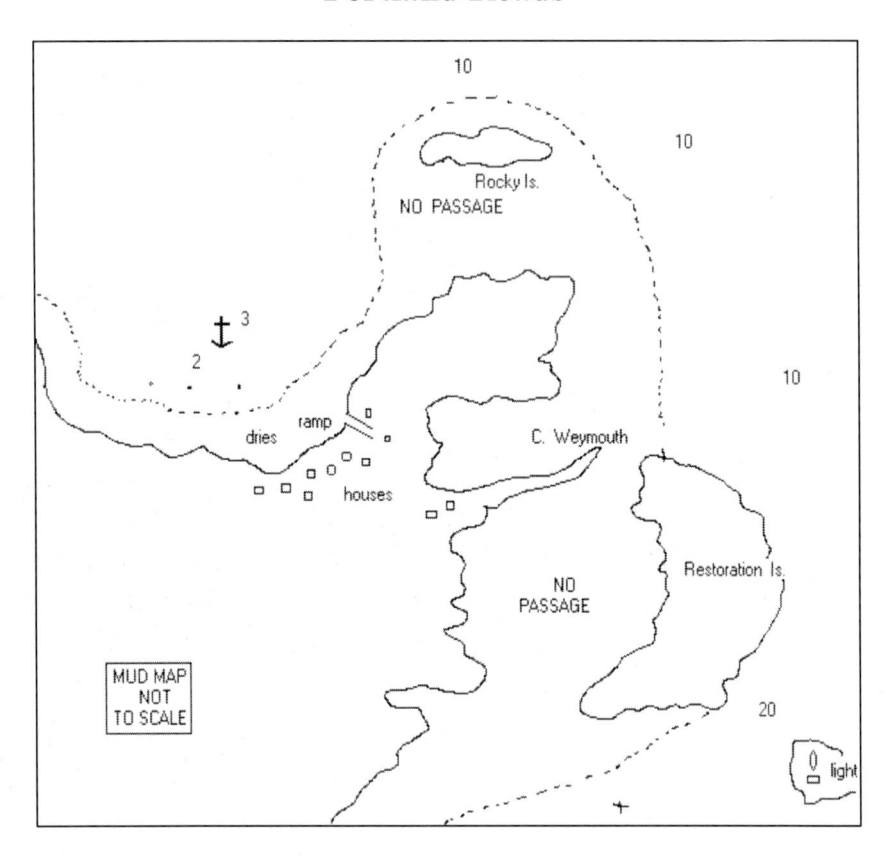

TEMPLE BAY

CHART   AUS 835
LIGHTS   **Piper Island** flashes 4 every 20 seconds, visible 8 miles. **Inset Reef** flashes 7 seconds. visible 8 miles.
TIDES   Leggatti Island (Piper Island) ANTT

Temple Bay is 25 miles north of Portland Roads. Entry is on a track to the north of Andrews Reef in 10 metres. Then south of Daniel and Lion Reefs in 9–10 metres. In Temple Bay, there are two creeks. The first is Hunter; further in is Glennie. Both have barred entrances with 0.8 metres of water. Anchorage outside is not very comfortable, but is suitable while waiting for the tide. A tide of ship's draft plus 1 metre is necessary to enter. Once inside, depths ranging from 2–5 metres are found in both creeks. The fishing and crabbing is excellent, but as with all mangrove-lined creeks, the sandfly and mosquito population are very friendly.

Temple Bay

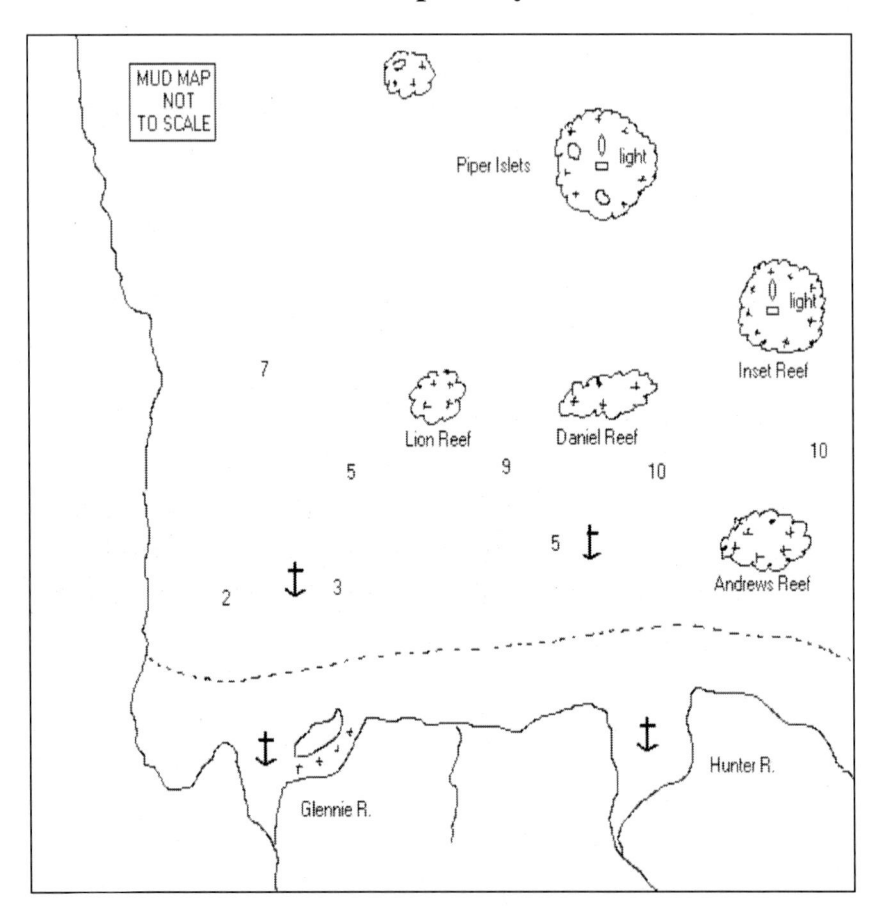

BEESLEY ISLAND

CHART   AUS 835
LIGHTS   Piper Reef flashes 4 every 20 seconds, visible 10 miles.
TIDES   Leggatti Island (Piper Islands) ANTT

Beesley Island is the westernmost island of the Piper Islands. Anchorage is in 4 metres out from the northwest corner. The water shoals, so it is possible to go in closer. There are a few coral patches, so take care. The anchorage has a sandy bottom and is reasonably comfortable in winds up to around 10 knots. It is better than nothing late in the day, as there are no other places nearby. The fishing is quite good. The reef area to the south is filled with sand, the same as Morris Island, and allows a large area to be explored.

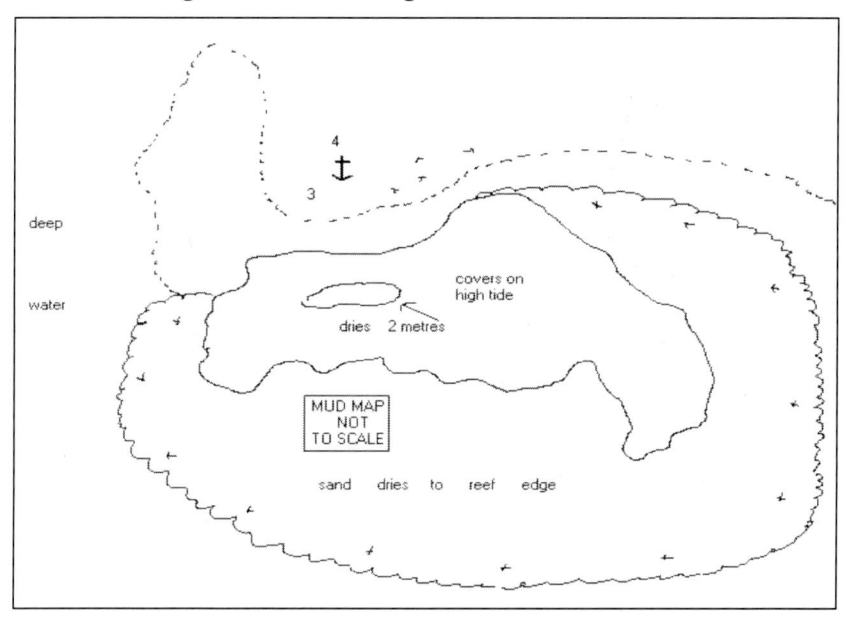

FORBES ISLAND

CHART   AUS 835
LIGHTS   Nil
TIDES   Leggatti Island (Piper Island) ANTT
CAUTION These are unsurveyed waters.

Forbes Island is to the east of Gallon Reef and is in uncharted waters. I chose to motor rather than sail; it's safer. The only entry is to the northern end of Gallon Reef and to the south of Kay Reef. There are numerous coral patches, so be careful. Anchorage is over sand at the skipper's discretion. I anchored on the northern side out from the nice beach in 6 metres. It can get uncomfortable in heavy winds, but is both secure and tolerable. There is also a great beach on the southern side; both are a beachcomber's paradise where the fishing is out of this world. The lease option was not taken up and the island has now reverted to National Park.

Forbes Island

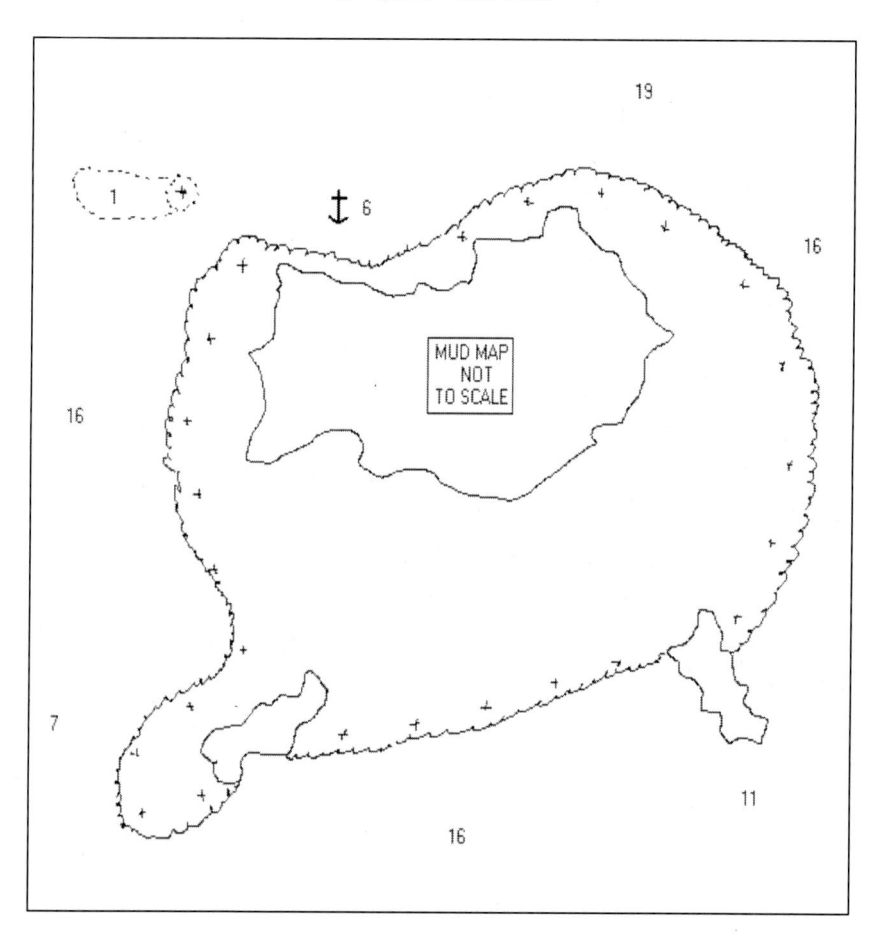

GORE ISLAND – (New)
Home Island Group

CHART AUS 835
LIGHTS Clerke Island has green/white sector lights (see chart for sectors) flashes 2.5 seconds, visible white 10 miles, green 7 miles.
TIDES Leggatti Is. (Cape Grenville) ANTT

This is one of the few anchorages protected from all winds. It is a beautiful anchorage and is worth the stop. There is a beach with dinghy access over the reef on a rising tide. Anchor out from the reef face in 20 metres. From here it is an easy passage north; the channel is as marked on the chart.

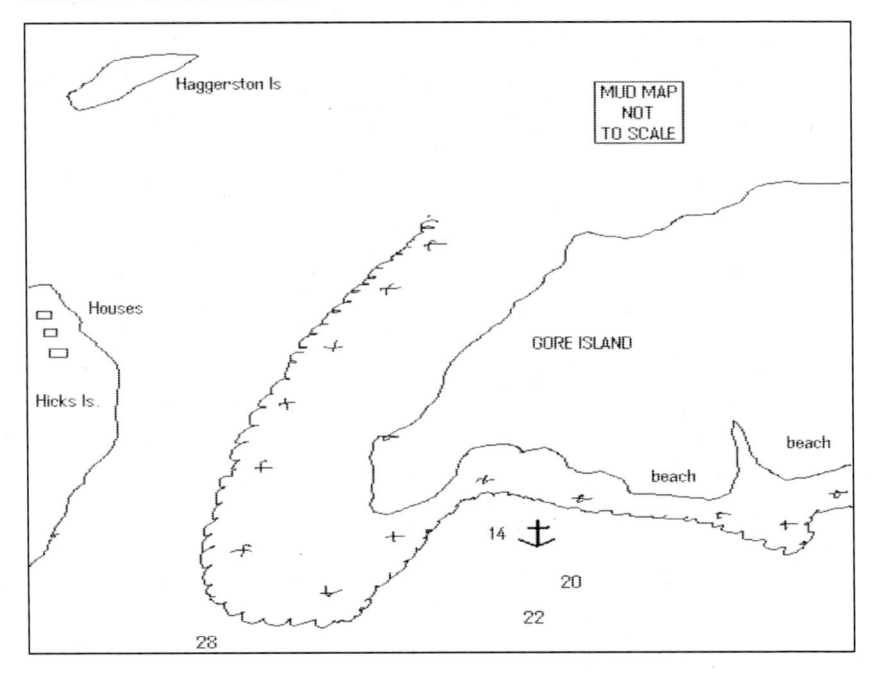

CAPE GRENVILLE

CHART AUS 835
LIGHTS Clerke Island shows a green/white sector light (see chart for sectors) flashing every 2.5 seconds, visible white 10 miles, green 7 miles.
TIDES Leggatti Island (Cape Grenville) ANTT

Cape Grenville offers secure anchorage from southerly winds in **MARGARET BAY**, and from northerly winds in **INDIAN BAY**. Although channels exist amongst the Home Islands, it is the captain's choice whether to use them or to go around the outside of Clerke Island. In either case, be aware of the Bremner Shoals that run for some distance to the north of Cape Grenville. Anchorage within Margaret Bay is secure in 2–4 metres, but be aware of shoaling water that extends out from the shore for some distance and has 1.2 metres.

Cape Grenville

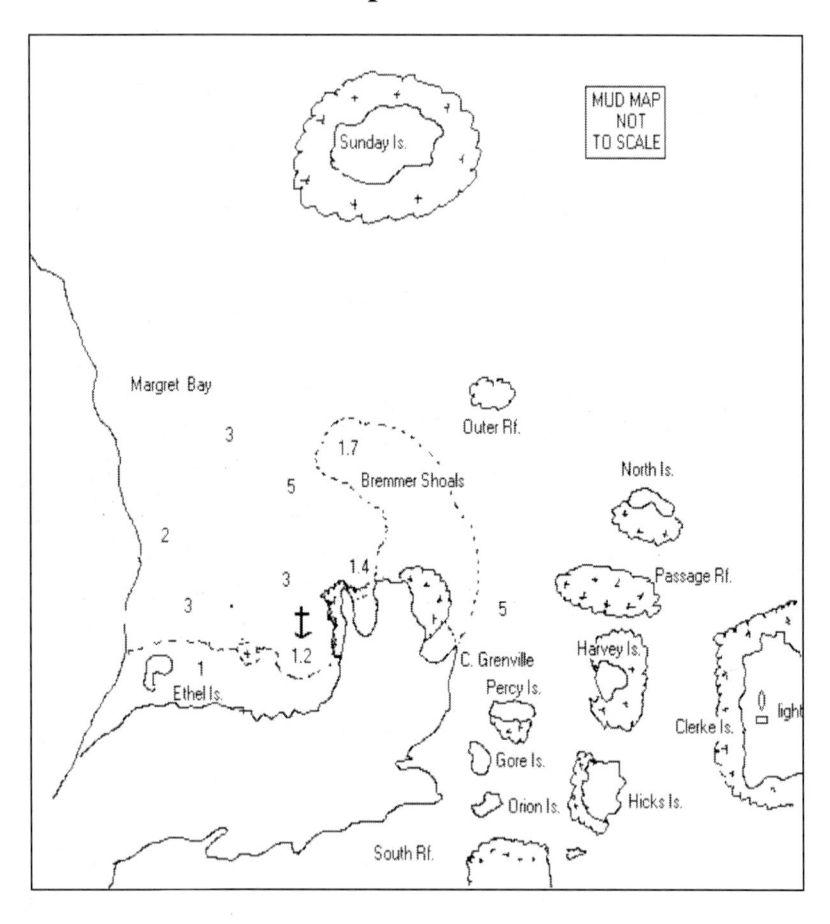

SHELBURNE BAY

CHART AUS 835
LIGHTS Nil
TIDES Leggatti Island (Shelburne Bay) ANTT

Shelburne Bay is 11 miles north of Cape Grenville and has no offshore dangers. After clearing Sunday Island, lay a course around the north of Rodney Island in 11 metres, which quickly decreases to 3 metres abeam of Round Point. Shelburne Bay has a number of scattered reefs. A lookout should be posted if going further west than the indicated anchorage. This beautiful area, full of white silica sand, is secure from all southerly winds. Anchorage is under Round Point in 2–4 metres. The water close in is shoal and the area is poorly surveyed.

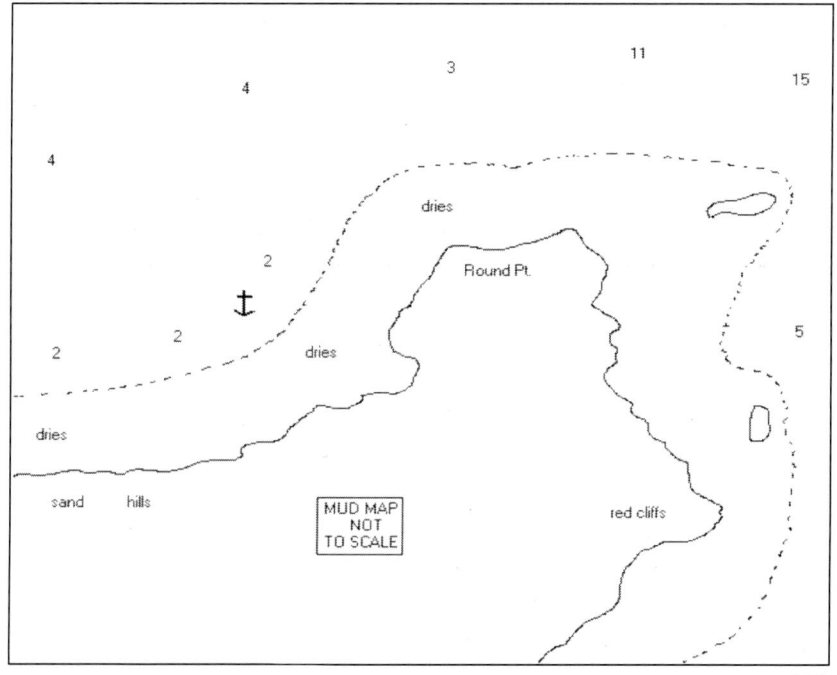

MACARTHUR ISLAND – (New)

CHART   AUS 835
LIGHTS Nil
TIDES   Leggatti Is. (Hannibal Island) ANTT

A good anchorage 20 miles north of Margaret Bay. It is a useful stopover to break the distance to Escape River. Anchor in 10 metres out from the face of the reef. Anchor with reef to the east and the sand cay on the other side. Comfortable in winds to 25 knots, it should remain secure in a strong wind warning.

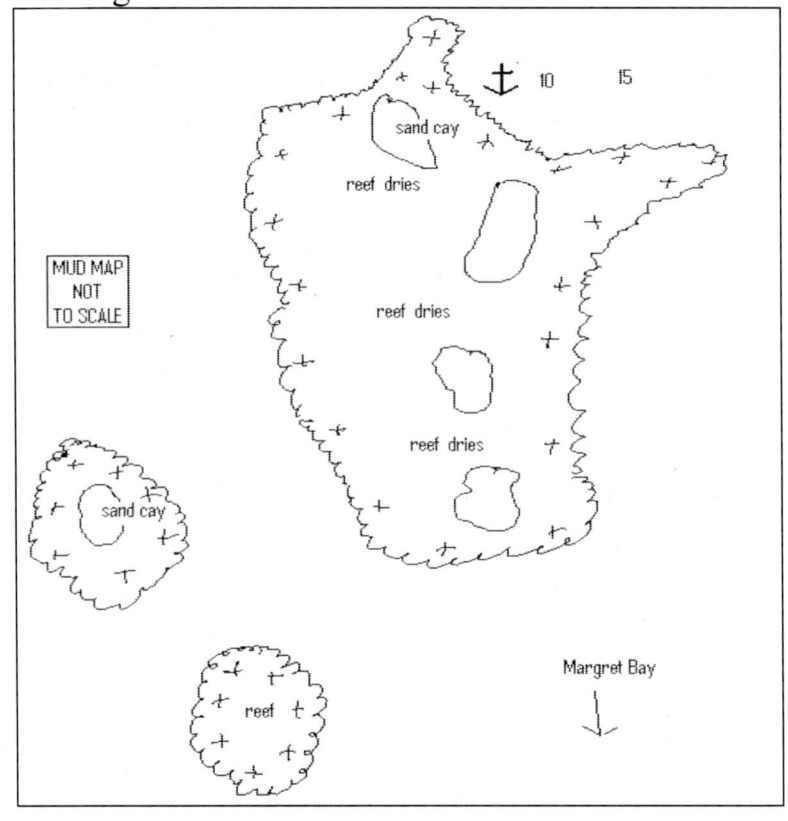

HANNIBAL ISLETS

CHART AUS 835
LIGHTS The eastern islet flashes 2 every 8 seconds, visible 10 miles.
TIDES Leggatti Island (Hannibal Island) ANTT

The anchorage is at Hannibal Island north of Macarthur Island. There are two islets at the northern end of the large reef area, a bent tree and a few boulders on the southern end. The smaller islet supports the light, which is partly hidden by scrub. The best anchorage is over sand in 3 metres in the small wrap around beach off the northern side. The beach connects to a northwest running sand spit. The holding is good, but can become uncomfortable as the winds and seas increase.

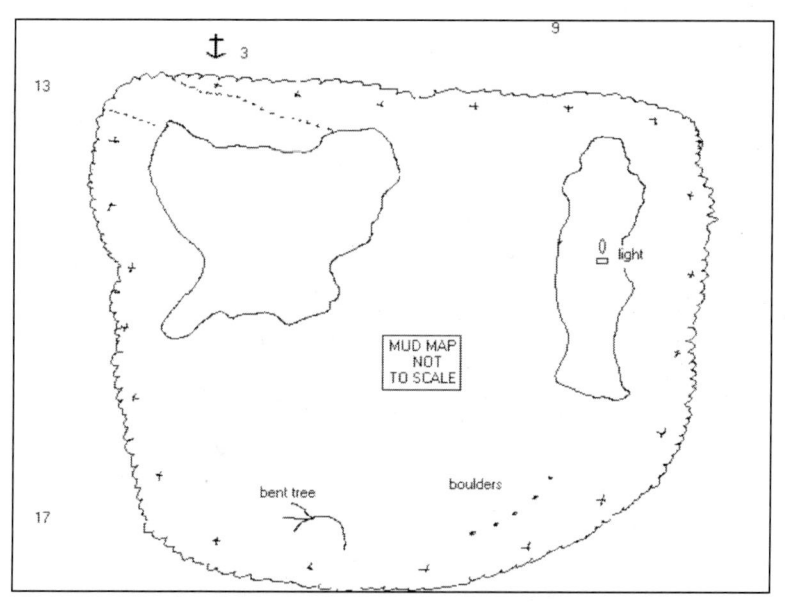

BUSHY ISLET – (Updated)

CHART AUS 835
LIGHTS Cairncross Island flashes 3 every 15 seconds, visible 10 miles.
TIDES Leggatti Island (Cairncross Island) ANTT

Over the past cyclones, Bushy Islet anchorage has improved considerably. It is secure and reasonably comfortable in 20-knot southerly winds. The islet is surrounded by a vast drying reef area. Anchor in 5 metres at the northwest corner in a bend in the reef, with the islet on one side and the sand cay and reef on the other. From here, it is clear of dangers. The imprint of a very large crocodile was seen on the sand cay, so take care.

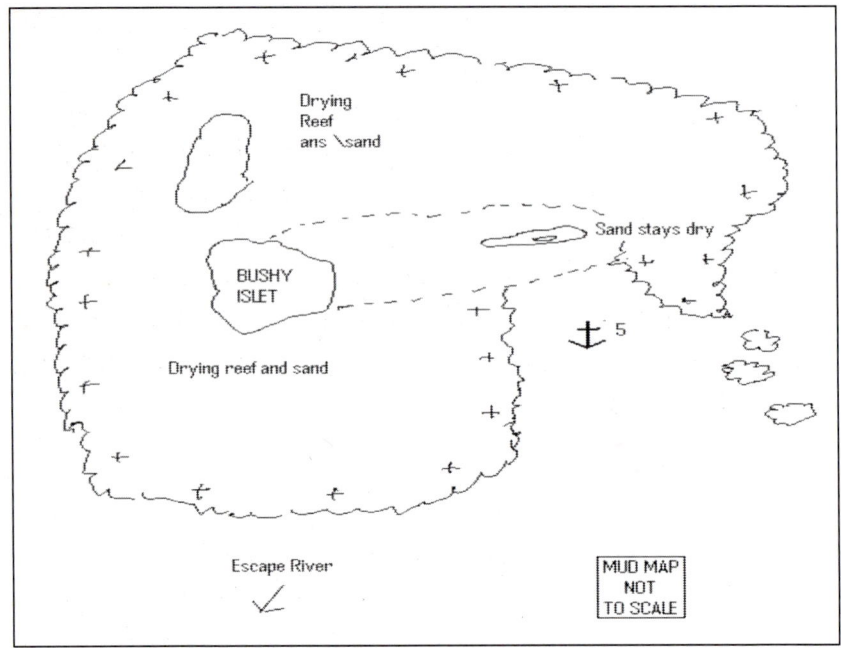

ESCAPE RIVER

CHART AUS 835
LIGHTS Nil
TIDES Ince Point (Turtle Head Island) ANTT
CAUTION The new owners, Arrow Pearls, have filled the area with pearl rafts.

An early start from Shelburne Bay may be necessary, as Escape River is 60 miles to the north, and there are no worthwhile anchorages in between. Lay a course to clear Macarthur Island, then the light on Hannibal Island will be seen, after which there is clear passage. Entry to Escape River is between Sharp Point and Turtle Head Island. Both have low red bauxite cliffs. The bar carries 2 metres, making an all-tide entry. Stay in mid channel until past Turtle Head Island, then anchor where desired. Turtle Head Island has a pearl farm with pearl rafts scattered throughout the area. Visits are possible, after gaining permission from the management. Anchorage off the pearl farm suffers from a swell in developed onshore conditions, and may get unpleasant. Anchorage can be found further upstream, but take care not to interfere with pearl rafts. Escape River would make a secure cyclone anchorage. There are rocky patches along the banks and crocodiles.

Escape River

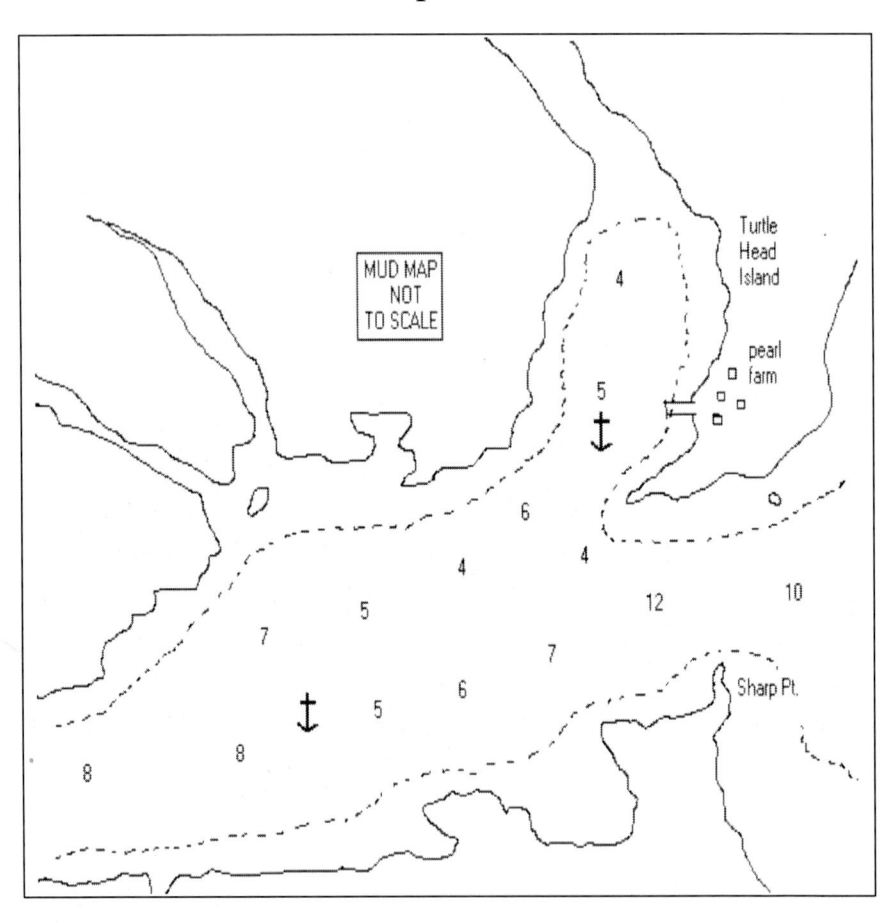

ALBANY PASSAGE

CHARTS AUS 839, 292
LIGHTS Albany Rock has a red/white/green sector light (see chart for sectors) flashing 5 seconds, visible white 11 miles, red and green 8 miles.
TIDES Ince Point (Albany Island) ANTT

Albany Passage is 14 miles north of Escape River and is found between the mainland and Albany Island. It is a deep, fast-running channel. The tide floods north at 5 knots and ebbs south at the same speed. From Escape River, lay a course to clear Ariel Bank, and the shoal area to the south, by at least 2.5 miles. Owing to the fast current and deep water, there are not any safe anchorages available. Albany Passage should only be attempted in daylight and on a suitable tide. There are pearl rafts in the only anchorage. However, the bay to the south does give acceptable anchorage.

Albany Passage

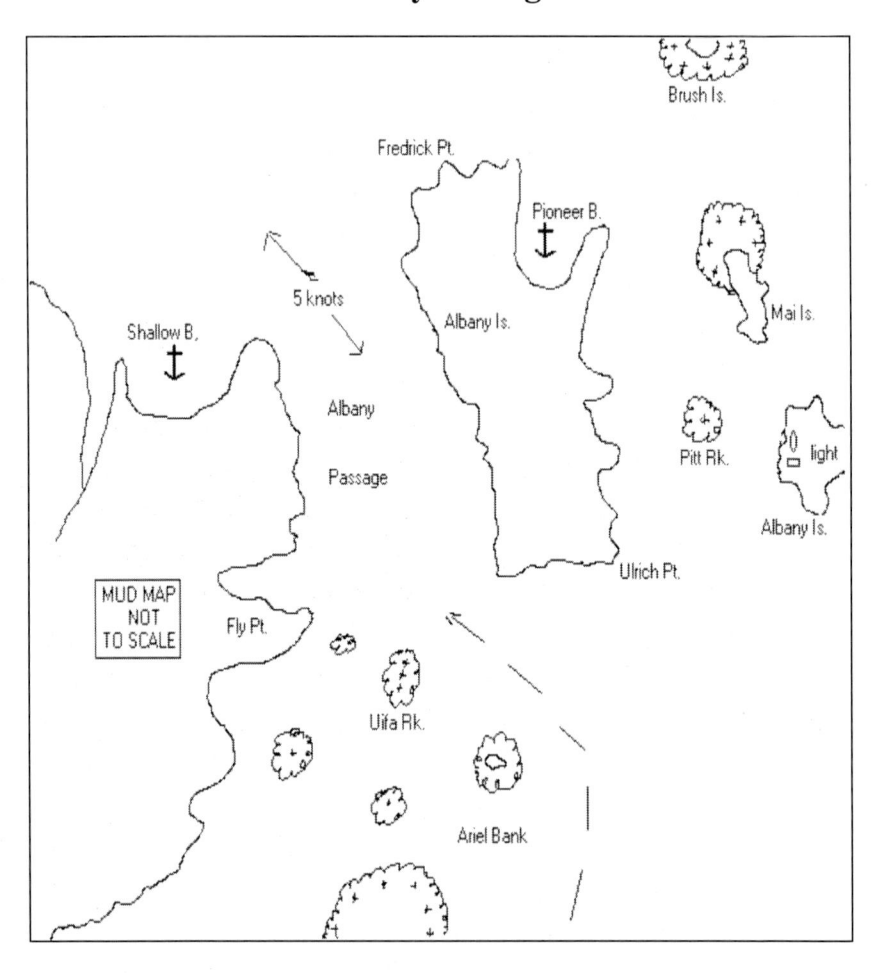

PIONEER BAY

CHARTS AUS 839, 292
LIGHTS Albany Rock has a red/white/green (see chart for sectors) flashing 5 seconds, visible white 11 miles, red and green 8 miles.
TIDES Ince Point (Albany Island) ANTT

Pioneer Bay is on the outside of Albany Island. It is a pretty place, with clear water and a white beach. The best water is between Charlotte Point and Pitt Rock. I found more than 20 metres. After clearing Alfred Point, be aware of the shoal area that runs north from the point. Anchor in 2 metres over sand. It is a good spot if you do not want to use Albany Passage. This is a reasonably comfortable anchorage, but a swell does invade in wind against tide conditions. A more comfortable anchorage can be found in Blackwood Bay, on Mount Adolphus Island, 5 miles to the north.

Pioneer Bay

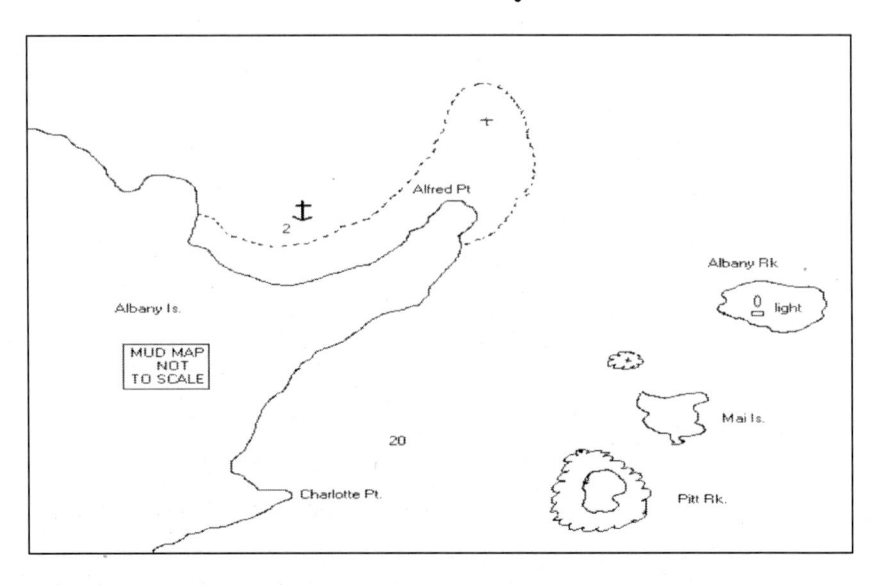

SHALLOW BAY

CHARTS AUS 839, 292
LIGHTS Nil
TIDES Ince Point (Albany Island) ANTT

Shallow Bay is to the west of Osnaburg Point at the northern end of Albany Passage. There is a low tide beach of sandy mud backed by mangroves. Anchor in 2 metres over mud. Holding is good, but is invaded by a beam swell in strong winds. This is a good anchorage if not enough light to make Cape York. There is a small creek at the western end of the bay, where the fishing is good. Shallow Bay is not troubled greatly by the strong tides through Albany Passage.

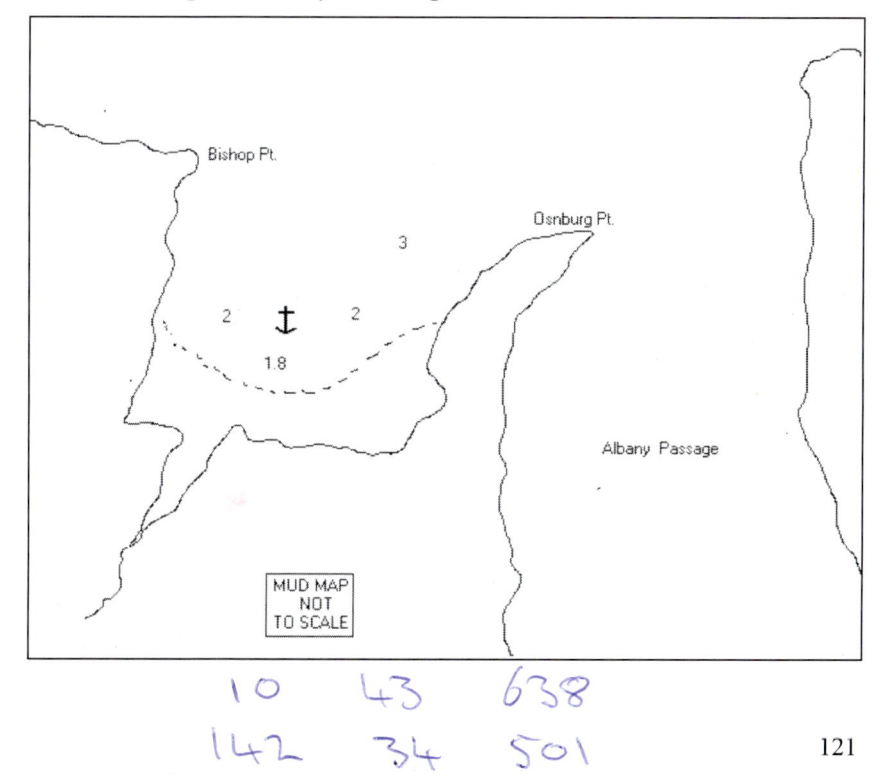

MOUNT ALDOPHUS ISLAND

CHARTS　　AUS 839, 292
LIGHTS　　Nil
TIDES　　Ince Point (Albany Island) ANTT

Mount Aldophus Island is 5 miles north of Pioneer Bay. A flat-topped mountain can be seen about 20 miles away. Blackwood Bay, on the western side of the island, gives a secure anchorage in moderate to fresh winds, and remains comfortable. Anchor in 3–4 metres out from the fringing reef in clean water. Coming from Pioneer Bay, take care to clear Quetta Rock, which has less than 3 metres of water. The historic wreck of the *Quetta* lies to the northwest. Beware of the strong currents in the area between here and Pioneer Bay.

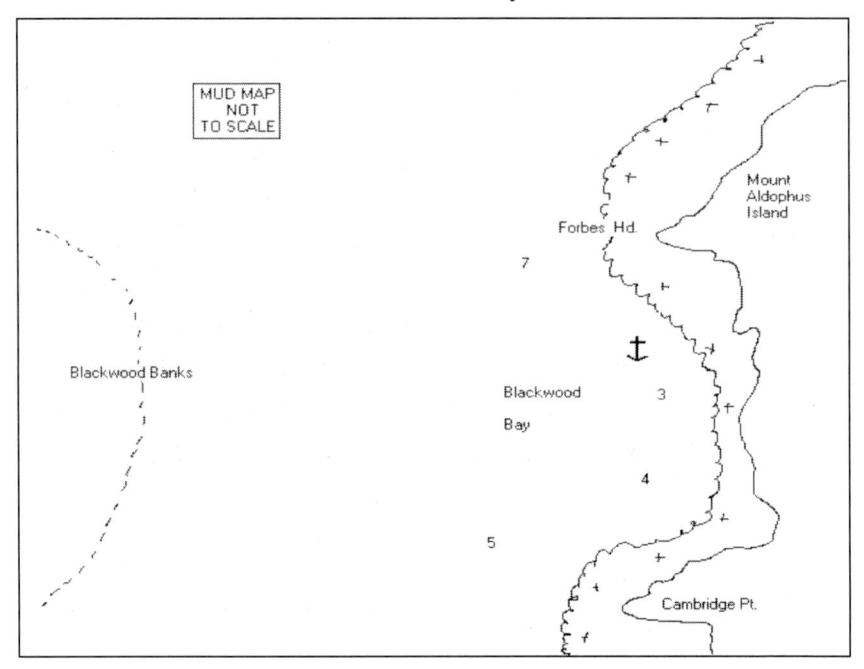

CAPE YORK

CHART AUS 292
LIGHTS Eborac Island has a red/white/green sector light (see chart for sectors) flashes 2 every 10 seconds, visible white 10 miles, red/green 7 miles.
TIDES Ince Point (Albany Island) ANTT

Cape York provides an acceptable anchorage, and extreme satisfaction that the northern tip of Australia has been reached. Anchorage is to the west of the cape, and can be entered between Cape York and York Island in calm weather. Favour the cape side of the channel, as a rocky patch exists on the southern side of York Island. At other times, the passage to the outside of Eboc Island and York Island should be taken. On rounding York Island, it should be held close in 4–6 metres to avoid drying and shallow sandbanks. Also, be aware of the 2–3 knot current running west on a flood tide. Near the anchorage, there is a 22-metre deep boil hole. Anchorage is clear of this and the obvious rock in 2–3 metres. Do not go any closer in than a line between the rock and Cape York. Dinghy landing can be difficult, as the distance between high and low is large and you may have to drag your dinghy for some distance. The Wilderness Lodge has closed and is now derelict.

Cape York

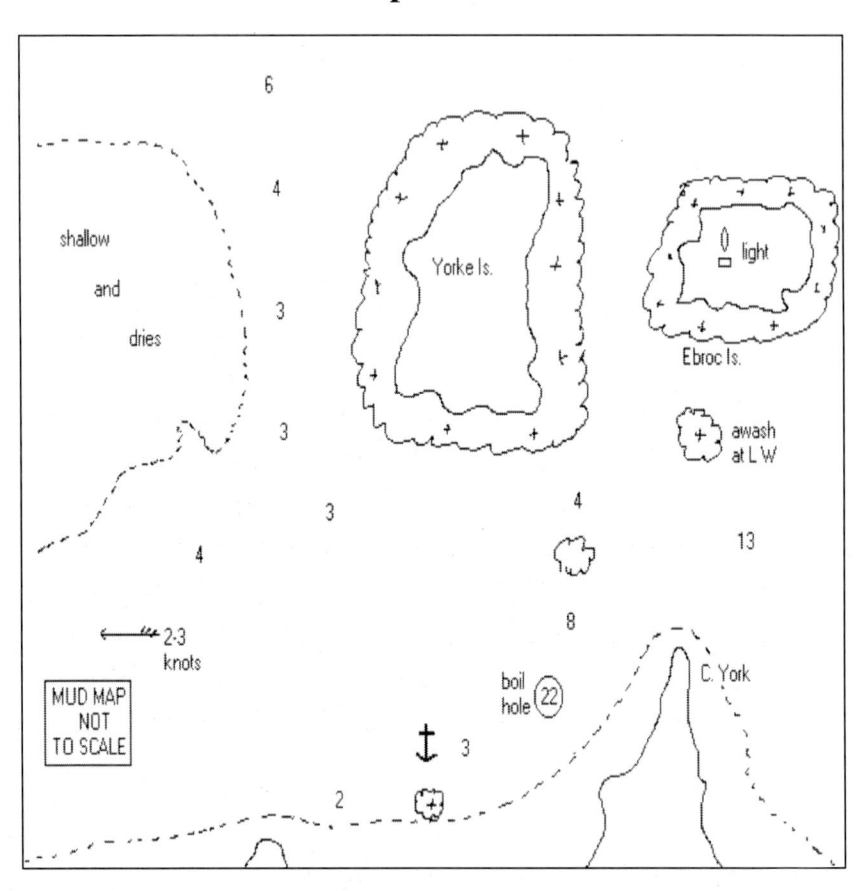

POSSESSION ISLAND (ROONGA CREEK)

CHARTS   AUS 292, 294
LIGHTS   Nil
TIDES   Ince Point (Possession Island) ANTT
RESCUE   Coast Guard Bamaga VMR 424
             Coast Guard Thursday Is. VMR 422

From Cape York, the best course to Possession Island is to travel north along the western side of York Island. Hold this until in deep water, then turn west, making sure to clear the shoals around York Island. Entry to the anchorage at Roonga Creek is easy by following the mainland between High Island and then between Little Roko Island and the mainland. Currents here can reach 8 knots. A hut and some palm trees are at the back of the beach, south of Roonga Creek. Anchorage is out from the hut in sand, weed and rock patches. Once anchored, it remains secure. A change of anchor may help.

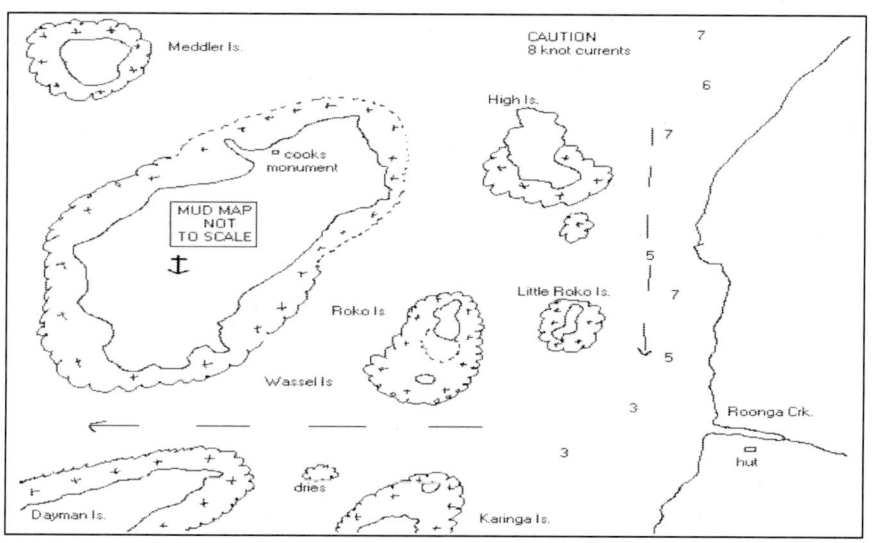

POSSESSION ISLAND (OUTSIDE)

CHARTS AUS 292, 294
LIGHTS Nil
TIDES Ince Point (Possession Island) ANTT
RESCUE Coast Guard Thursday Island MR 422
Coast Guard Bamaga VMR 424

This anchorage is on the outside of Possession Island in 2–3 metre, off the beach and out from the fringing reef. There is a constant swell, however this depends on wind strength and tide. There is also a 3–5 knot current. Dinghy landing is possible through the reef. At the north end of the island is a monument to Captain Cook taking possession of the east coast. If too uncomfortable here, the anchorage out from Roonga Creek is more secure.

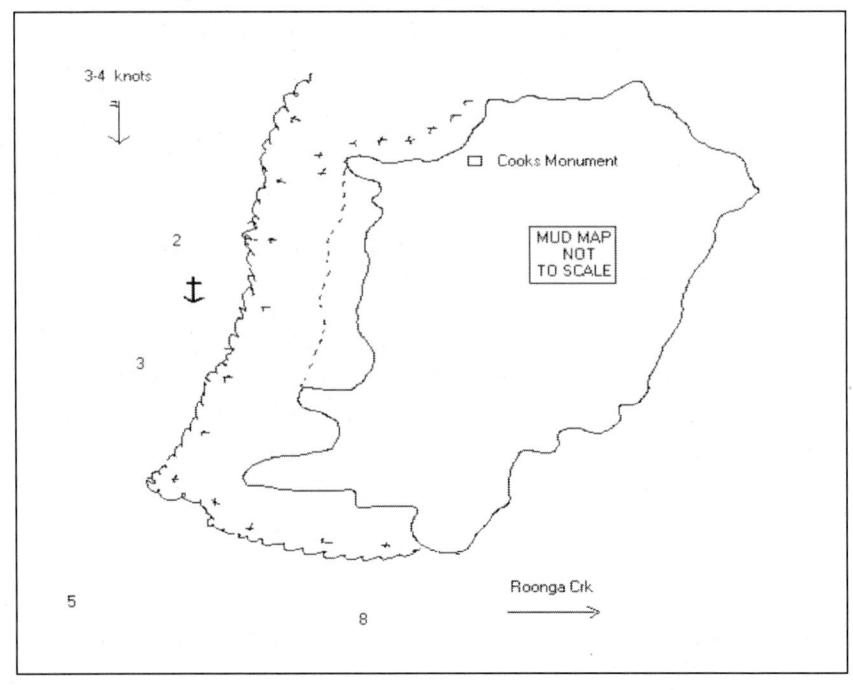

BAMAGA (SEISIA)

CHART   AUS 294
LIGHTS   Red buoy, green buoy and white triangle leads flashing 2 seconds.
TIDES   Ince Point (Red Island) ANTT
RESCUE   Coast Guard Bamaga VMR 424

It is recommended to clear Possession Island from Roonga Creek between Dayman Island and Possession Island before laying course for Bamaga. Approach Bamaga by keeping the red buoy to port, at which time the white triangle leads should be seen, but if not a green buoy will be seen which should be passed to starboard. After rounding the green, a natural progression between Red Island and Red Island Point takes the boat past the jetty. Anchor in 3 metres well clear of the jetty. The water shoals rapidly in this area, so watch your sounder. The jetty cannot be used without permission. Fresh water is available at a tap on the outside of the Sea Swift Shed. The water at the jetty was found to have a strong diesel taste. There is a small kiosk and a supermarket at Seisia and a servo. Fuel is close to Port Douglas prices. The supermarket is not recommended, except for bread. There is a large supermarket at the Bamaga township, 13 kilometres away. You need to hitchhike both ways into Bamaga.

Bamaga (Seisia)

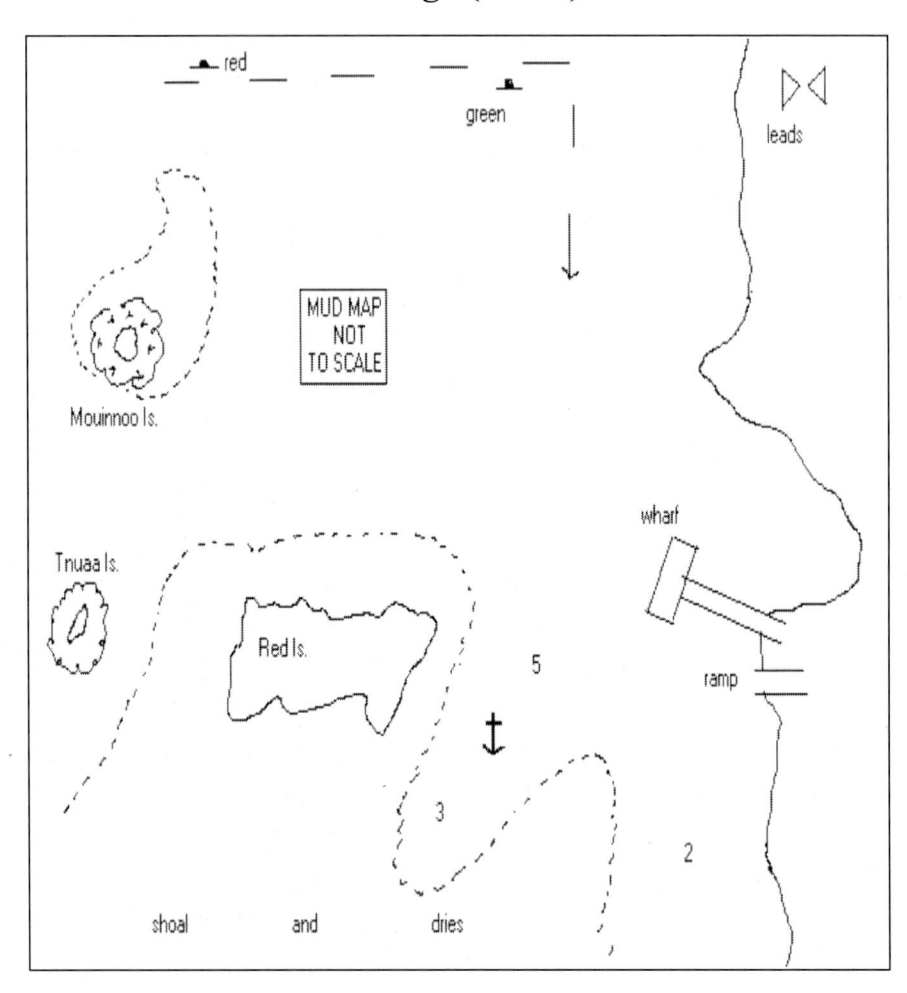

PASSAGE NOTES

From Bamaga, there are two possible courses available. The first is through Boat Passage and Thursday Island. After leaving Thursday Island for Booby Island, a white light will be found – pass this to port. Next is a yellow light – keep this to starboard, at which time back-leads will be sighted. These will take boats on a track between Goods and Friday Islands, passing a red buoy kept to starboard. This will take you to Booby Island, but take care to clear the shoals of Larpent Bank.

Booby Island has a light that flashes white every 4 seconds and is visible for 25 miles. Booby Island is not a comfortable anchorage, but can be tolerated. Anchorage is out from the northwest corner in 2.5 metres. From Booby Island, set a course to clear the shoals of Endeavour Straits. This extends out into the Gulf for some distance. An outward distance of at least 5 miles is recommended, and should be held for at least 25 miles, after which time it is reasonably safe to close the coast. Constant navigation is necessary. Keep the sounder running and a constant lookout.

The second course is via the Endeavour Straits. This is the shortest route. Extensive sandbanks are encountered at the southwest end. Travel is definitely daylight only, and requires exact navigation and an alert lookout. An early start is required from Bamaga, or an overnight anchorage can be found out from the mouth of the Jardine River. A rising tide is necessary to travel this area. A careful and detailed study of AUS Chart 294 is also necessary.

SECTION 2

The Gulf of Carpentaria

This section covers suitable anchorages from Slade Point south to Karumba, across the bottom, then up to Gove.

From Booby Island to the light on Veronica Island (Gove) is a distance of about 300 miles. The gulf is low and regular along its eastern shore, with numerous offshore hazards. In general, anchorage can be found close in where depth allows while the southerlies are blowing. While the southern end is more exposed and cannot be closed too close, anchorage can be found around most offshore islands. The shallows extend for quite some distance offshore and extreme care is necessary. The west coast rises steeply, and provides more anchorages in sheltered bays, rivers and islands, but extreme care is still necessary, as there are many hazards and unsurveyed waters to trap the careless.

Commercial shipping is quite busy, as are the prawn trawlers in the prawn season. Navigation aids are rare except around the towns. In the prawn season, night travel is hazardous owing to the number of trawlers working. Do not take it for granted that you will be seen. It cannot be stressed enough that constant vigilance and constant navigation updates in all detail is vital in this area.

Towns in the gulf are oriented to mining and a few to fishing. Therefore stores etc. can be expensive and facilities just about non-existent.

The sense of achievement on cruising the gulf safely is great – one of the last great adventures where the fishing and crabbing are unbelievable.

The coordinates shown from Slade Point to Darwin are chart positions only, and are NOT to be used as waypoints.

Owing to the smoke from fires lit by the Aboriginals, travel south from Bamaga is not recommended if you suffer from any breathing problems. I have had times, when I have had to use radar in daylight. At these times, I have been around 1 mile offshore.

CAUTION
Crocodiles are prolific throughout the entire gulf area.

PASSAGE NOTES

When leaving Bamaga (Seisia), instead of going back via the shipping channel, and around Red Island, it is possible to travel along the beach. There is a channel that has 2 metres L.W. To enter, it is necessary to go close to the wharf and head for the ramp; you will see the sandbank on your starboard. Once past this, you will find deeper water. Anchor wherever you want in this channel, however the top half of the tide is needed to enter.

When leaving, keep travelling west. You will see a rocky headland at the end of the beach, when you get here. As a general direction, head for the headland on the horizon. Keep a close eye on your sounder! Again, the top half of the tide is needed.

As a rising tide is necessary to cross Endeavour Straits, a suitable anchorage will be found at the back of Muttee Head. Leave here at low tide to navigate Endeavour Straits.

The waypoints I use are as follows:

1	Entry to Endeavour Straits	10°55–60'S 142°05–55'E
2	West of Crab Island	10°58–50'S 142°03–40'E
3	Exit Endeavour Straits	11°01–80'S 41°59–30'E

From here, it is safe to change course for Vrilya Point. However still keep a close watch on the sounder.

A final word of advice. Treat all river and creek entrances as having a drying sandbank across its mouth. Anchor out wide and check out the entrance before attempting to enter.

MUTTEE BAY

12°55.00′S – 142°13.90′E

CHART   AUS 294
LIGHTS   Nil
TIDES   Booby Island (Crab Island) ANTT

Muttee Bay lies to the west of Muttee Head and is 8.5 miles from Seisia (Bamaga). This is a useful place to wait for the tide to travel through Endeavour Straits and on into the gulf. Anchorage is in 2 metres over sand, well in behind Muttee Head. It is secure in 15 knots of easterly winds and 20 knots in southeast to southwest, however in east winds a swell may invade in wind against tide conditions. Anchor towards the centre of the beach to avoid rocks around Muttee Head and to the west. You will need to leave here just after low tide to clear Endeavour Straits on a rising tide. Also, beware of the 6–8 knot current on spring tides that flood west.

Muttee Bay

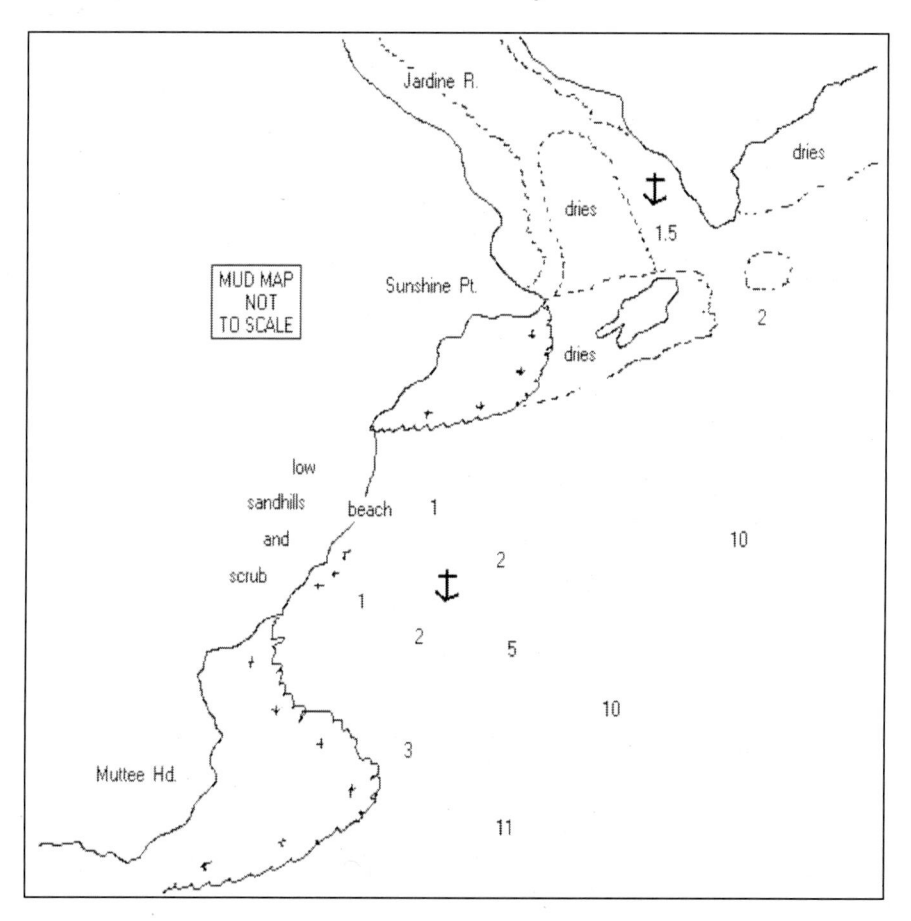

UNNAMED BAY (south of Crab Island)

11°32'S – 142°05'E

CHART AUS 301
LIGHTS Nil
TIDES Booby Island (Crab Island) ANTT

After clearing Endeavour Straits, set a course for Vrilya Point as a general direction. This anchorage is 6 miles to the north of the point. I anchored in 2 metres in the entrance of the unnamed waterway. I did not take the yacht any further in, but exploring by dinghy showed it possible to enter, as there was sufficient water, and the fishing was good. The wreck shown on the chart has been removed.

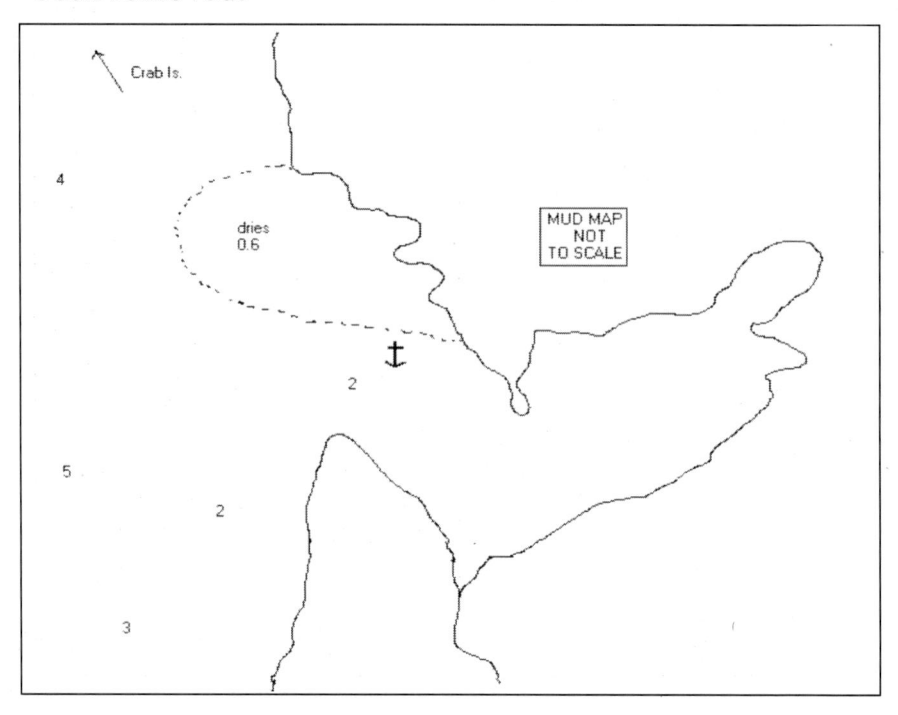

VRILYA POINT

11°14′S – 142°07′E

CHART   AUS 301
LIGHTS   Nil
TIDES   Weipa (Vrilya Point) ANTT

Vrilya Point is 15 miles south of Crab Island and Slade Point. The point is fringed by high cliffs and a bare hill, about 30 metres in height. The best anchorage is on the northern side in 4 metres. Take care to avoid the drying rock to the north.

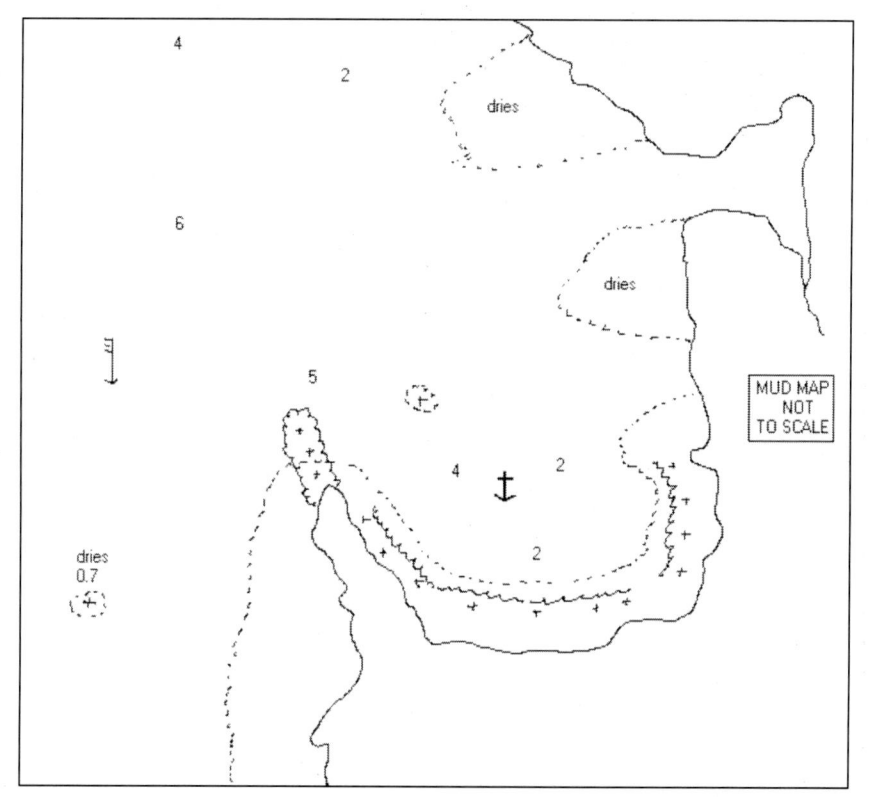

COTTERELL RIVER – (New)

11°21–62′S – 142°06–51′E

CHART   AUS 301, 701
LIGHTS   Nil
TIDES   Weipa (Vrilya Point)   ANTT

There is a drying sandbank across the mouth that extends out for some distance and into the river. The top of the tide is needed to enter. While waiting for the tide, anchor in 2–3 metres out from the mouth. Once inside the river, the main flow is to the north. Anchor anywhere, however, I don't recommend going much further than the large bend to the right. Anchor inside the mouth of the south arm.

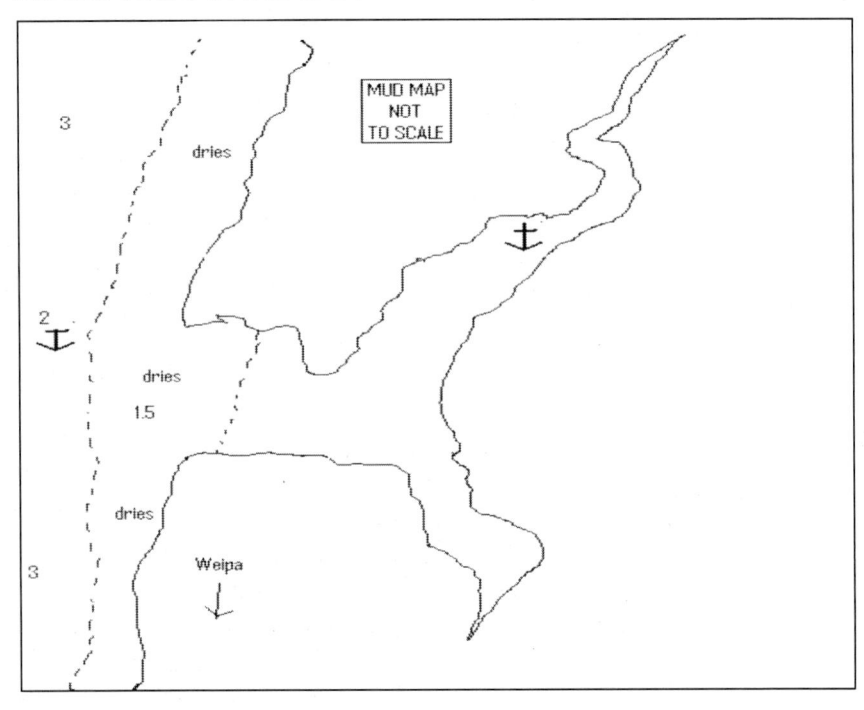

DOUGHBOY RIVER – (New)

11°27–60′S – 142°05–45′E

CHARTS   AUS 301, 701
LIGHTS   Nil
TIDES   Weipa (Vrilya Point) ANTT

The mouth of the river has extensive sandbanks that dry 1.8 metres, making slack water high to enter. There is an extensive waterway here to explore. The river turns and runs north for some miles. I found no underwater dangers, but don't recommend going any further than the island in the middle of the river. The creek to the south has only been explored by dinghy. While waiting to enter, anchor out from the mouth in 5 metres or to the north behind the sandbank in 2 metres.

Doughboy River

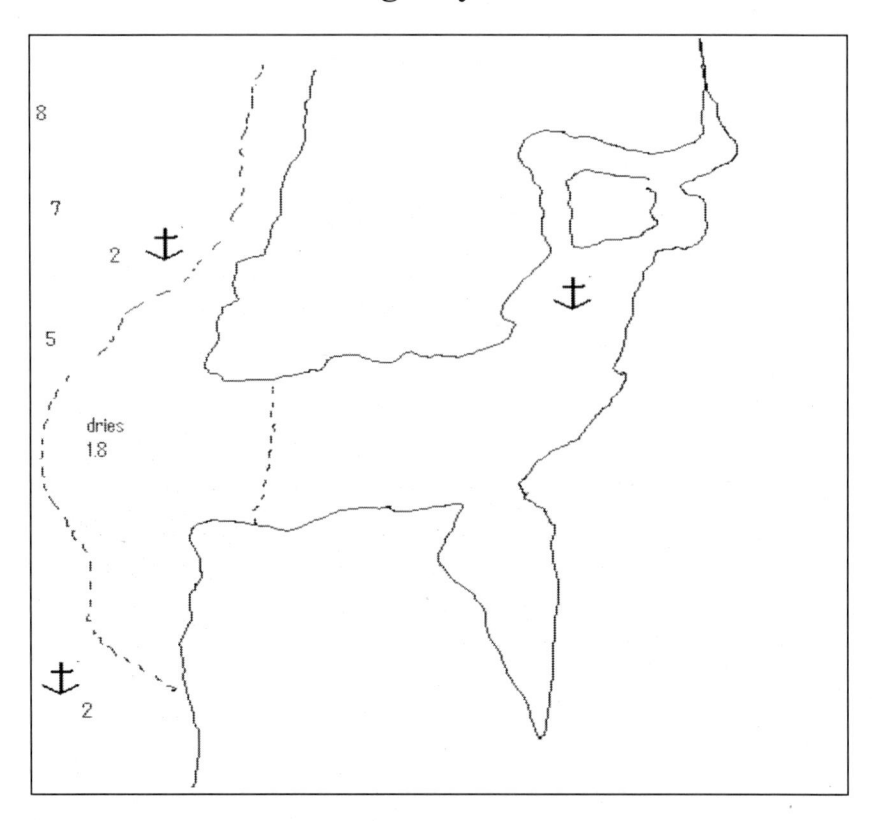

MACDONALD RIVER

11°32'S – 142°05'E

CHART AUS 301
LIGHTS NIL
TIDES Weipa (Vrilya Point) ANTT

The Macdonald River is 18 miles south of Vrilya Point. There is a bar that dries 1.5 metres. Entry is at the top of the tide with a height of ship's draft plus 1.5 metres. Once inside, deep water will be found. The best anchorage is in mid-stream, to stay clear of the friendly sandfly community. A forward lookout is necessary when entering or navigating the river. However, if entry is not possible, anchor outside 2 miles to the north and about 0.75 mile offshore in 3 metres.

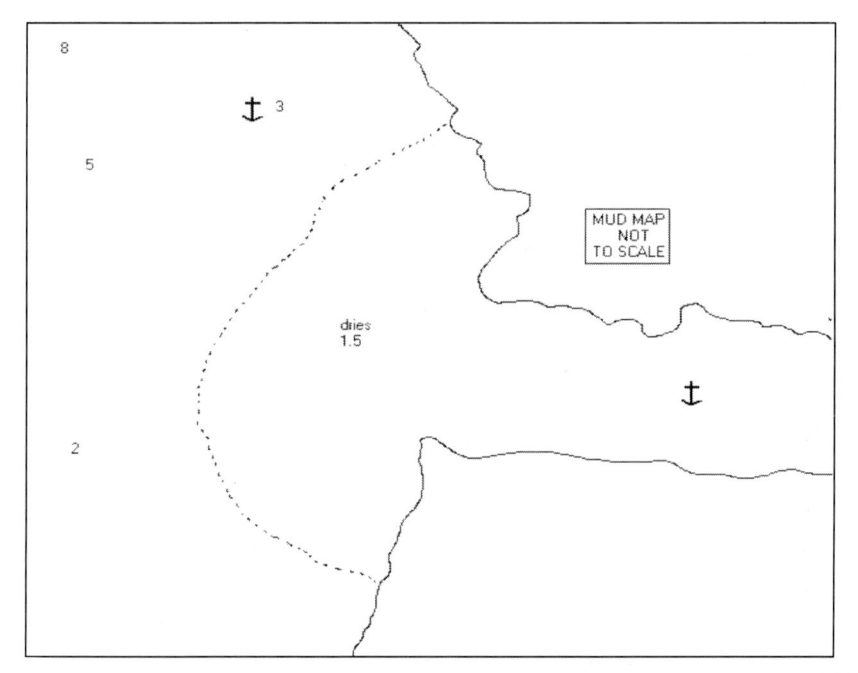

JACKSON RIVER

11°40′S – 142°01.5′E

CHART AUS 301
LIGHTS Nil
TIDES Weipa (Vrilya Point) ANTT

Anchorage can be found anywhere depth allows. I anchored to the side in 4 metres. Holding is good in mud. If unable to enter, anchorage can be found 1.5 miles north of the entrance, in 3 metres, 0.75 miles offshore. This will clear the shoal area at the mouth. There is also anchorage 0.75 miles to the south of the entrance, again 0.75 miles offshore.

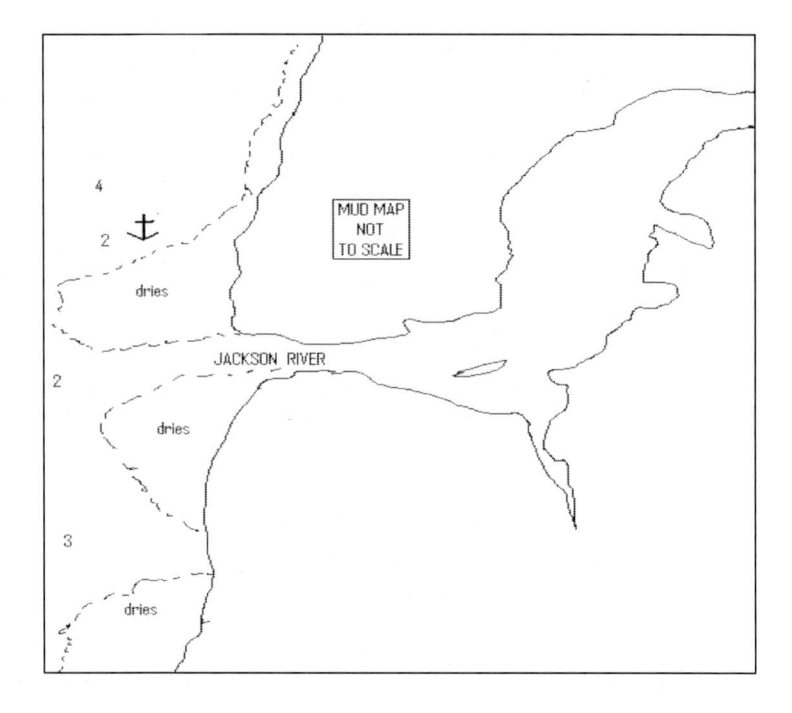

SKADON RIVER – (New)

11°45–40′S – 141°59–96′

CHARTS AUS 301, 701
LIGHTS Nil
TIDES   Weipa (Cullen Point) ANTT

There is an extensive sandbank out from the mouth for about a mile, drying 1.8 metres. Inside the river, there are miles of water to explore, with many tributaries. While waiting for the tide, anchor out from the mouth in 2–4 metres, but take care as there is a lot of shoal water in this area.

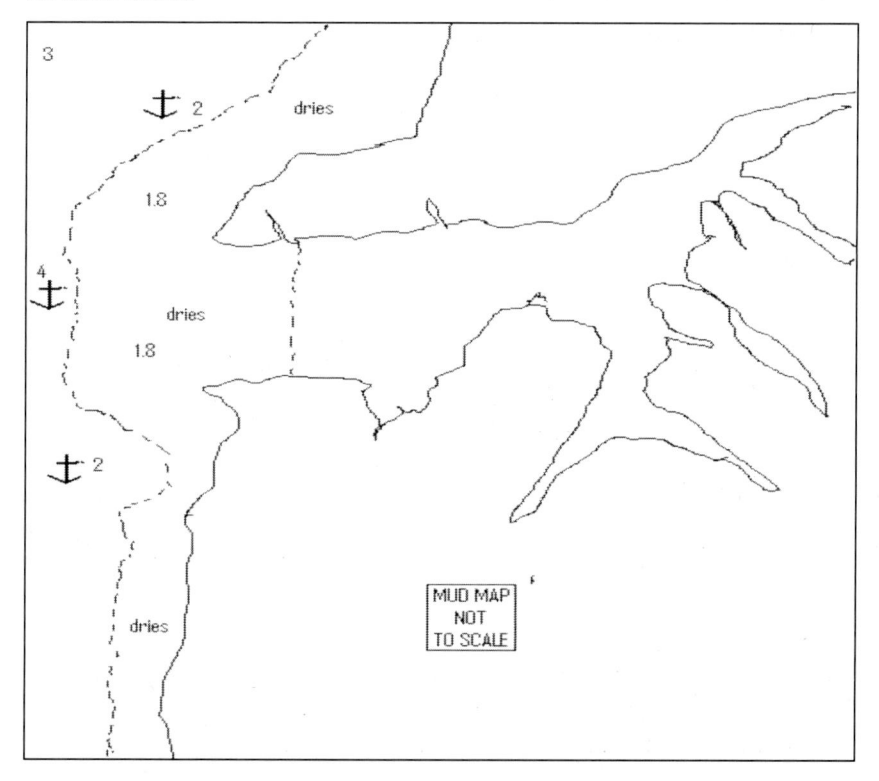

143

CULLEN POINT

11°57'S – 141°54'E

CHART AUS 301
LIGHTS NIL
TIDES Weipa (Cullen Point) ANTT

Cullen Point is marked by a conspicuous clump of trees that runs north. The point offers no anchorage, but marks the entrance to Port Musgrave. The stranded wreck shown on the Chart 2.5 miles to the north has gone.

PORT MUSGRAVE

12°00'S – 141°55'E

CHART AUS 301
LIGHTS Nil
TIDES Weipa (Cullen Point) ANTT

Travelling south from Jackson River, stand well out, as there are numerous shoals and other dangers, in particular Kerr Reef, which dries 0.3 and lies approximately 9.5 miles north northwest of Cullen Point. The surrounding reef has 2 metres. Stand well out from Cullen Point in 5–7 metres. A rising tide is needed to enter, as the bar has varying depths from 0.3 to 2 metres. Once over, this anchorage is in depths from 4–12 metres in sand. Port Musgrave is a good natural harbour for small craft and gives good shelter. The Wenlock River enters from the south and the Ducie River from the east.

Anchorage can be found in both of these for some distance upstream, but post a forward lookout and travel slow on a rising tide.

Port Musgrave

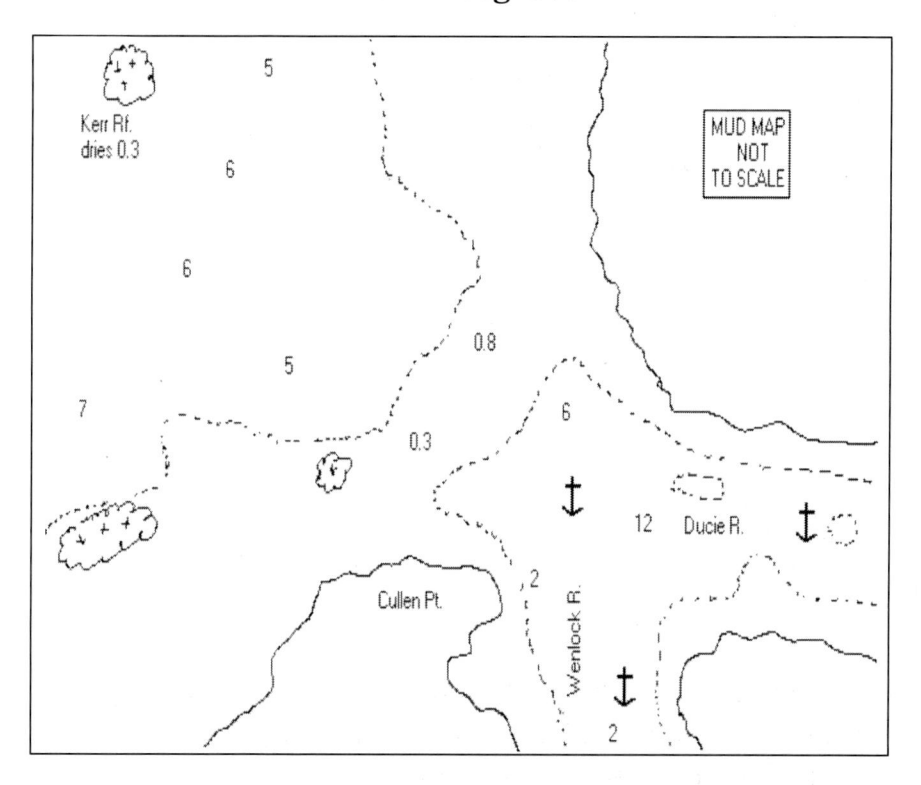

PENNEFATHER RIVER

12°13′S – 141°37′E

CHART AUS 301
LIGHTS NIL
TIDES Weipa (Pennefather River) ANTT

The Pennefather River is 19 miles south of Cullen Point. This extensive waterway provides good fishing and crabbing. As with other rivers, there is a drying bar across the mouth, which requires a rising tide to enter. Once inside, anchor anywhere depth allows. Days can be spent exploring in the dinghy, but watch out for crocodiles. While waiting for the tide to enter, anchor 1 mile offshore in 3 metres.

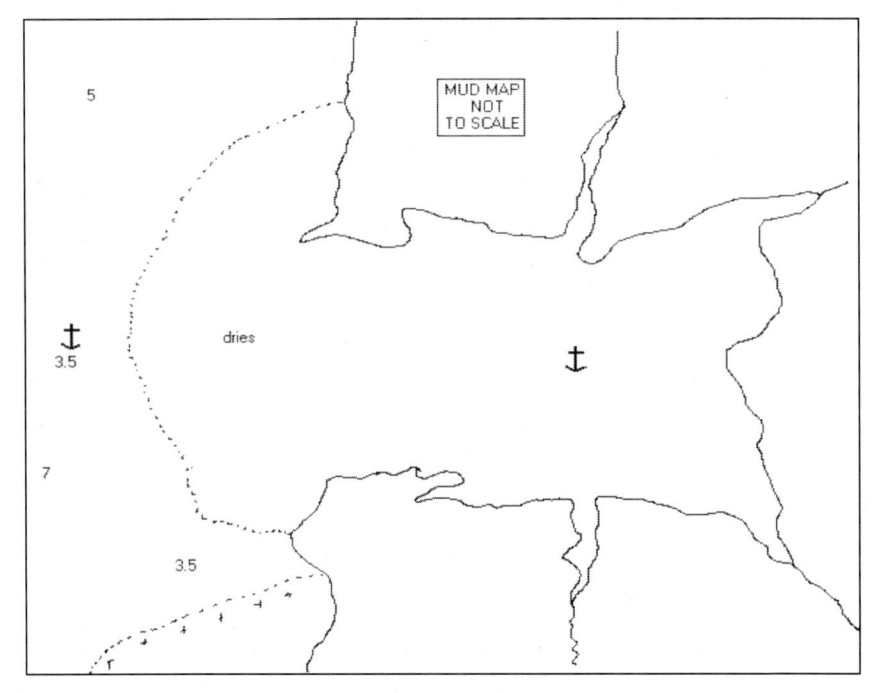

DUYFKIN POINT ANCHORAGE

12°34.00′S – 141°36.00′E

CHART AUS 301
LIGHTS Duyfkin Point flashes white every 5 seconds, visible 16 miles.
TIDES Weipa (Standard Port) ANTT

Anchorage here is close in to the beach in 2 metres over sand. Make sure to anchor to the north of the reef and drying rock. There is a large dead tree high up on the beach; in front of this is the best. A small swell does invade from around the point, but is no bother.

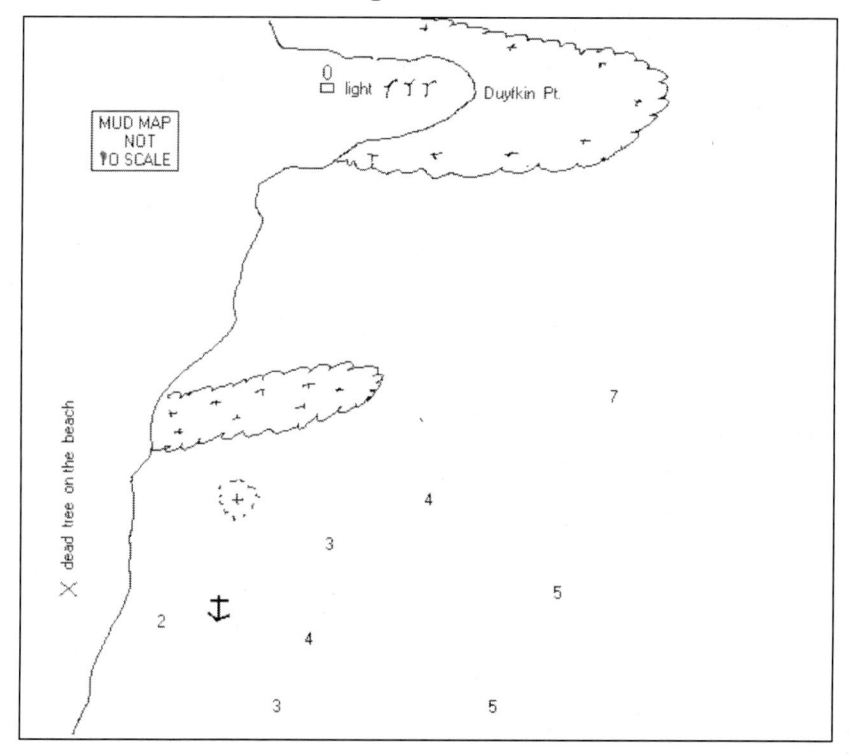

DUYFKIN POINT

12°34′S – 141°36′E

CHART	AUS 301
LIGHTS	Duyfkin Point flashes white every 5 seconds, visible 16 miles and can be difficult to see. It is at the southwest extremity of the point and carries a Racon.
TIDES	Weipa (Standard Port) ANTT

Duyfkin Point is 41 miles south of Port Musgrave. The coast is low sand-hills. Duyfkin Point consists of four low, sandy, tree-covered points, and low red cliffs on the southeast edge of the point. There are a few high hills along the southern end of the point. These are the only natural features along this part of the coast. Drying reefs and shoal ground extend up to 1 mile south and west of the point. In particular, Janssen Shoal, lies 2 miles southwest of the point. There is no passage between this and Duyfkin Point. No attempt should be made without local knowledge.

ALBATROSS BAY

After rounding Duyfkin Point, proceed into Albatross Bay, where anchorage can be found in varying depths of 1.6–3 metres, or where depth allows. The Normanade Creek can be entered on a rising tide. The Mission River is navigable up to the Road Bridge; anchor in 2 metres.

Duyfkin Point and Albatross Bay

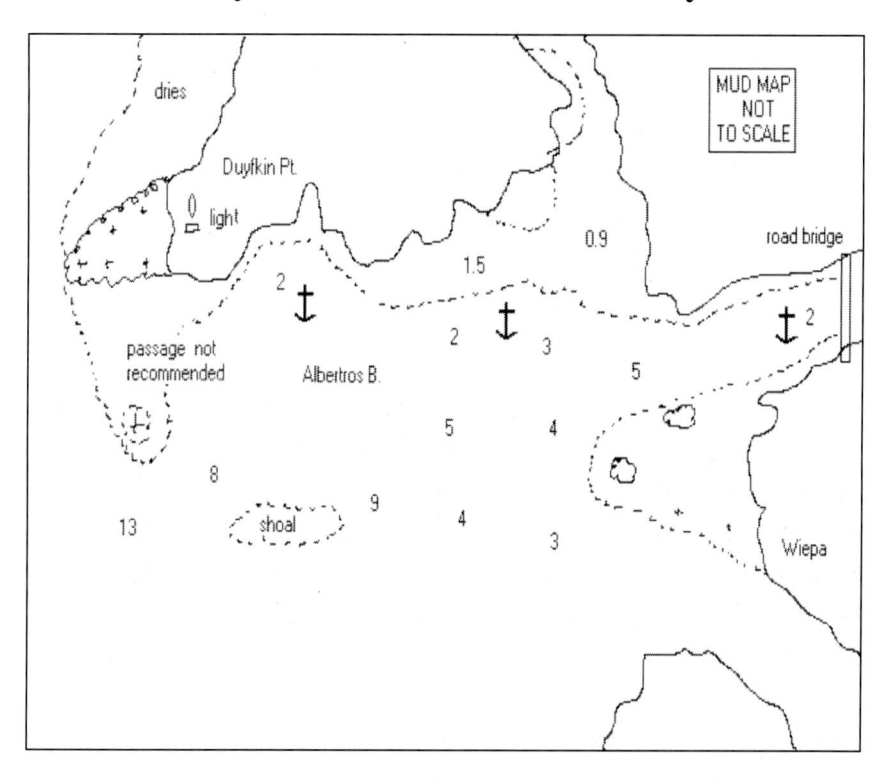

WEIPA

12°41'S – 141°53'E

CHARTS	AUS 301, 4
LIGHTS	Fairway Buoy on a red and white metal tripod, long flash white, visible 8 miles.
TIDES	Weipa (Standard Port) ANTT
RESCUE	Weipa Air Sea Rescue VMR 430

Entry to Weipa is either by the Jackson Channel or by the Main Channel to the south. The Jackson Channel is reasonably easy for small craft in daylight, as there is a minimum depth of 2.5 metres L.W. The Main Channel to the south is easier; it is beaconed its full length. There are lead lights on Gonburg Point and behind the wharf area. A lookout must be kept for ore carriers entering and leaving, as there is no room to manoeuvre and limited area outside. Once inside the port the anchorage is at Evans Landing. There is a shoal area in the port entrance (CORA BANK). This divides the river into 2 channels the one to the north leads to the main ore loading facility. The southern channel gives an alternate route into the river. Evans Landing has a public jetty just inside Gonburg Point and a tanker berth off Humbug Point. The water shoals to 5 metres well out and provides good anchorage for visiting craft, but you must anchor behind the main channel buoys and clear of all shipping. Weipa is a port of entry; the quarantine line is west of 140°40' E. Weipa has reasonable facilities where stores, fuel etc. can be purchased for the run across the gulf. Unfortunately, the town is 5 km away.

Weipa

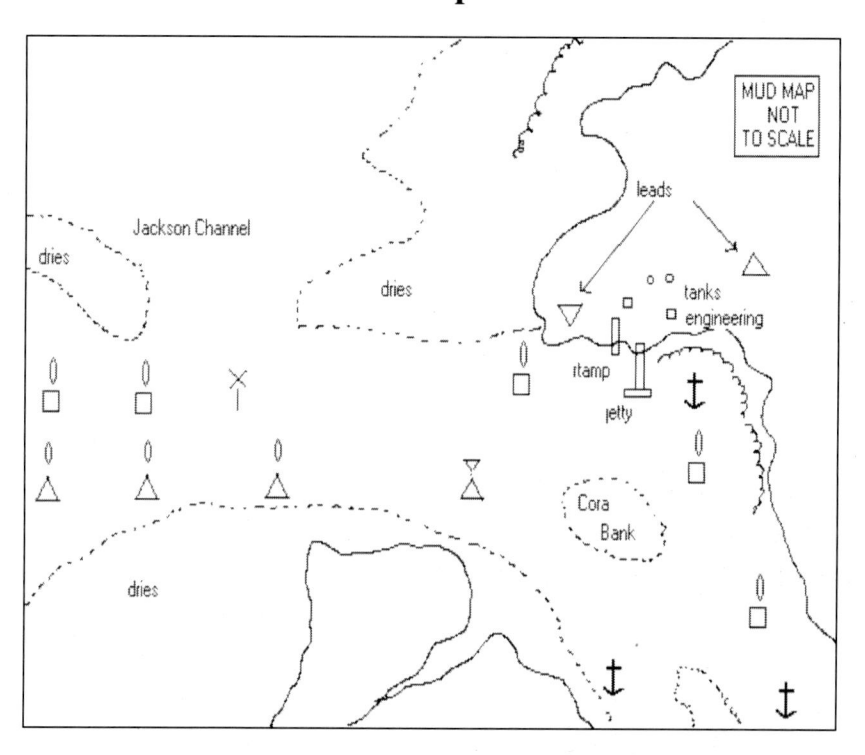

BOYD POINT

12°55′S – 141°38′E

CHART AUS 301
LIGHTS Nil
TIDES Weipa ANTT

Leaving Weipa by the south channel, exit is midway along, then Boyd Point lies 17 miles to the south. It is the only reasonable anchorage between Weipa and Archer River, a further 32 miles to the south. The coast is low, sandy and tree covered with some red bauxite cliffs. Anchorage is in 4 metres on the eastern side of the point.

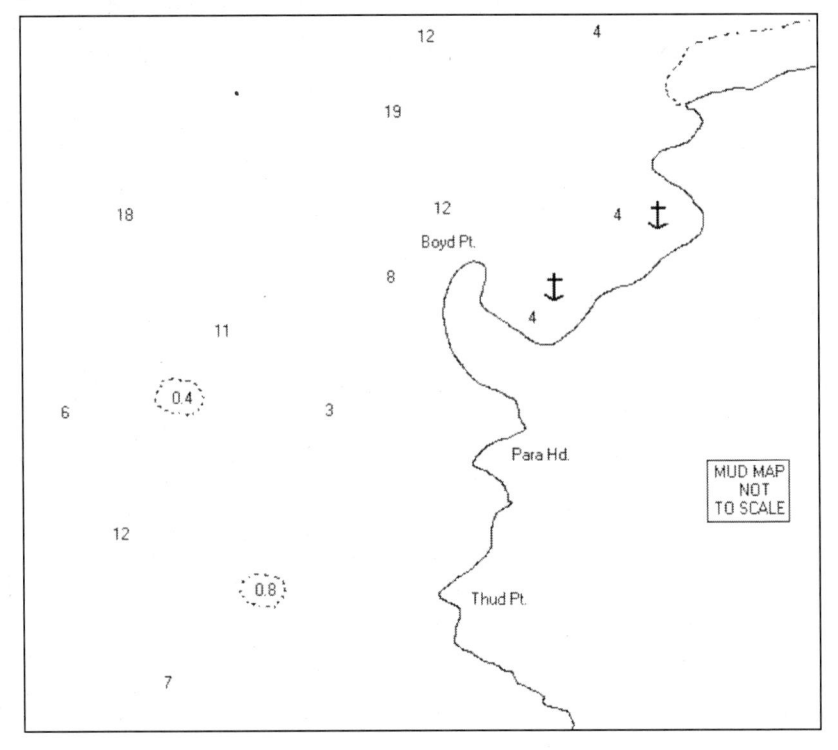

FALSE PARA HEAD

13°05′S – 141°37′E

CHART   AUS 301
LIGHTS Nil
TIDES   Weipa (Archer River) ANTT

This is a useful anchorage to cut the distance between Boyd Point and Archer River, 16 miles to the south. It bears a striking resemblance to Para Head to the north. The best anchorage was found in 4 metres on the northern side of the point. Anchorage can also be found in 2.5 metres on the southern side of the point, but is more exposed. If anchoring on the northern side, take care to avoid the 1.2-metre patch out from the head and the drying reef to the north. There are also two shoal areas between these two, but they gave no problems.

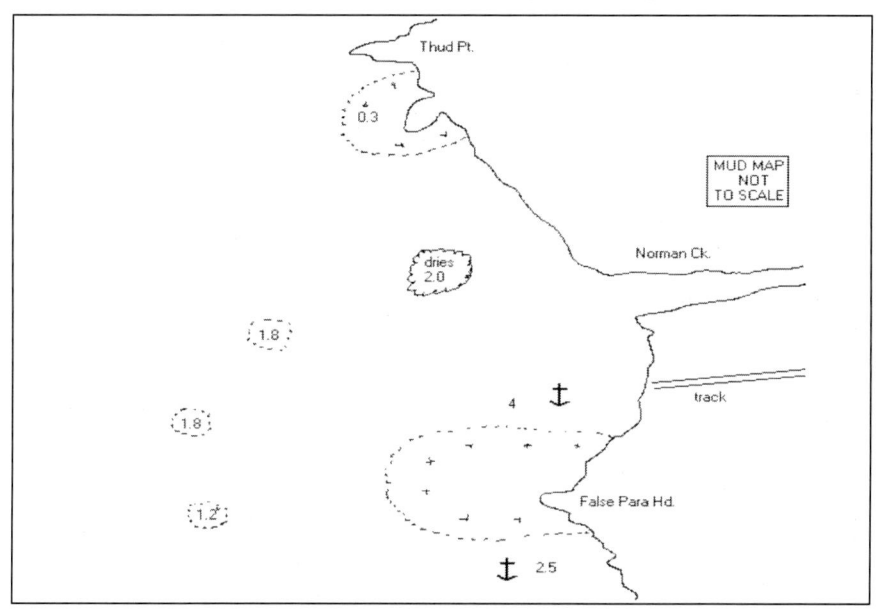

ARCHER RIVER

13°20.5′S – 141°38.5′E

CHARTS AUS 301, 302
LIGHTS Nil
TIDES Weipa (Archer River) ANTT

The entrance to the Archer River is 32 miles south of Boyd Point. The entrance is found between Worbody Point and Wallaby Island. There is a 0.5-metre bar in the entrance that requires ship's draft plus the bar. Also, a rising tide is needed to enter. The river can be navigated as far as the Aurukun Mission, 5 miles upstream from the mouth. Anchorage can be had anywhere depth allows, including in Archer Bay. Limited supplies are available at the mission, but prices are very high.

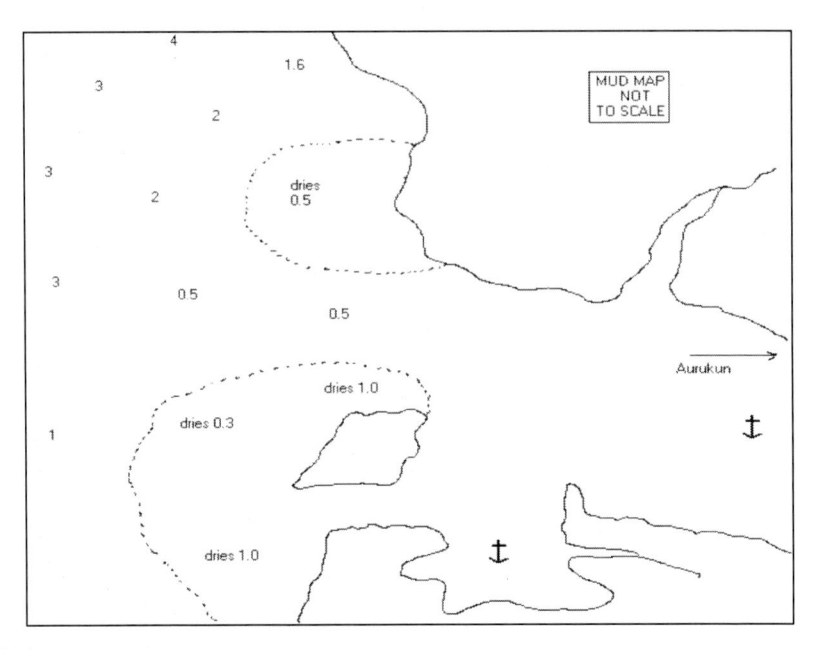

CAUTION
Mariners should be advised that the area south of the Archer River is unsurveyed or only partly surveyed. Extreme care should be taken at all times.

CAPE KEERWEER

13°55.5′S – 141°28′E

CHART AUS 302
LIGHTS NIL
TIDES Weipa (Archer River) ANTT

Cape Keerweer is 36 miles south of Archer River. The Kirke River runs along the inside of the cape, opening into a large lake system. Entry to the river is on high tide only. A survey by dinghy first is strongly recommended. Overnight anchorage can be had in 3–5 metres out from the cape.

KENDALL RIVER

14°09.5′S − 141°35.5′E

CHART AUS 302
LIGHTS Nil
TIDES Weipa (Archer River) ANTT

The Kendall River, 15 miles south of Cape Keerweer, is a handy stopover on the trek to the Edward River, 40 miles further south. A rising tide is necessary to enter the river. While waiting for the tide, I anchored out in 5 metres with no problems. The river is navigable for three miles up to Kuchendoopen, then a further 2 miles with care to the junction of the Kendall and Holroyd rivers. Anchorage can be found anywhere depth allows. I did not go any further than the junction of the two rivers.

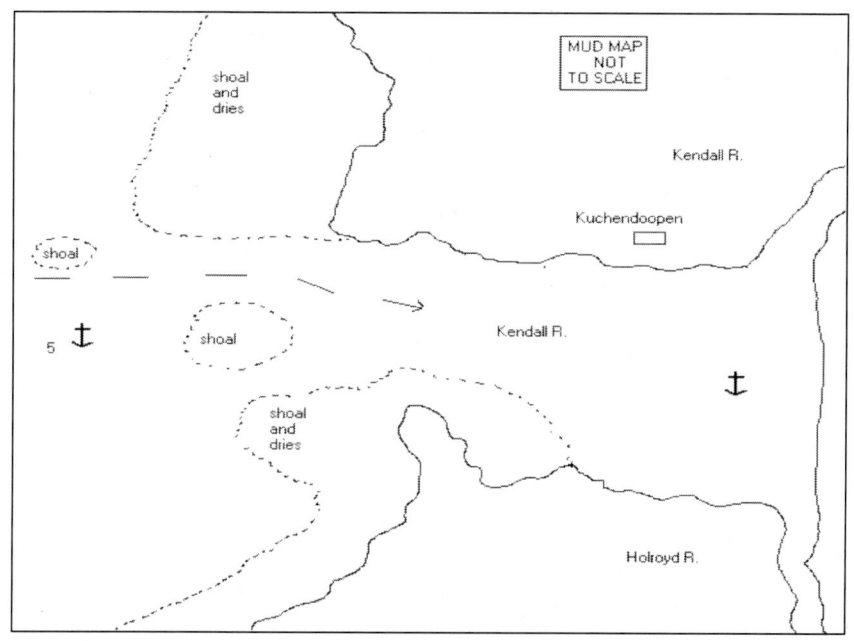

EDWARD RIVER

14°46'S – 141°34.5'E

CHART   AUS 302
LIGHTS   Nil
TIDES   Karumba (Nassau R. Offshore) ANTT

Edward River is 55 miles south of Cape Keerweer. There is a 0.6 bar across the river mouth. Once inside, the river is navigable with care as far as Edward River Mission. Limited supplies are available at the mission but expect to pay exorbitant prices. Anchorage can be found offshore, while waiting for the tide.

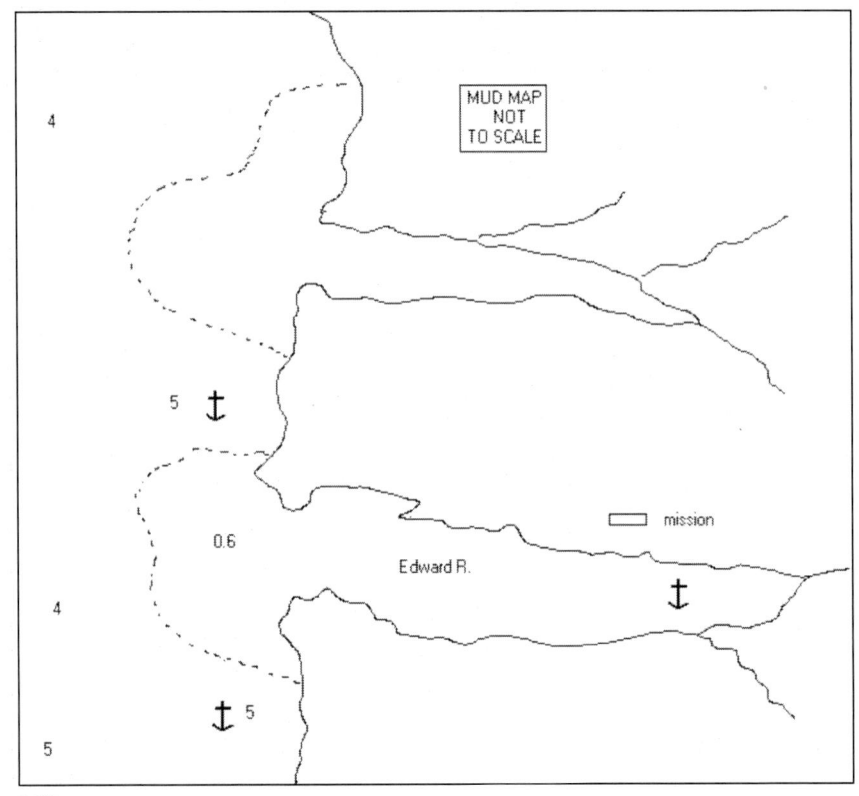

MUD MAP NOT TO SCALE

CHAPMAN RIVER

14°55′S – 141°37′E

CHART AUS 302
LIGHTS Nil
TIDES Karumba (Nassau River) ANTT

The community of Pormpuraaw is found north of the mouth. It is easily found by the large radio tower, visible for some miles. Landing is possible on the beach, but the best place is in the mouth of the river at the barge landing. A short walk will bring you to the community. There are extensive sandbanks around the mouth and seawards for some distance.

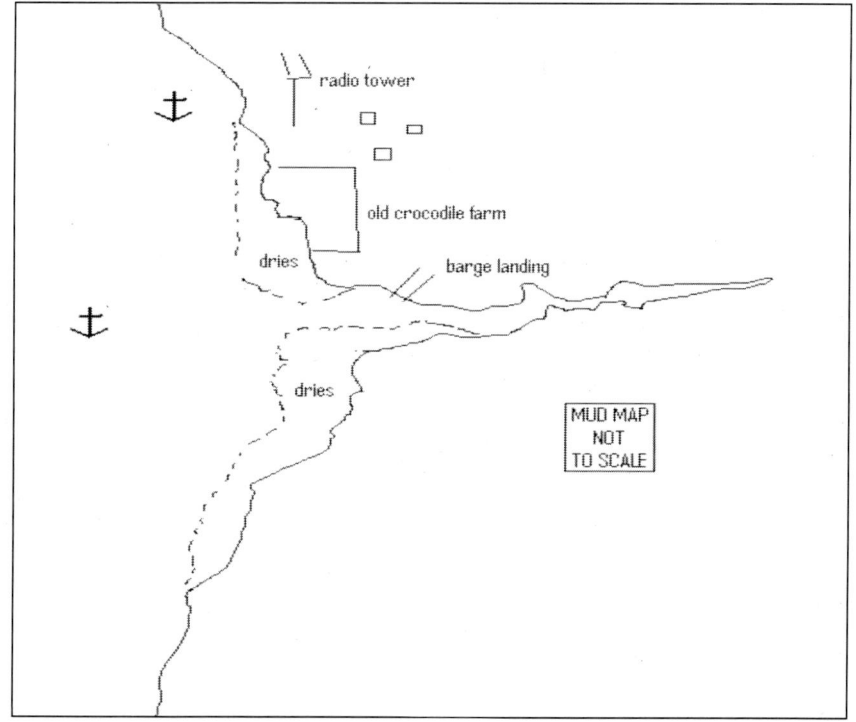

MUD MAP NOT TO SCALE

MITCHELL RIVER

15°12'S – 141°35'E

CHART   AUS 302
LIGHTS   NIL
TIDES   Karumba (Nassau River) ANTT

The entrance to the Mitchell River is 26 miles south of Edward River. The mouth is one mile wide, and carries a 0.6-metre sandbar, which extends right across the river mouth. The coast in this area is a lot lower than it is to the north. A number of creeks and rivers discharge to the north and south of the main river. Travelling south from Edward River, a distance of 1.25 miles out from the mainland is recommended, to clear the shoal area between the Chapman and Coleman rivers. There is a large mission on the South Mission River. The river is navigable without any trouble and anchorage can be found anywhere that depth allows. Water is available in Surprise Creek, further up from the South Mission River entrance. There is a tourist campsite here.

Mitchell River

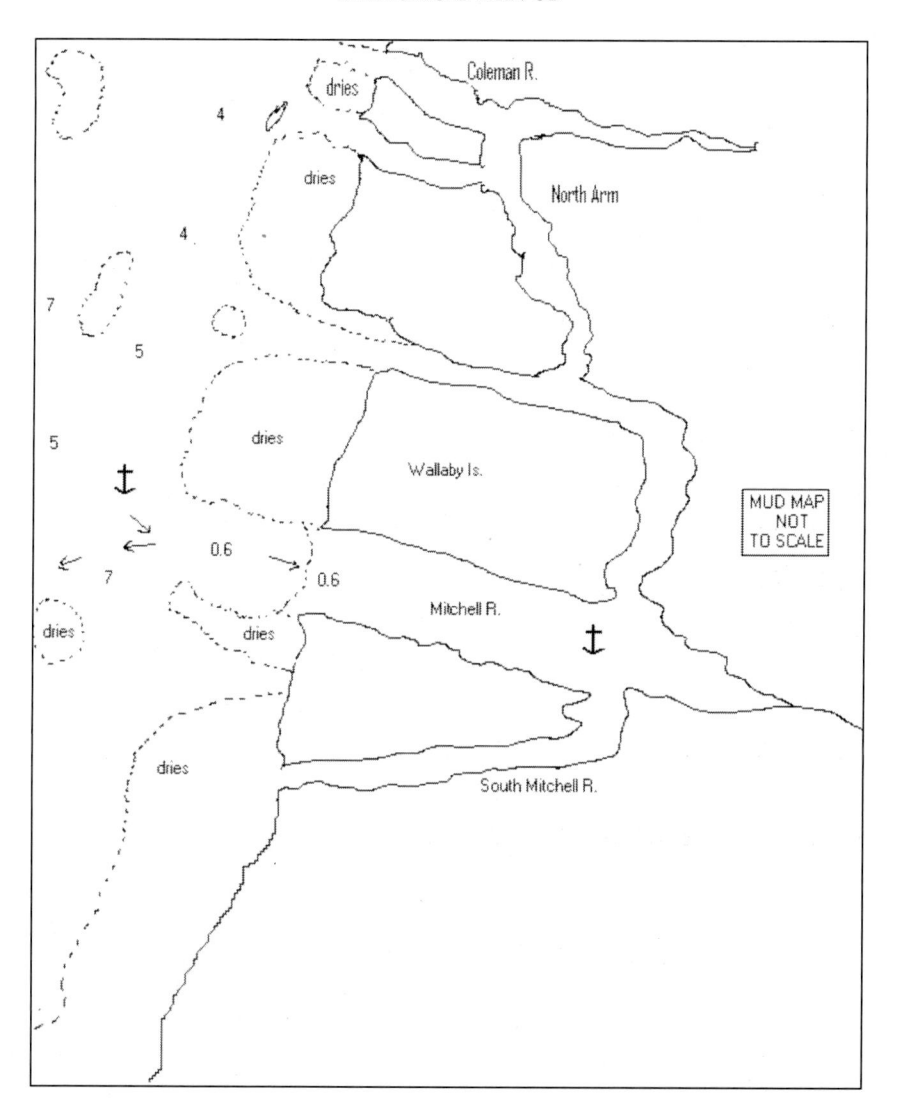

NASSAU RIVER

15°54'S – 141°23'E

CHARTS AUS 302, 303
LIGHTS Nil
TIDES Karumba (Nassau River) ANTT

The mouth of the Nassau River is 44 miles south of the Mitchell River. A bar of 0.6 metres requires a rising tide to enter. Once inside, the river swings to the north and is joined by Rocky Creek coming in from the south. The river itself is navigable for some distance. This area gives good fishing, crabbing and exploring in the dinghy. Anchor anywhere depth allows; I found mid-stream best.

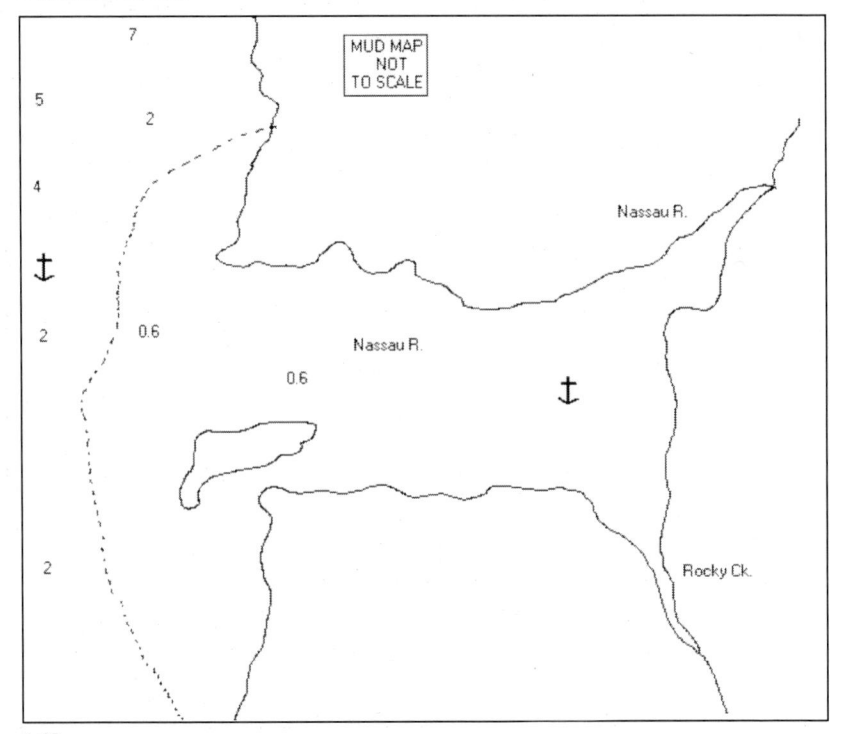

STAATEN RIVER

16°22′S – 141°16.5′E

CHART AUS 303
LIGHTS Nil
TIDES Karumba (Staaten River) ANTT

The Staaten River empties into the gulf 30 miles south of the Nassau River. It is navigable for approximately 12 miles. Anchor anywhere depth allows; I found it best to the side. As it was high tide and late in the afternoon when I entered, there did not appear to be a bar at the entrance, nor any other hazards. However, check before entering. As with other anchorages, the fishing was tops. After leaving to head south, be aware of the shoal area 8.5 miles south, and 4.25 miles offshore.

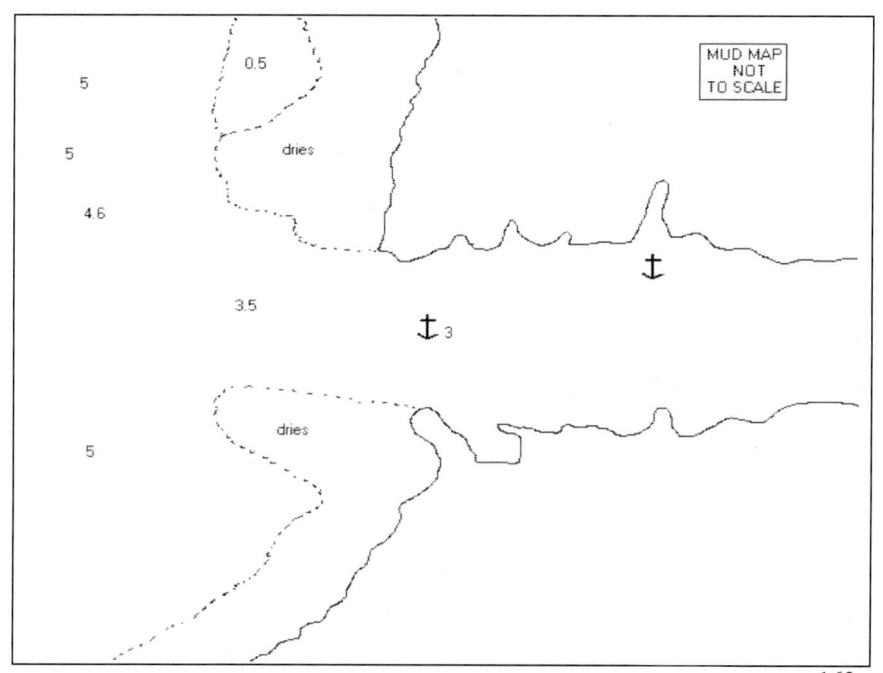

GILBERT RIVER

16°32′S – 141°16′E

CHART   AUS 303
LIGHTS   Nil
TIDES   Karumba (Staaten River) ANTT

Entrance to the Gilbert is 10 miles south of the Staaten River. I found no bar at the entrance, but check first. There are three entries. I used the westerly one with no problems. I was told that the river was navigable for most of its length. I only went as far as the first bend to the west with no trouble. There was plenty of water and holding was in mud. Fishing was good with plenty of bities and crocodiles.

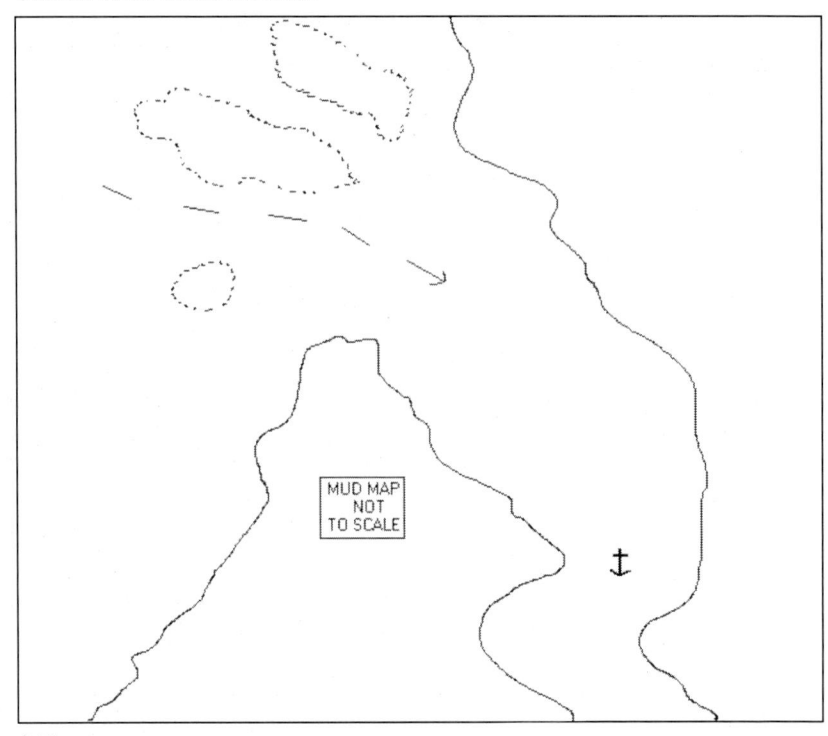

MUD MAP
NOT
TO SCALE

POINT BURROWS

16°58′S – 140°58′E

CHART   AUS 303
LIGHTS   Nil
TIDES   As for Karumba ANTT

Point Burrows is the southern entry point to Van Diemen Gulf, which is fronted by tidal mud flats. There is a bar of 0.5 metres in the entrance. Once inside the depth increases to average 3 metres, then the river quickly narrows but is navigable by boats with a 1.5-metre draft. Anchor where depth allows. If anchoring outside, anchor in 3–4 metres, the holding is good, but anchor 1.5 mile offshore. The river goes east for 2 miles then swings north, does a circle, and meets up again from the south.

KARUMBA

FAIRWAY BUOY 17°25.6'S – 140°43.5'E

CHART AUS 303
LIGHTS Fairway Buoy flashes red/white 10 seconds and is 5 miles offshore. Landfall light to the east of Alligator Point flashes every 2 seconds, visible 6 miles. Red/green/yellow channel markers light the channel, making entry easy.
TIDES Karumba (Standard Port) ANTT

Karumba is home to a large fishing fleet. There are all the facilities associated with a busy fishing port, but there are no haul-out facilities. Entry is over a bar of 0.6 metres, so a rising tide is needed. After rounding the Fairway Buoy, the channel is clearly marked. The first are red and green, the next is red, then red and yellow. Turn here for the next green, then between the next red and green, now turn southeast for the next two reds; keep these to port. Next there are two greens and a yellow; keep these to starboard. Between the fuel jetty and the last jetty there are two reds and a yellow. Pass these and anchor where possible. Vessels with up to 3-metre draft can navigate the Norman River as far as Double Island, about 11 miles upstream. Normanton is a further 17 miles and can be reached by small craft on most tides, but favour the outside of the curves and post a lookout. No real problems were encountered. Live cattle are exported from here as well.

Karumba

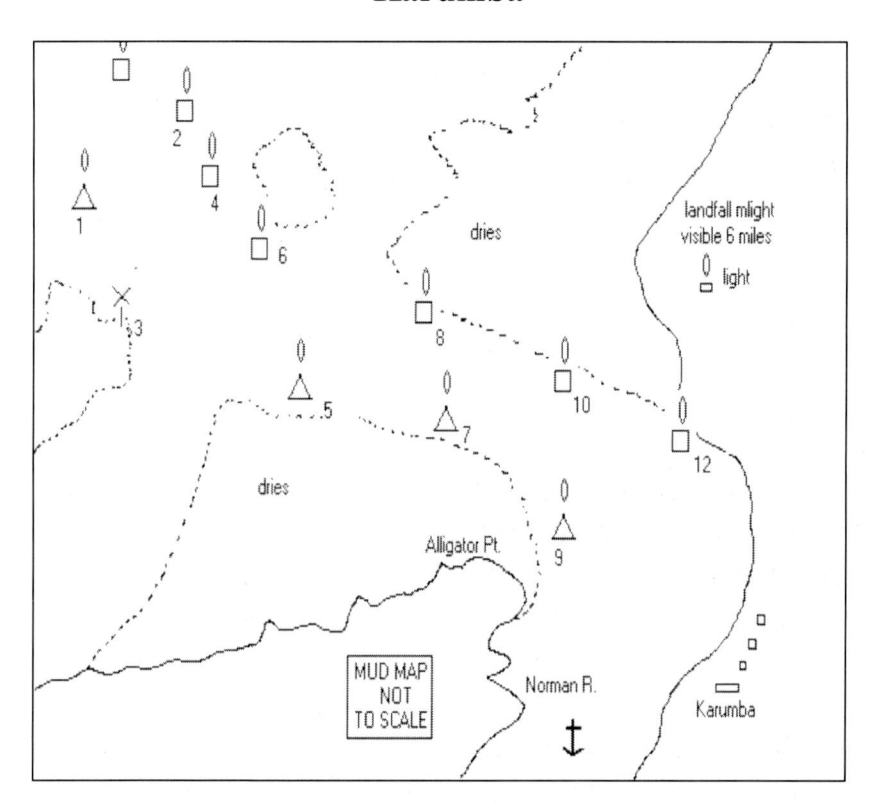

ALBERT RIVER

17°34′S – 139°45′E

CHART AUS 303
LIGHTS Kangaroo Point flashes 6 seconds, visible 10 miles.
TIDES Karumba (Sweers Island) ANTT

The Albert River lies 55 miles west of the Karumba Fairway Buoy. The bar extends 4 miles out from the light on Kangaroo Point, with a depth of 0.1 metres. Kangaroo Point can be identified by an odd shaped clump of trees. The river mouth is approximately 0.5 miles wide, and is entered between Kangaroo Point to the east and Stokes Point to the west. The river extends to Burketown some 30 miles upstream. Small craft can proceed up the river on most tides, as far as Truganini Landing, which is just below Burketown, where a depth of 1.5 metres will be found. Anchor anywhere in the river that depth allows.

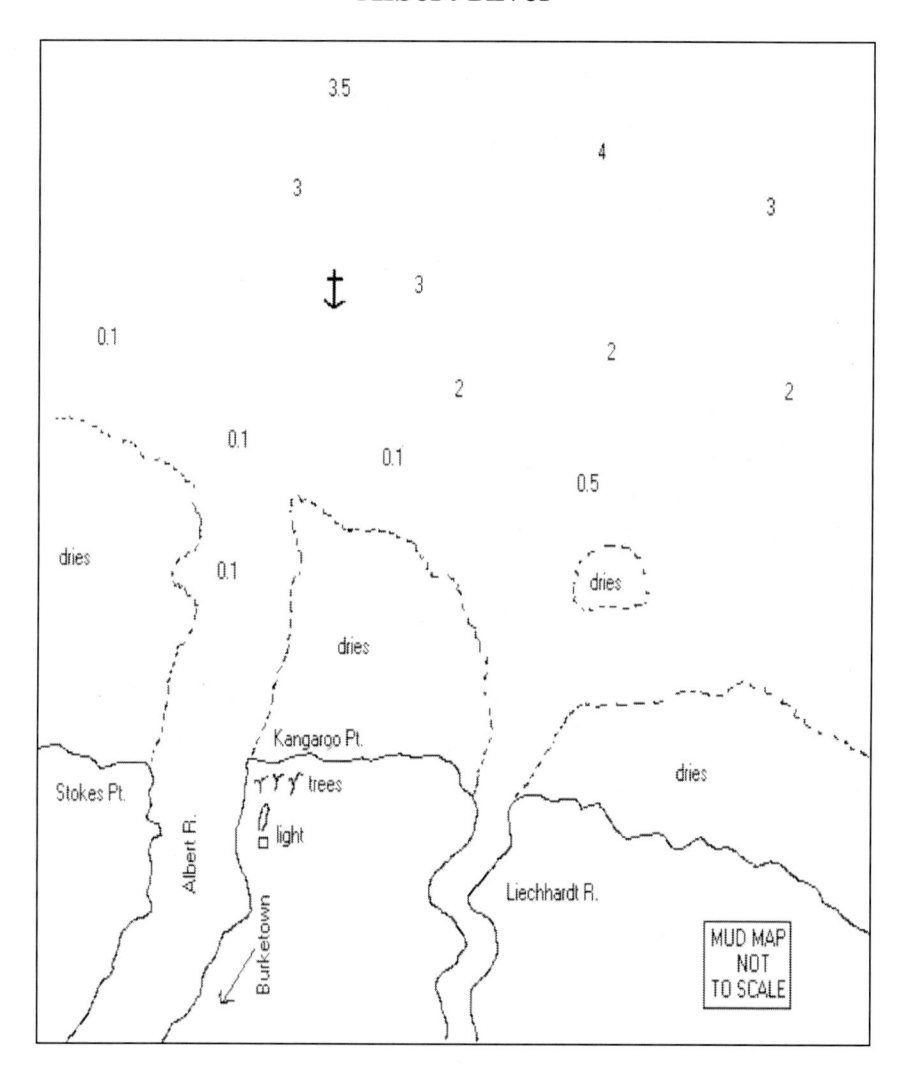

Albert River

SWEERS ISLAND

17°06'S – 139°37'E

CHART   AUS 303
LIGHTS   Nil
TIDES   Karumba (Sweers Island) ANTT

Sweers Island lies approximately 30 miles north-northwest of the Albert River. It is entered from the south through Investigator Road. Anchorage is on the western side of the island, between Macdonald Point in the south and Inscription Point in the north, in 7 metres. The tide here floods south and ebbs north at 1.0 knots. Owing to extensive shallows to the north of the anchorage, a course along the southern side of Bentinck Island is recommended. There is also a resort that is worth a visit. When approaching from the south, watch out for a large red buoy in the middle of the channel. This marks the end of a reef and should be kept to starboard. Continue and anchor in the clear area behind the next marker on a pole. Visitors are welcome.

Sweers Island

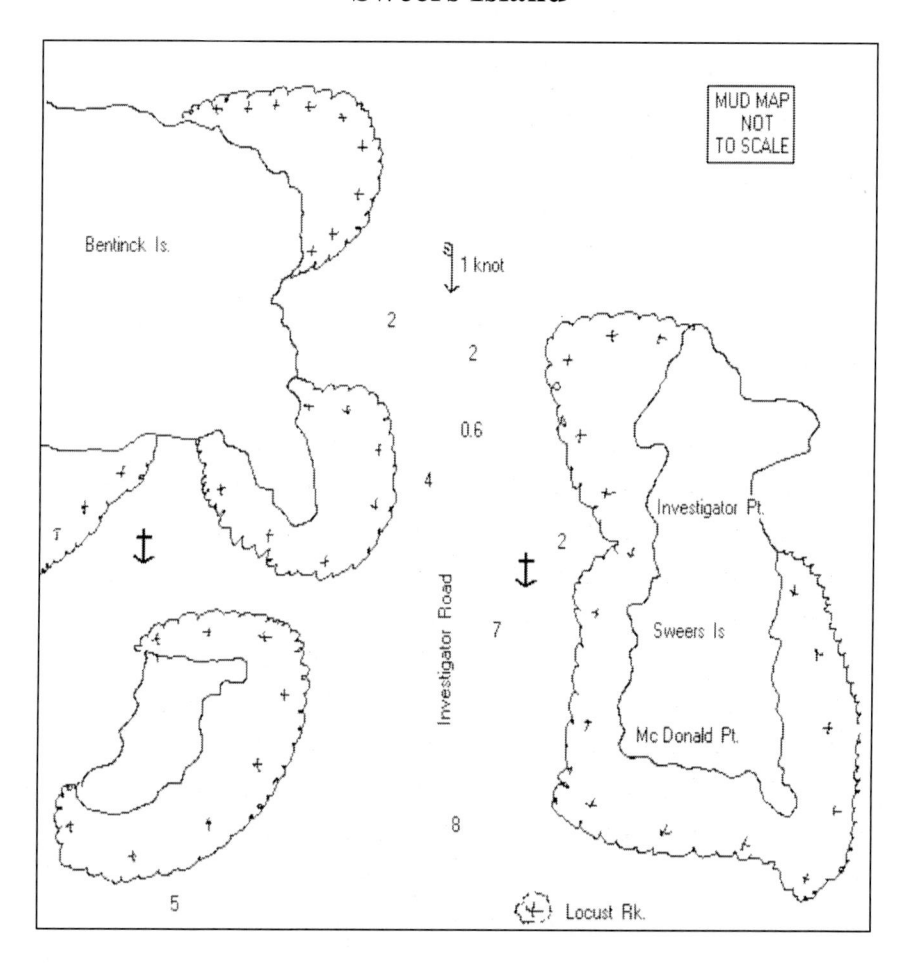

POINT PARKER

17°02'S – 139°09'E

CHART AUS 303
LIGHTS Nil
TIDES Karumba (Sweers Island) ANTT

Point Parker offers anchorage close to Allen Island in 4 metres, out from the northwest corner of the Island or close to Point Parker, in 2 metres. Approach from Sweers Island until clear of Bentinck Island, and then steer for Point Parker. The anchorage out from Allen Island was found to be best, as it is more protected from the southeast. The southern side of Horseshoe Island also offers shelter in 3 metres out from the fringing reef, but there is no passage further west. When leaving Point Parker and Allen Island, take care to give Little Allen Island a wide berth. From Allen Island, there is passage between Forsyth Island and Pains Island. However, the top half of a rising tide is needed to cross the mud flats to the channel. Keep a close eye on the sounder and motor; not recommended to sail. Keep a close visual lookout while in the channel, as well as sounder. There is a large sand area with a bar running north from it which not shown on the chart. It is not advisable to close the coast from here, as there are scattered shoal areas.

Point Parker

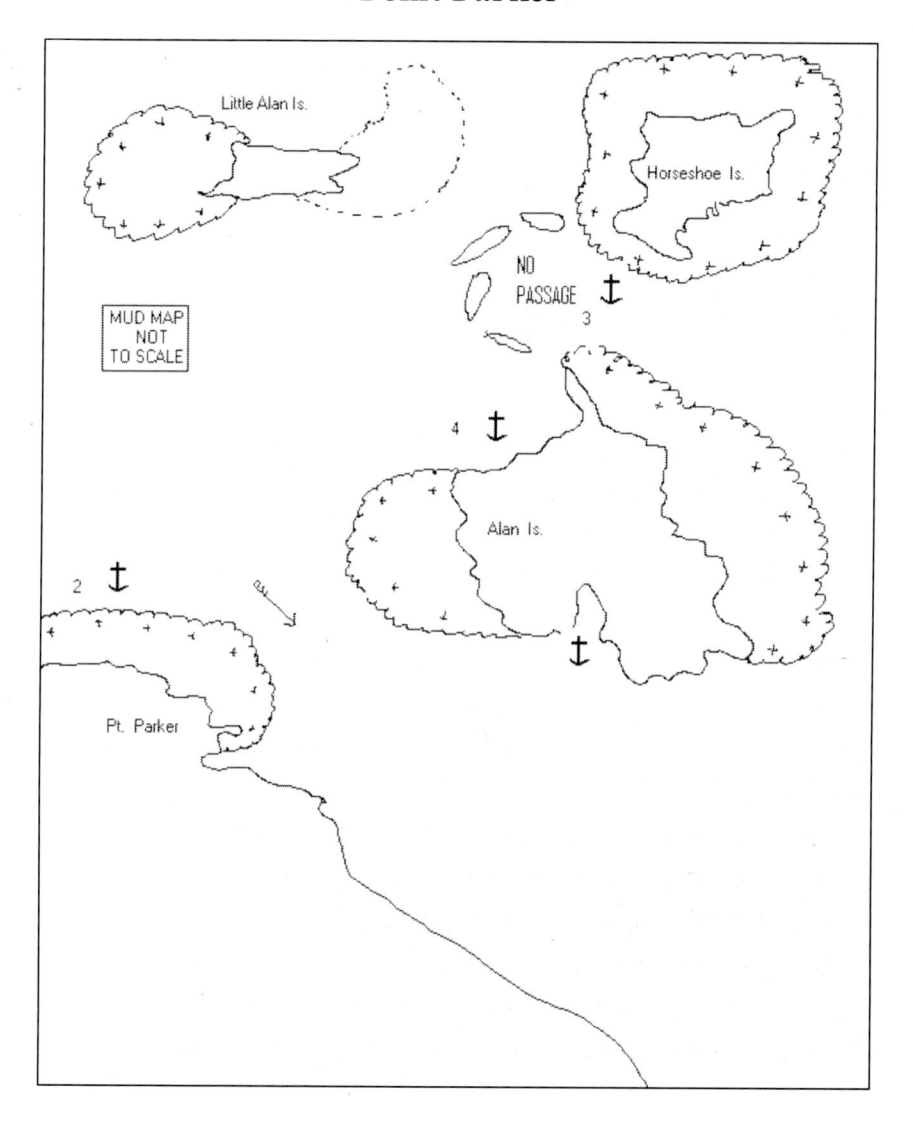

MORNINGTON ISLAND – (Updated)

DUBBAR POINT 16°40'S – 139°10'E
APPEL CHANNEL entrance 16°47.25'S – 139°15.60'E

CHARTS	AUS 303, 304
LIGHTS	Nil
TIDES	Karumba (Mornington Island) ANTT
RESCUE	Air Sea Rescue Mornington Island VMR 457

Mornington Island is 45 miles from Sweers Island. There is a large mission on Dubbar Point, at the north end of Appel Channel. Extreme care is a definite must in this area, owing to many offshore dangers. Once in the channel, the depth I found was 3.6 metres L.W. The mission services the entire Wellesley Islands. There is an airstrip and other facilities, including post office and supermarket. Owing to the lack of navigation aids, the following waypoints are required, and are as supplied by the barge service to the island. Ships draft plus top half of a rising tide is necessary, owing to a rock bar and a sand bank at the other end. Coming from Sweers Island the first waypoint is:

1	16°47.250'E	139°15.600'S
2	16°44.908'E	139°12.261'S
3	16°44.194'E	139°11.727'S

SAND BAR

4	16°43.783'E	139° 11.622'S
5	16°44.341'E	139° 11.431'S

6   16°41.036'E   139° 11.598'S
7   16°40.651'E   139° 11.631'S
ROCK BAR
8   16°40.337'E   139°11.640'S

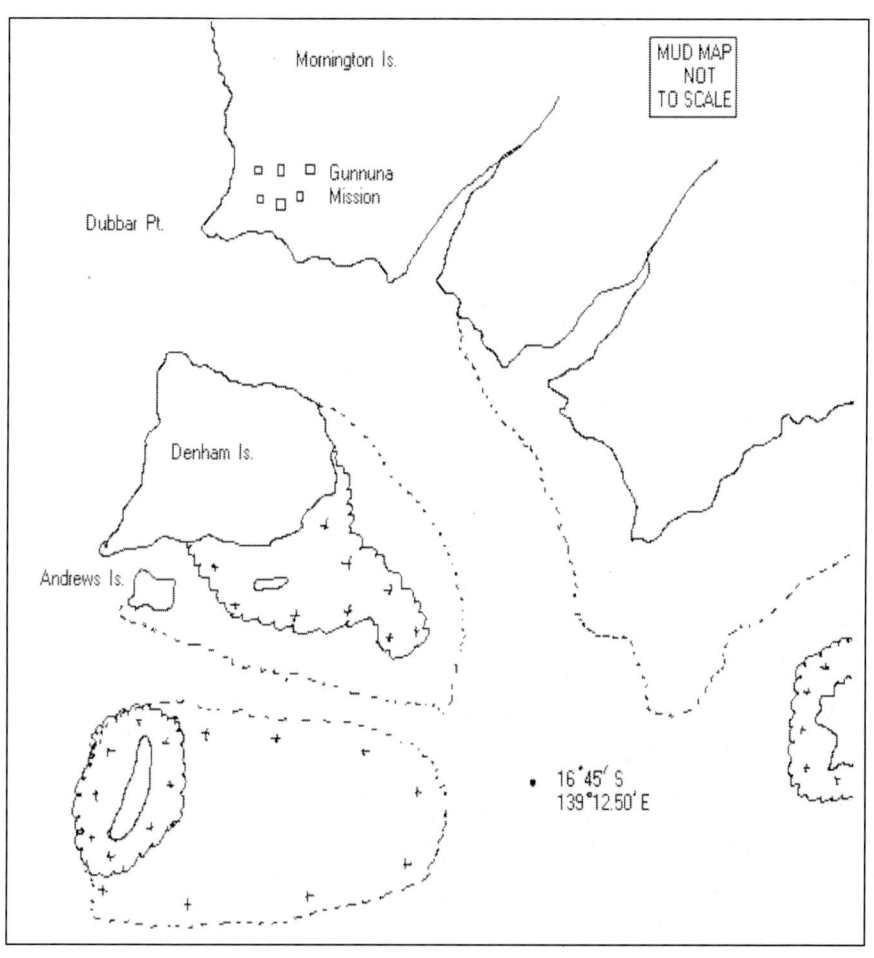

TULLY INLET

16°40′S – 138°09.5′E

CHART   AUS 304
LIGHTS   Nil
TIDES   Karumba (Mornington Island) ANTT

Tully Inlet is 55 miles west of Mornington Island; this is the last anchorage in Queensland. The border to the Northern Territory is 12 miles further on. There is a drying bar across the entrance. It extends 1.5 miles offshore, and depths of 1.5 metres extend a further 3.5 miles out. Anchor inside the inlet in 2.5 metres in mud.

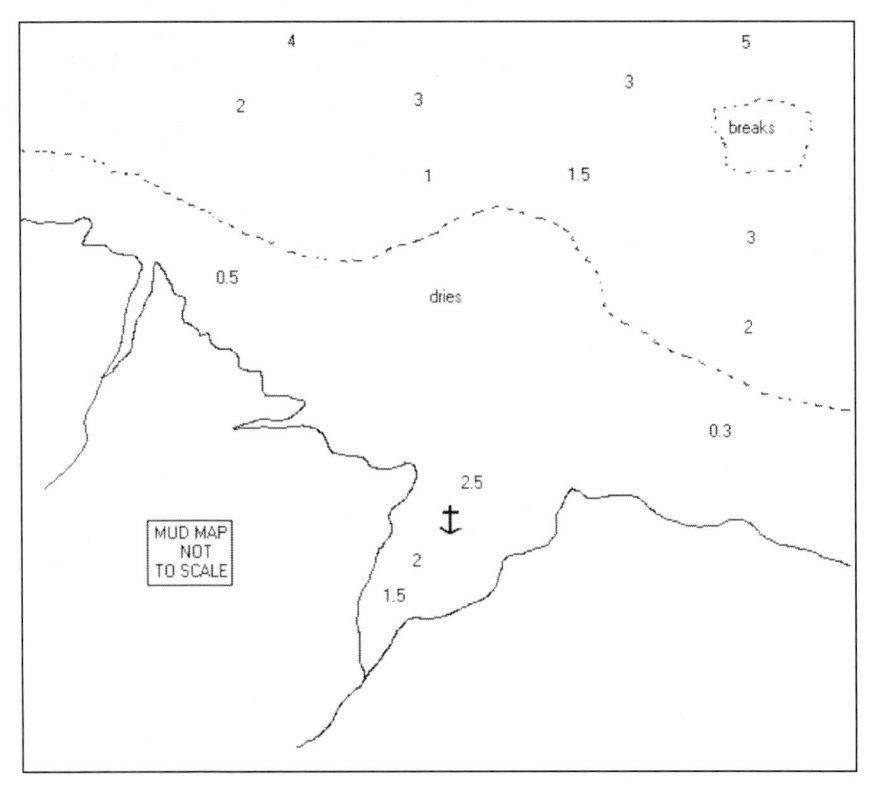

CALVERT RIVER

16°16′S – 137°45′E

CHART	AUS 304
LIGHTS	NIL
TIDES	Karumba (Mornington Is.) ANTT
TIME	Welcome to the Northern Territory. Turn your clocks back 30 minutes.
CAUTION	There is an uncharted reef close inshore centred at 16°12′S – 137°45.50′S and extending 2.5 miles from centre.

The Calvert River is 38 miles northwest of Tully Inlet. There is a drying bar across its entrance. The entrance is 1 mile wide. There are patches of 1.5 to 1.8 in the bar. The river is shallow. I anchored in 4 metres over mud just inside the mouth.

Calvert River

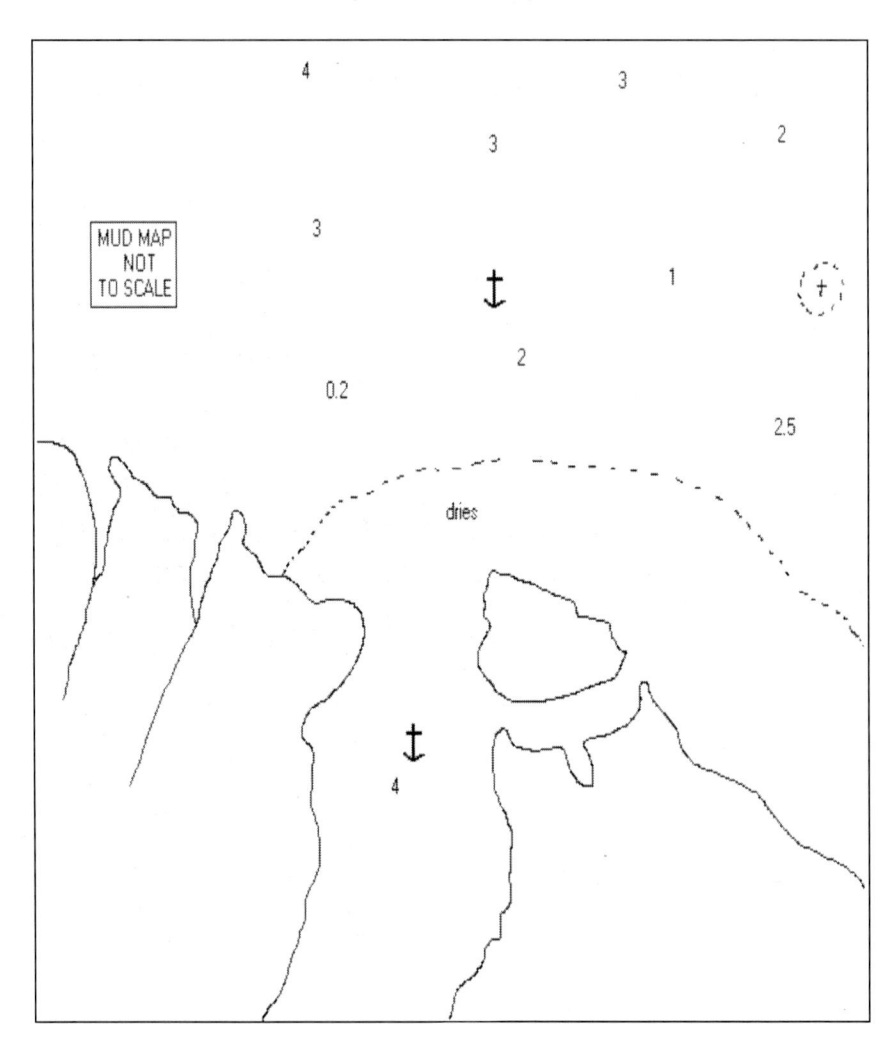

ROBINSON RIVER

16°02.5'S – 137°16'E

CHARTS   AUS 304, 305
LIGHTS   Nil
TIDES   Milner Bay (Centre Island) ANTT

The Robinson River is located 32 miles west-northwest from the Calvert River. Keep at least 4 miles offshore to clear the patch of rocks about halfway along the coast. The entrance bar has 1 metre on it and can be crossed without difficulty on a rising tide. Once inside the river it divides into three and rejoins 2 miles upstream. At this point, there are varying depths of 6–9 metres. The river can be travelled for some distance, depending on draft.

UPDATE 2004 showed the bar has extended out for around 2 miles. Keelboats will not be able to enter.

Robinson River

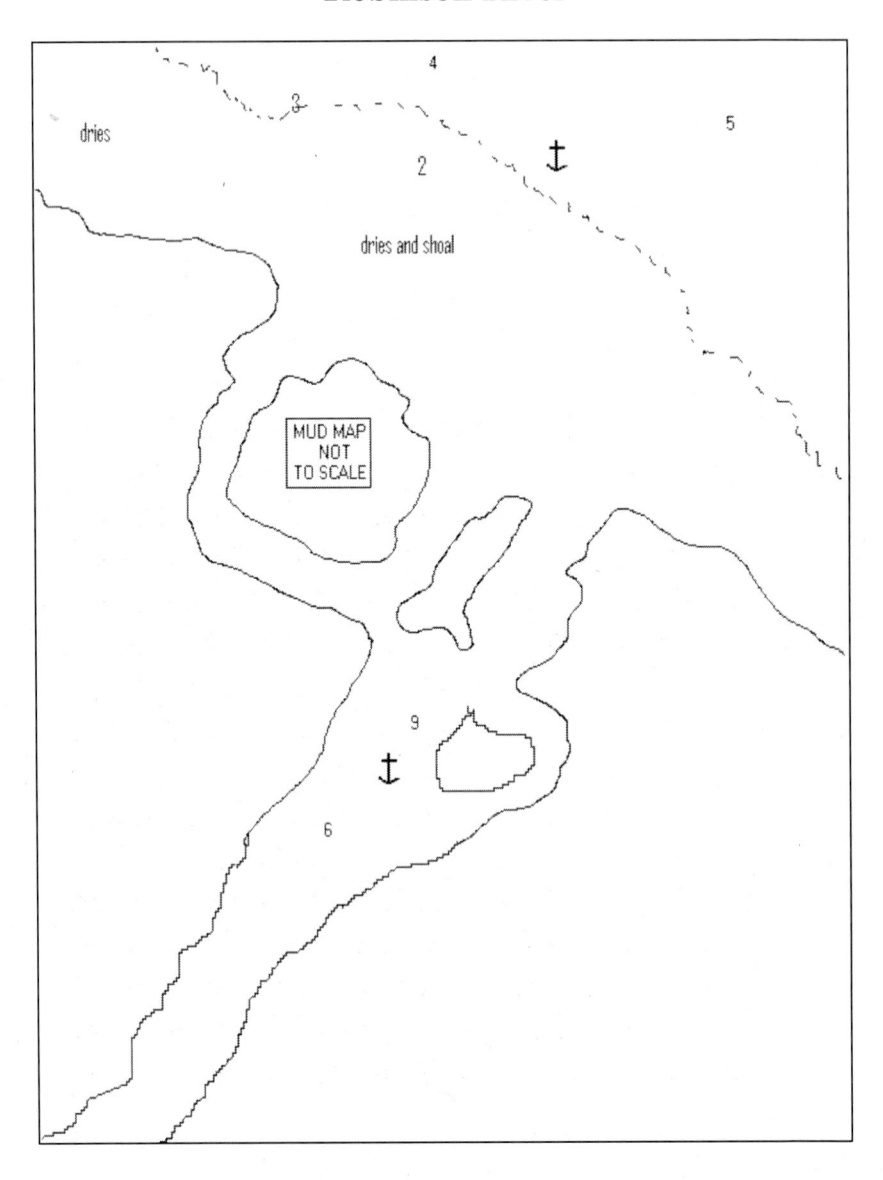

dries

4

3

5

2

dries and shoal

MUD MAP
NOT
TO SCALE

9

6

VANDERLIN ISLAND

15°43'S – 137°0'E

CHART　　AUS 305
LIGHTS　　Nil
TIDES　　Milner Bay (Centre Island) ANTT

Directly under the eastern side of Cape Vanderlin is **REFUGE COVE**, providing good shelter for small craft. Cape Vanderlin has a very distinctive yellow sandhill. Around the cape and to the south lies **SECOND BAY**. This is an anchorage used by trawlers in the prawn season. There is a sandy beach here and a freshwater lagoon over the sandhills behind the beach. **BARBARA COVE** is a pleasant stopover, but needs further investigation. Further south lies **GERANIUM BAY**. A secure anchorage is found well out in 3 metres; the holding is good. Around Charles Point, the bay on the southern side also gives good anchorage in 3 metres. I did not look at the next bay, but went on to **CLARKSON POINT**, the southern point of the island. To the west of the point, anchorage can be found in 2.5 metres. **INVESTIGATOR BAY** is at the northeast corner of the island and is entered between Three Hummocks Point and Mesially Point, 2 miles to the northwest, giving good shelter in winds from the south and west. Anchor well out in 3 metres.

Vanderlin Island

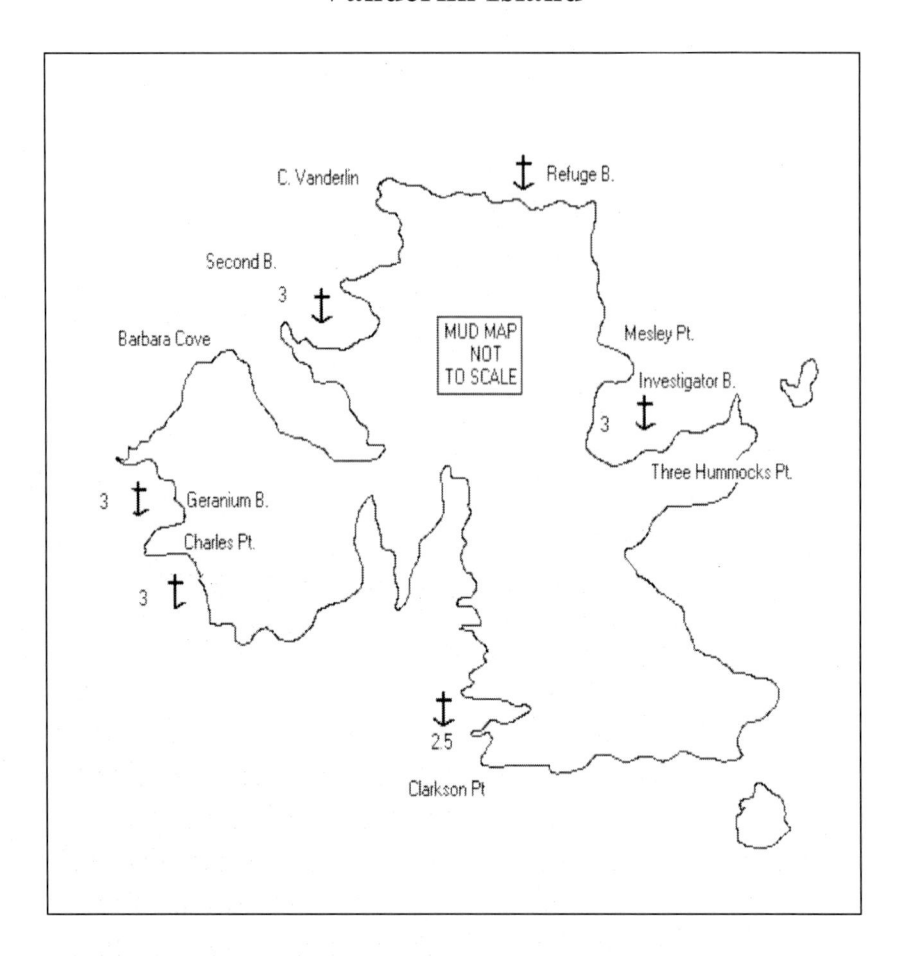

OBSERVATION ISLAND

15°37'S – 136°54'E

This island lies between Vanderlin Island and North Island in the Addison Channel. It has a monument 5 metres high that commemorates the visit by Matthew Flinders in 1802. There is no place to anchor, but it is possible if you want to.

NORTH ISLAND

15°35'S – 136°52'E

CHART	AUS 305
LIGHTS	Nil
TIDES	Milner Bay (Centre Island) ANTT

After Observation Island I went to North Island, rounding Cape Pellew on the inside of North Rock, but favour North Rock, or go around the outside if unsure. Carry on to Ross Point, round this and enter Paradise Bay. This bay provides excellent shelter in strong southeast winds. Anchor in 2–4 metres in mud. There is a good beach at the head of the bay. Trawlers use this bay during the prawn season. Ashore is the residence of a barra fisherman. The passage further south is blocked by extensive reef.

North Island

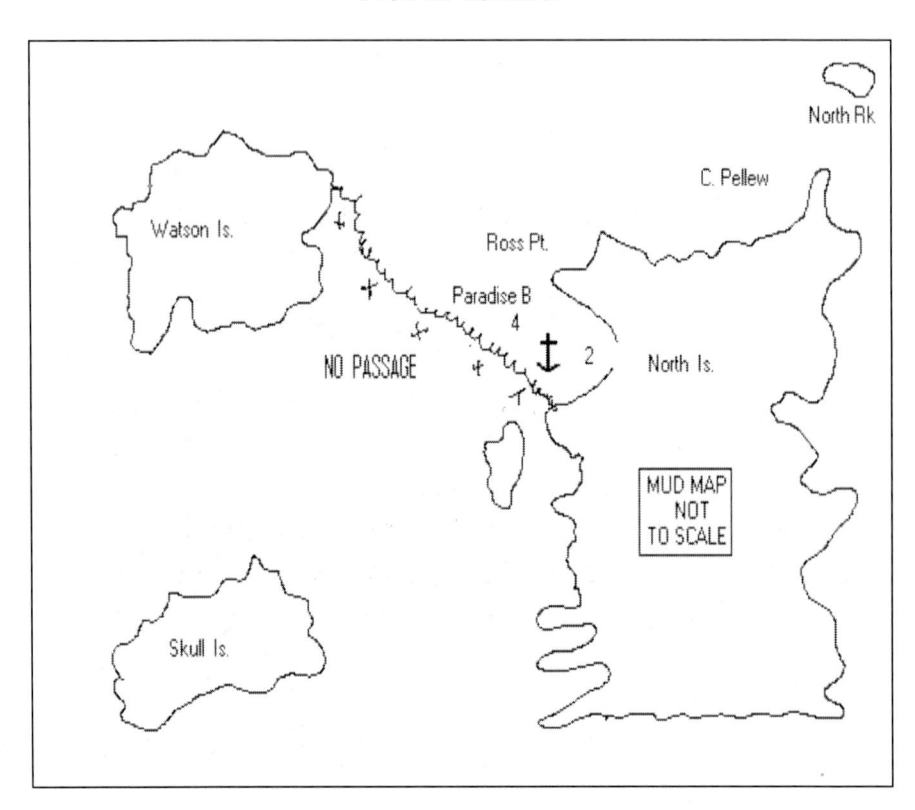

Map labels: North Rk, C. Pellew, Watson Is., Ross Pt., Paradise B, NO PASSAGE, North Is., Skull Is.

MUD MAP NOT TO SCALE

WEST ISLAND and BING BONG

15°35'S – °33'E

CHART   AUS 305
LIGHTS   At Bing Bong a green flashes 10 seconds leading to a green/white/red sector flashing 17 seconds, visible 10 miles.
TIDES   Milner Bay (West Island) ANTT

On the western side of West Island, there is an unnamed bay. Where anchorage can be found in 3 metres over mud, the holding is good. Be on the lookout for barges taking ore out to load on ships at 15°21.57'S – 136°29.94'E. In 1995, mining commenced in the Macarthur River area and the port of Bing Bong was established. If there are no ships being loaded, it may be worth a look. There may also be water. They will not sell fuel or stores.

West Island and Bing Bong

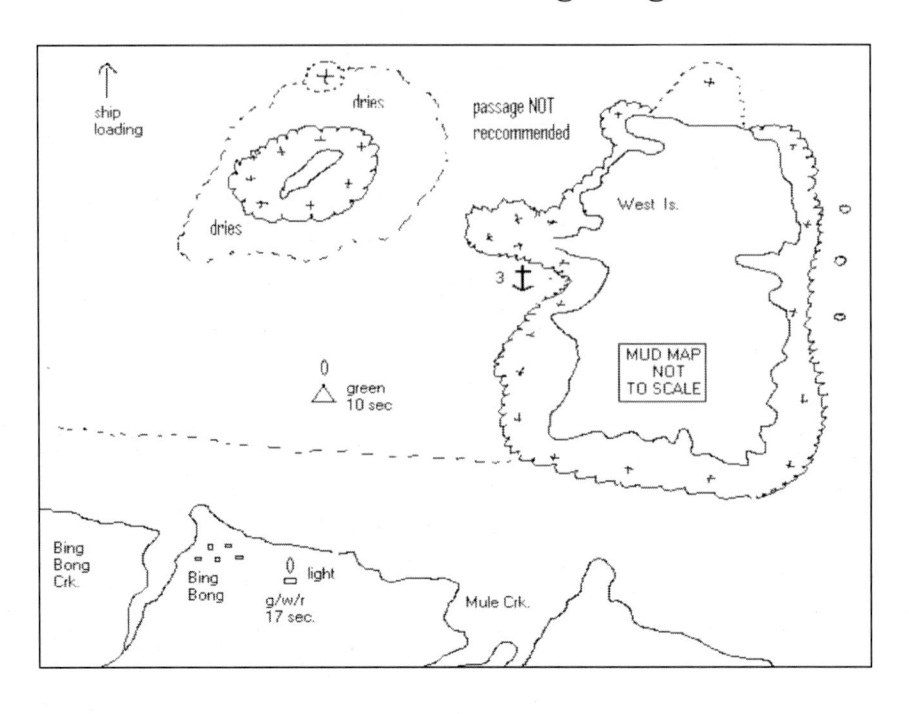

CAUTION

The reef shown on chart AUS 305 at 15°26.20′E and 136°24.75′S is not as shown. It extends a further 3 miles west and extends further north and south than shown.

LIMMEN BIGHT RIVER

15°06'S – °43'E

CHART　　AUS 305
LIGHTS　　Nil
TIDES　　Milner Bay (Rose River) ANTT

Limmen Bight River is 55 miles from West Island. After clearing Labrynthian Shoals, a distance of 5 miles offshore is recommended, to clear Beatrice Island and its Satellite Island to the north. At this point, depths of 2 metres will be encountered. This will hold to the entrance of the river. The shoal water extends out for 3.5 miles. The barred entrance was found to have 0.75 metres in it, but can be crossed on a high tide. I used the middle entrance with no trouble. The river is narrow and shallow at low tide, but there are some deep holes to be found or sink in the mud. It is hardly worth the trouble.

Limmen Bight River

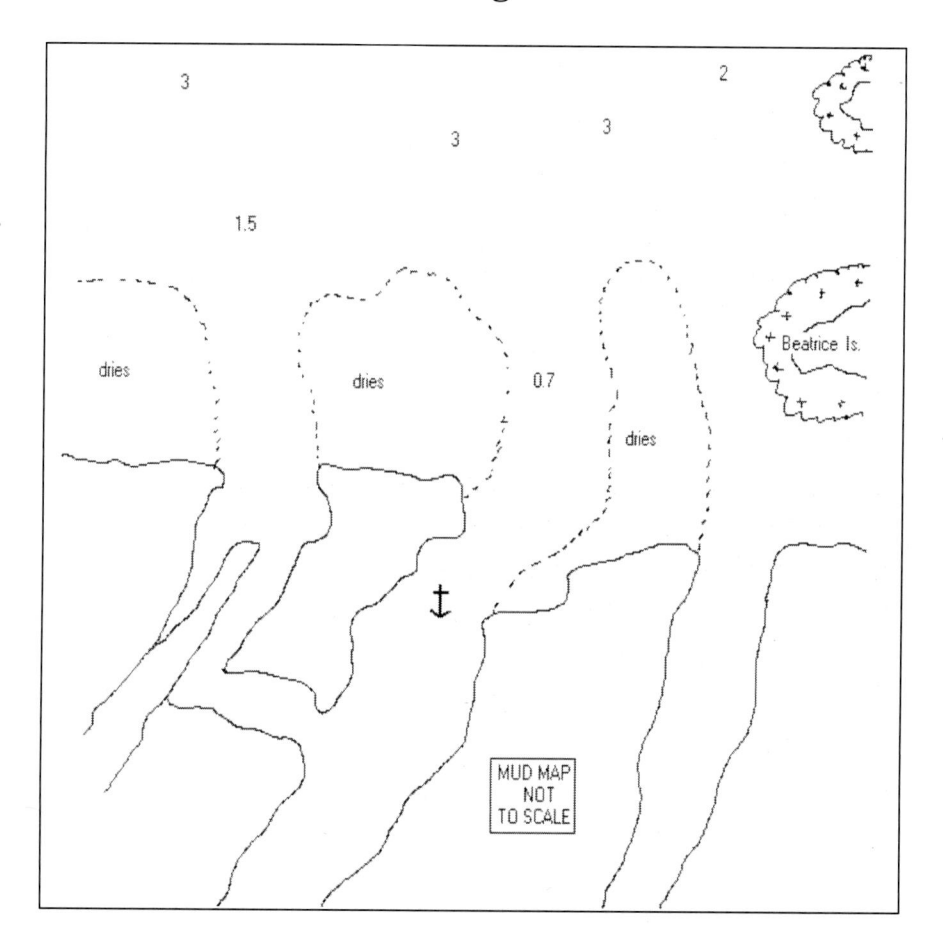

MARIA ISLAND

14°52'S – 5°44'E

CHART AUS 305
LIGHTS Nil
TIDES Milner Bay (Rose River) ANTT

Maria Island is 65 miles from West Island anchorage. There are not any decent anchorages along this part of the coast. It is possible to enter Limmen Bight River by the middle entrance, but is hardly worth the effort. The only anchorage on Maria Island is on the western side in Eagle Bay in 3–4 metres over good holding thick mud. Beware of the rock northwest of the anchorage; it only has 1.6 metres. The southern side of the island appeared to be clear of dangers. The western shore has shallows and rock patches. Careful navigation is necessary. A track west-northwest of Eagle Bay is the entrance to the mighty Roper River.

Maria Island

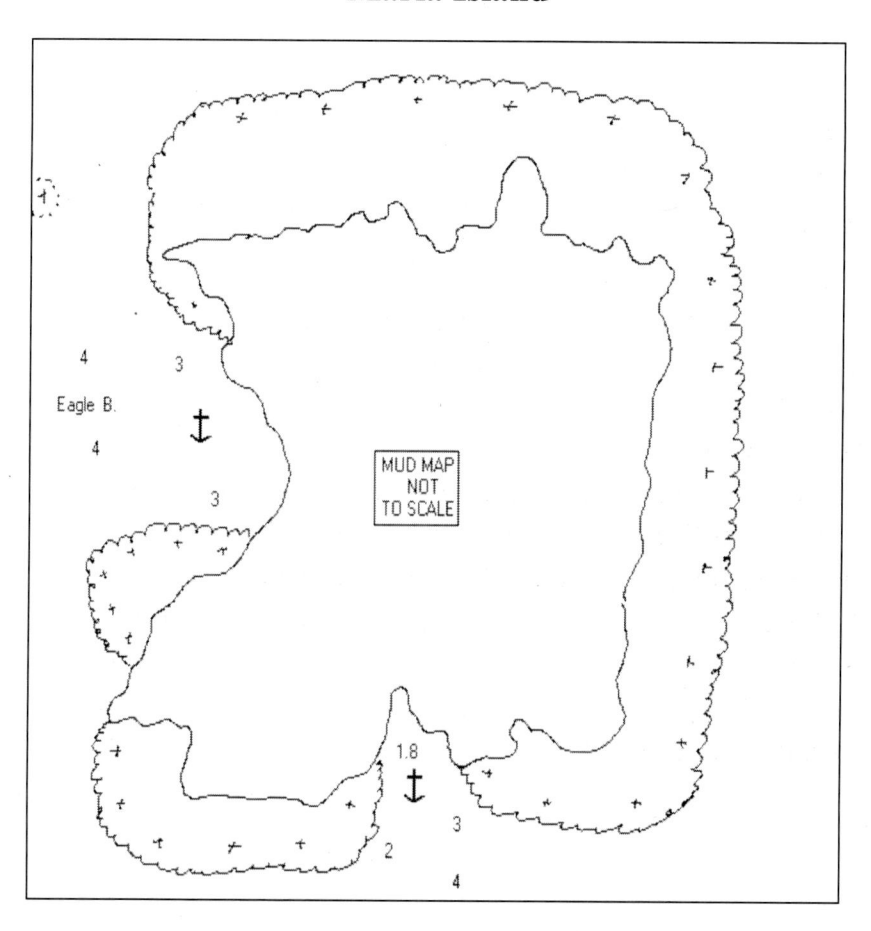

ROPER RIVER ENTRANCE

14°45'S – °25'E

CHART AUS 305
LIGHTS Nil
TIDES Milner Bay (Rose River) ANTT

The mouth of the Roper River lies 20 miles west-northwest of Eagle Bay. However, there is a bar 7 miles out from the river mouth, which has 1 metre. There is a small patch of 0.5 near the outer end. The river mouth is identified by a high bluff, which terminates in a range of hills to the north. The channel after crossing the bar carries 1.8 metres, then 3 metres; this holds until 5 metres is reached. The river is navigable for around 100 miles to the Police Station at Roper Bar. This is a stone's throw away from the highway to Darwin. There is a small town 10 miles upstream from the river mouth, and a further 30 miles upstream is a mission. Tides rise about 1 metre on the bar. Vessels with a 2-metre draft should not have any difficulty entering.

Roper River Entrance

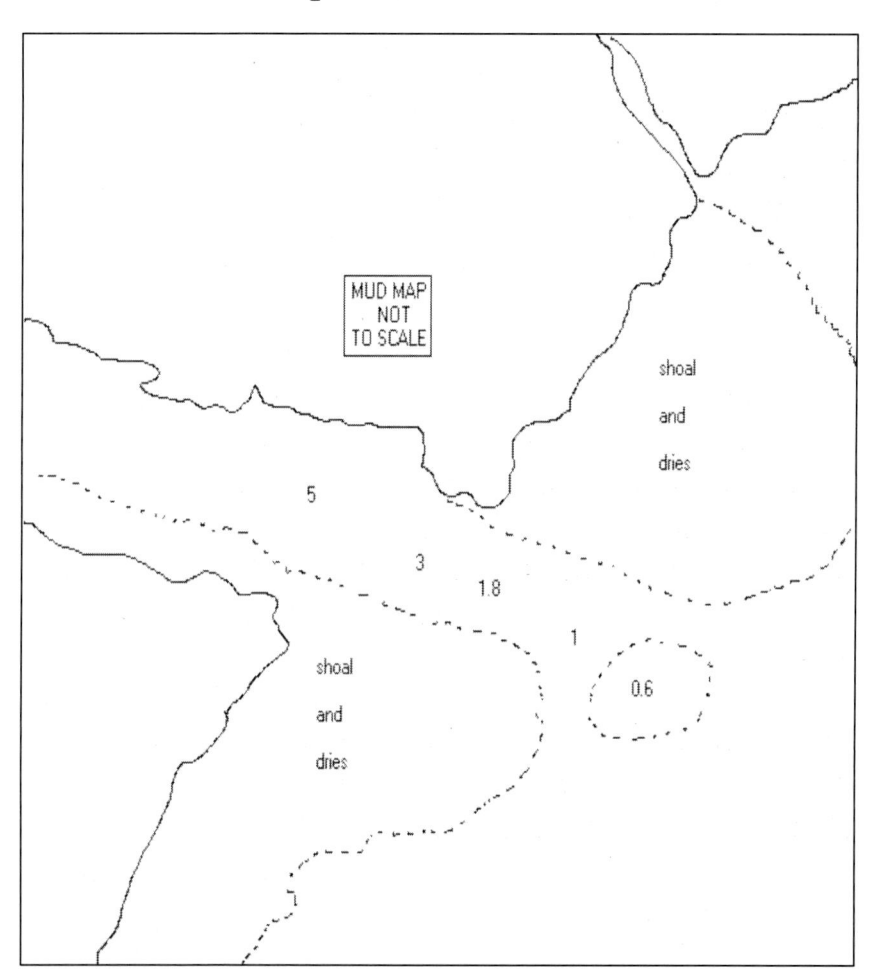

UNNAMED BAY
EAST OF TASMAN POINT

14°11'S – °21.5'E

CHART AUS 305
LIGHTS Nil
TIDES Milner Bay (Standard Port) ANTT

This is an unnamed and unsurveyed area found to the east of Tasman Point. I anchored about mid-way along towards Salt Creek. It can be uncomfortable, as it is in the area where the two currents meet. The amount of roll depends on the tide and wind strength. I anchored well out in 6 metres, but no doubt it is possible to anchor in closer. I did not worry, as I was only here for the night. I intended to travel along the southern shore early next morning. If going this way, stay well out to sea, as there are many dangers around Tasman Point, South Point and along to and around Cape Beatrice.

Tasman Point

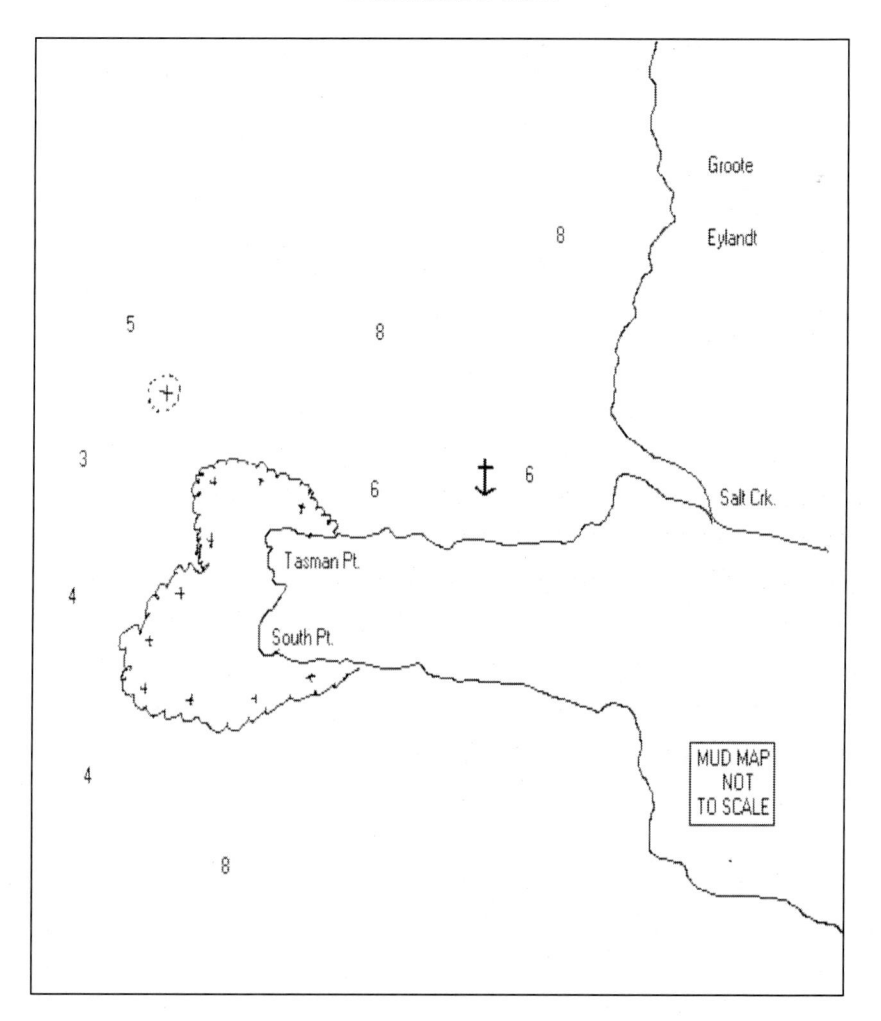

DALUMBA BAY

14°07'S – °49'E

CHART   AUS 305
LIGHTS   Nil
TIDES   Milner Bay (Hawk Island) ANTT

This bay offers a very secure anchorage in winds from east through south to northwest. When entering I suggest that vessels travel at least 3 miles past Adilyagba Point, before turning into the bay. I did not like the look of the passage to the east of the off-lying island. I crossed the reef to the west of the island; as it was high tide I had 4.5 metres. It may be safer to travel a further 2 miles to avoid the reef area altogether, as I did when I was leaving. The best anchorage was in 3 metres in the southeast corner.

Dalumba Bay

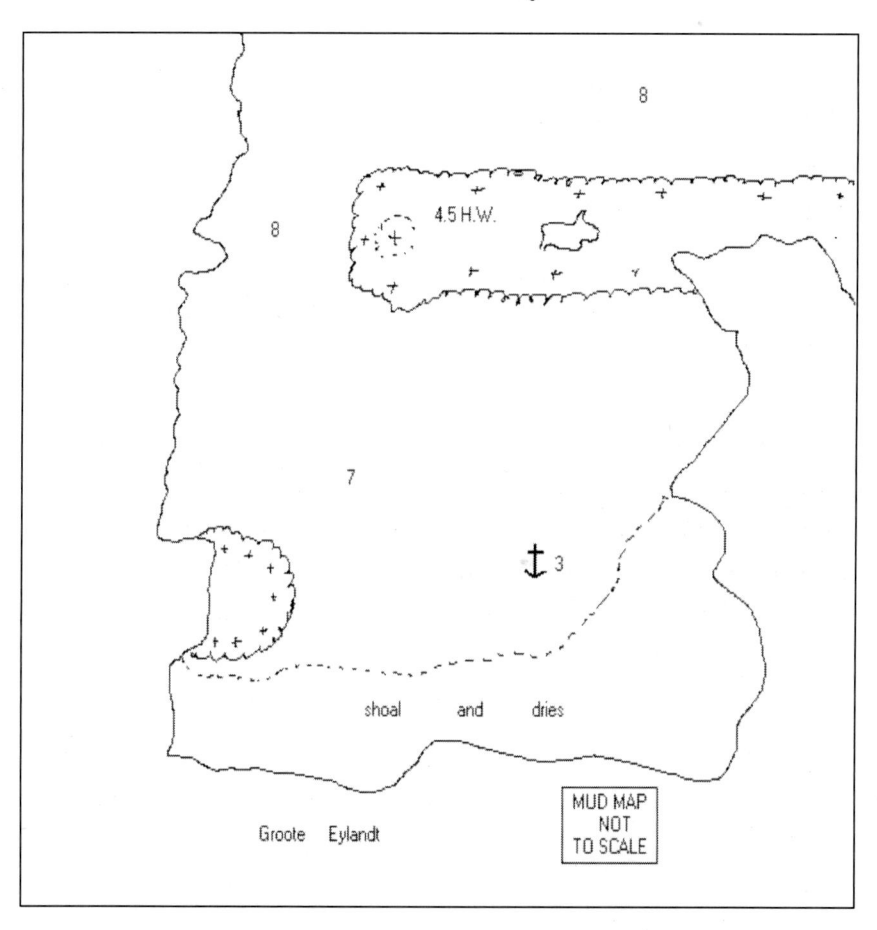

8

8   4.5 H.W.

7

⚓ 3

shoal   and   dries

Groote   Eylandt

MUD MAP
NOT
TO SCALE

SCOTT POINT

$13°45'S - °51'E$

CHART AUS 305
LIGHTS North East Islet flashes every 5 seconds, visible 15 miles.
TIDES Milner Bay (Hawk Island) ANTT

The channel around Scott Point has not been fully surveyed, so if not sure, go around North East Islet. I used the channel and found 5 metres to be the average depth. There are some 3-metre patches and some coral heads. I maintained a distance of around 2 miles offshore, until past Scott Point, but keep a good lookout. Scott Point is low, sandy and fringed by rocks. There are some large pink, yes pink, sand hills along the shore to the east of Scott Point. Travel south of Scott Point for about 1.5 miles and anchor over mud in 3 metres. You will still be about 1 mile offshore.

Scott Point

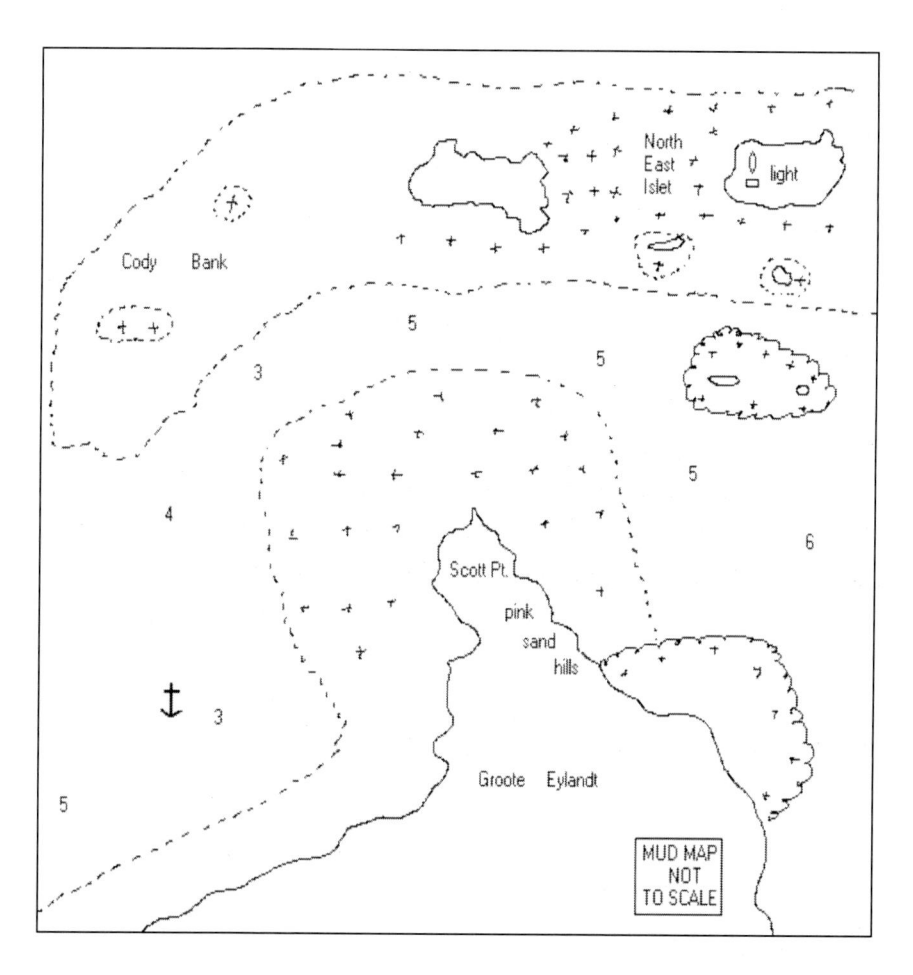

North East Islet
light
Cody Bank
Scott Pt.
pink sand hills
Groote Eylandt

MUD MAP
NOT
TO SCALE

PORT LANGDON

13°48′S – °46′E

CHART   AUS 305
LIGHTS   Nil
TIDES   Milner Bay (Port Langdon) ANTT

Port Langdon is entered between Jaggard Head to the west and Scott Point to the east. If coming from the north, or from around North East Islet, the track shown on the chart should be used. I found the average depth to be around 10 metres. Good anchorage will be found here from winds east through south to west. At the southern end, about 6 miles to the south of Scott Point, will be found a sand spit nearly 3 miles long. This protects the anchorage in Little Lagoon, where average depths of around 5 metres will be found. Barges unload here for the large mission of Umbakumba. There are only a few buildings visible behind the sand hills. There are two white lead boards, which will access to the beach. Little Lagoon should only be entered at high tide – favour the end of the spit.

Port Langdon

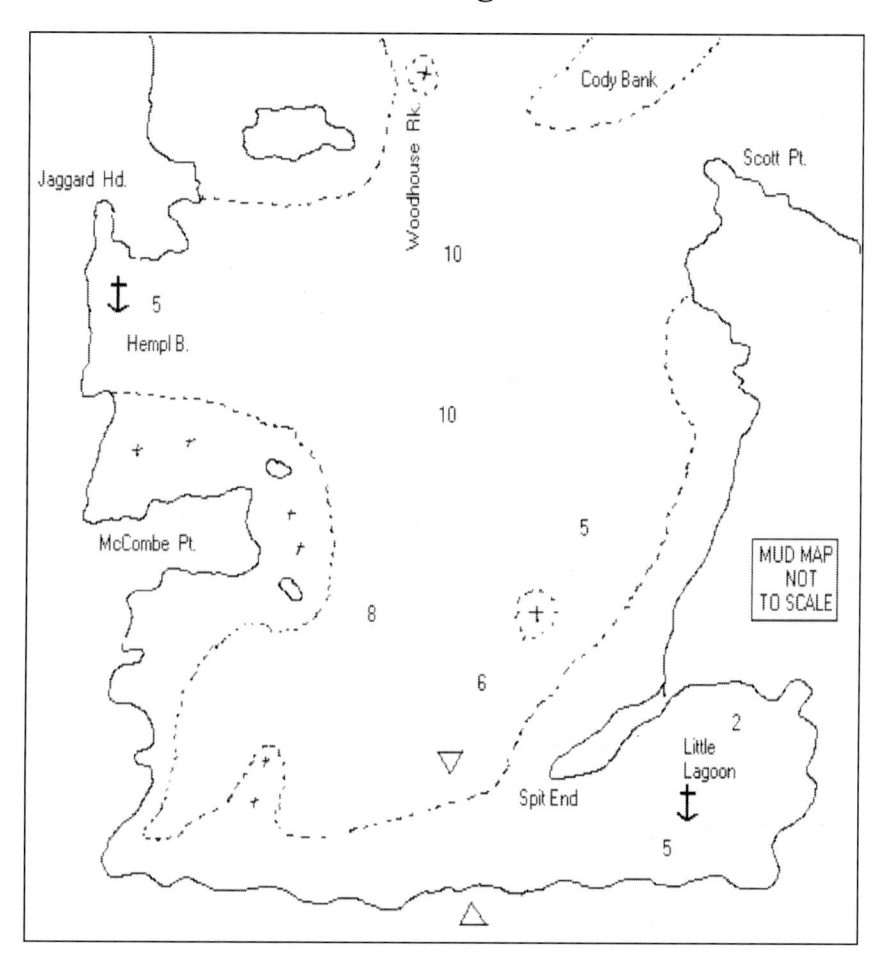

NORTH WEST BAY

13°41'S – °33.5'E

CHARTS   AUS 305, 14
LIGHTS   Nil
TIDES   Milner Bay ANTT
CAUTION Unsurveyed

From Port Langdon, I decided to go around to North West Bay. It is only about 35 miles. Stay well clear of North Point Island and Chasm Island. I found an average depth of 4 metres, but extreme care is needed. Yarranya Island lies to the southern end of the bay, and is surrounded by rocks and drying banks for some distance all round. Anchor anywhere, but take care.

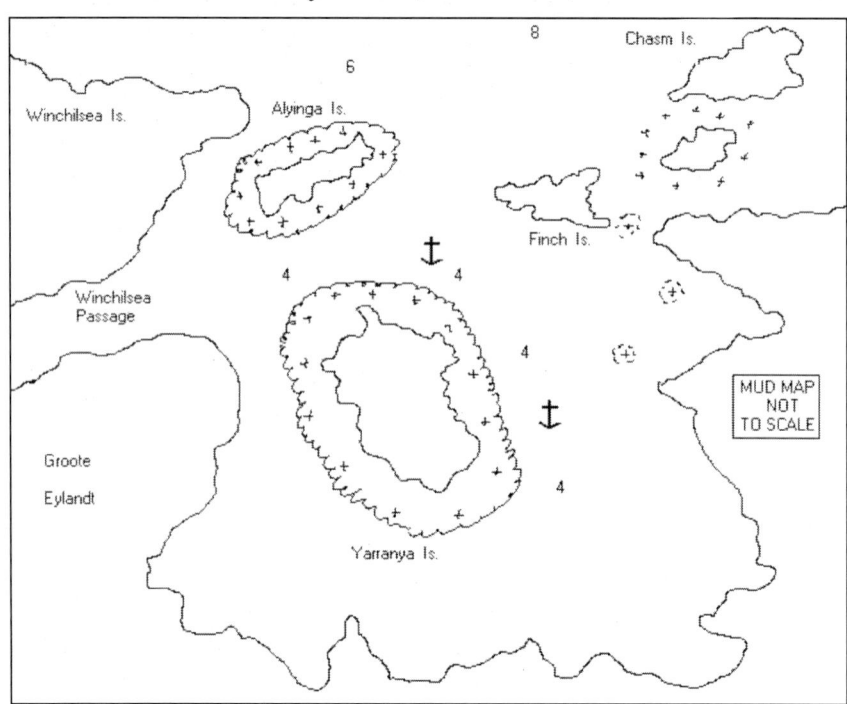

BARTALUMBA BAY

13°48′S – °30′E

CHARTS AUS 305, 14
LIGHTS Brady Rock flashes 3 times every 12 seconds, visible 8 miles.
TIDES Milner Bay ANTT
CAUTION Unsurveyed

From North West Bay, I travelled the Winchilsea Passage. A tide of at least ships draft is needed to get through. An inlet lies southeast of the conspicuous yellow patch on North West Bluff. There was a prawn-fleet base located on the eastern side of the small lagoon. Anchorage in the bay can be taken to the east of the jetty. Take care, as an underwater rock lies to the north of the jetty. There is a wreck northeast of the jetty with masts showing. I found an average depth in the bay of 5–7 metres.

Bartalumba Bay

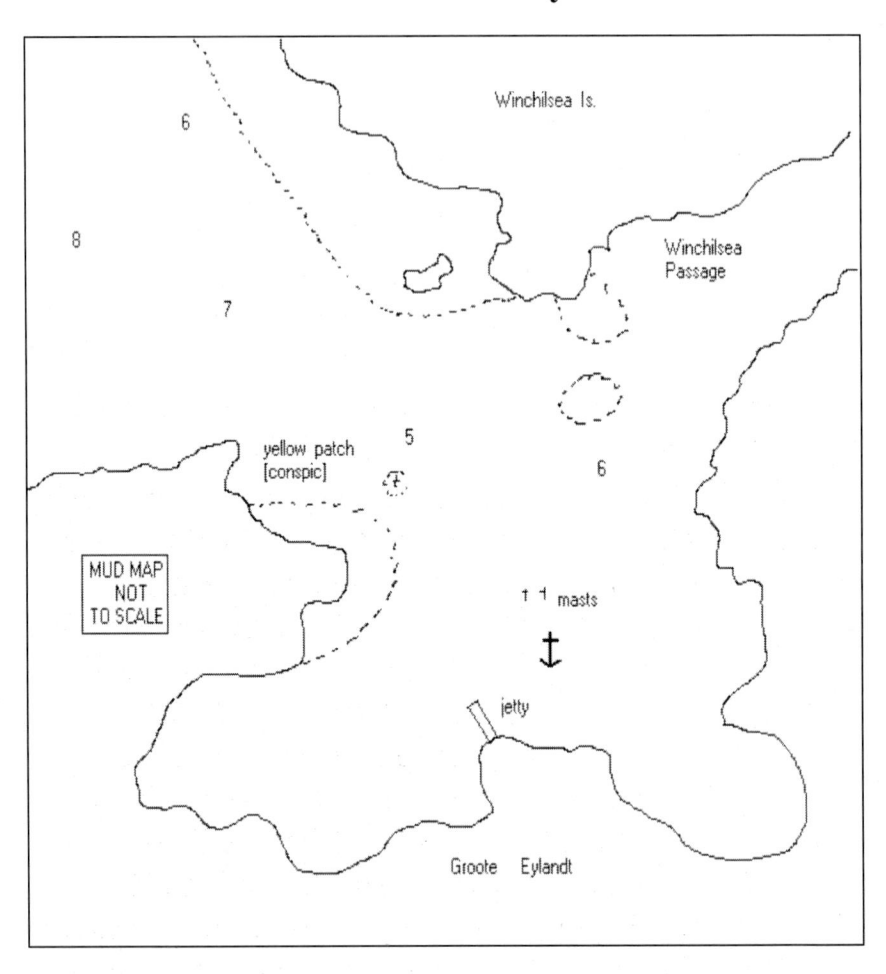

MILNER BAY

13°52′S – 136°25′E

CHARTS	AUS 305, 14
LIGHTS	Fairway Buoy flashes every 2 seconds.
TIDES	Milner Bay (Standard Port) ANTT

Milner Bay has one conveyor belt and one pier leading to a T-wharf for loading manganese ore. There is a rock wall at 13°51.4′S – 136°25′E. The light towers shown on the chart have been removed. A number of tanks are visible at the end of the pier.

Milner Bay is a Port of Entry. A small cargo wharf with 4.6 metres alongside is on the northern side of the pier root. A barge landing and a boat ramp are located nearby. The township of Alyangula is found north of the port facilities. It also has a boat ramp. Small craft will find secure anchorage in sandy mud out from here. The ramp is close to the main shopping centre; most items are available, but expensive. Water is available at the jetty. There is a small hospital and other facilities associated with a busy town. It is worthwhile to check here for work. Fuel is available, but difficult. You have to go to the Spotless Cleaning office located behind the supermarket. You estimate how much you need and pay for it there, then you are then given fuel cards to that value. Take the fuel cards and your drums to the servo at the wharf area. You need to do this by dinghy.

Milner Bay

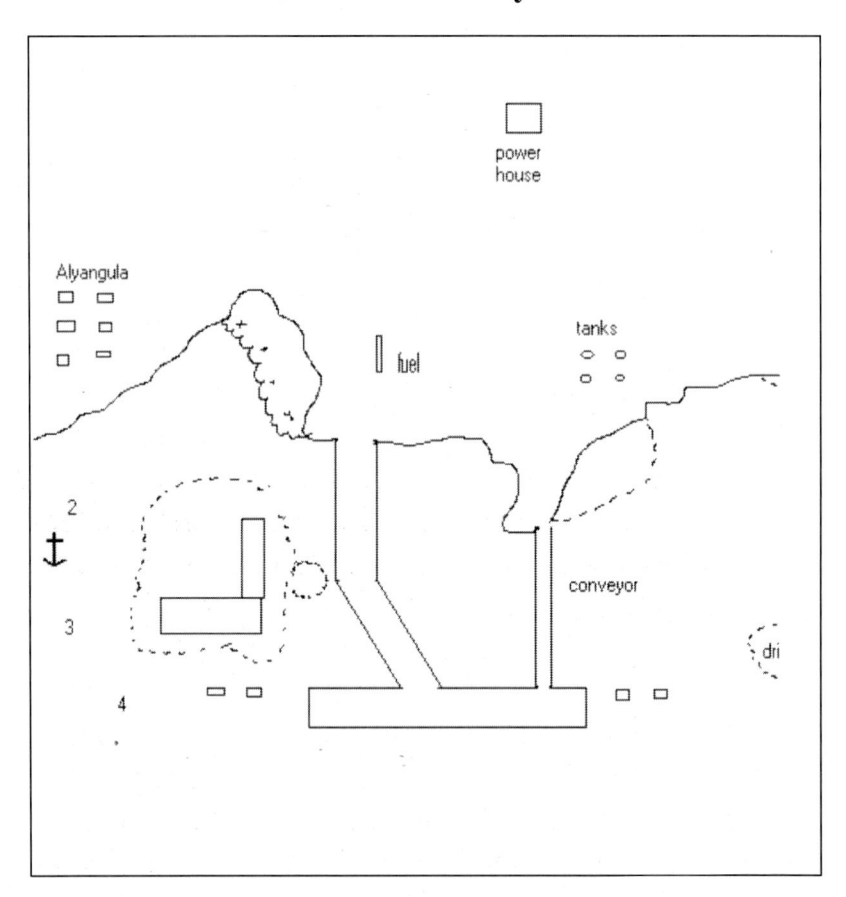

BICKERTON ISLAND

(NORTH BAY)

13°42.5′S – 136°10′E

CHART	AUS 305
LIGHTS	Nil
TIDES	Milner Bay ANTT
CAUTION	Unsurveyed

North Bay is at the northwest corner of Bickerton Island, and lies to the eastern side of Lowrie Channel. There is a small creek in the southeast corner and a series of beaches along the Eastern Shore. I found no underwater dangers, but this does not mean that they are not there, so take care. The average depth, I found, was 3–7 metres. When entering, it is suggested to favour the southern headland. Good shelter is to be had here from east to south winds. However, the bullets can be strong, owing to the hilly nature of the island. In northerly conditions, a secure anchorage will be found in the bay on the southern side of the island. There is an Aboriginal community here, so watch your petrol.

Bickerton Island (North Bay)

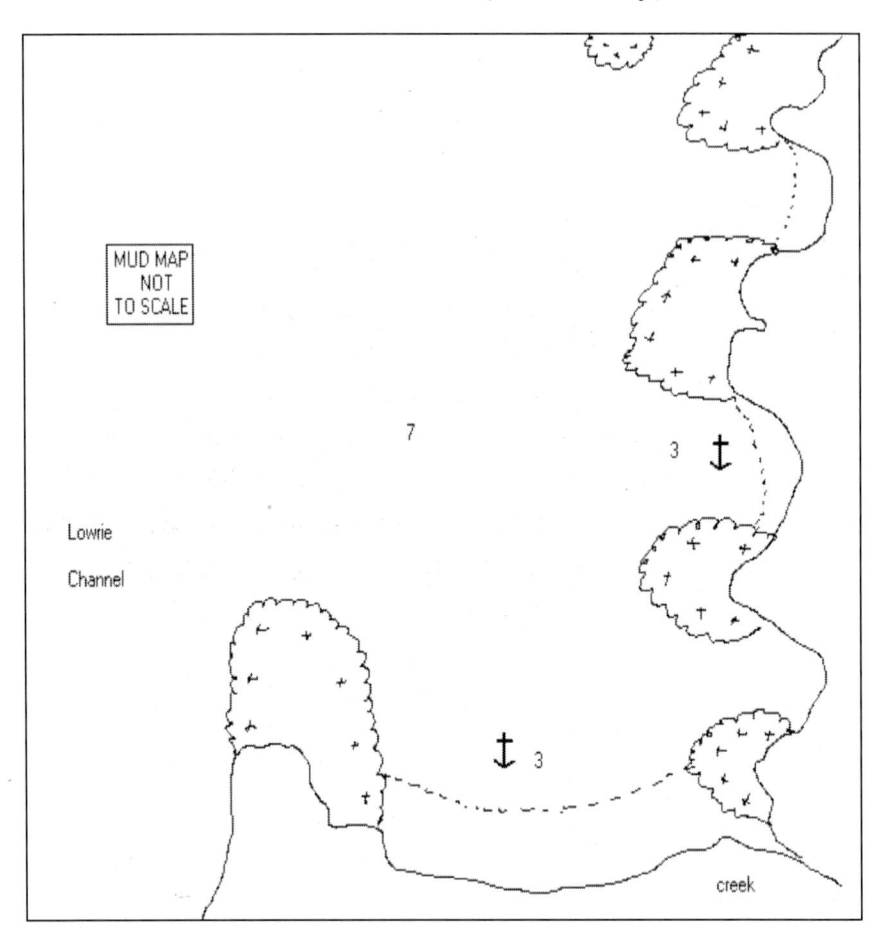

MUD MAP NOT TO SCALE

7

3 ⚓

Lowrie Channel

⚓ 3

creek

BUSTARD ISLAND – (New)

13°42.10′S – 136°22.80′S

CHART	AUS 305, 14
LIGHTS	Nil
TIDES	Milner Bay ANTT
CAUTION	Inadequately surveyed

From Milner Bay it is an easy run north via the Connexion Channel, however, be aware of the tide, as there is a strong current with eddies and overfalls, but which is perfectly safe. I did not like the look of the channel between Arruwa Island and Bustard Island. I went around Arruwa Island. Anchorage is out from the drying beach in 4 metres, and is reasonably protected from both north and south winds.

Bustard Island

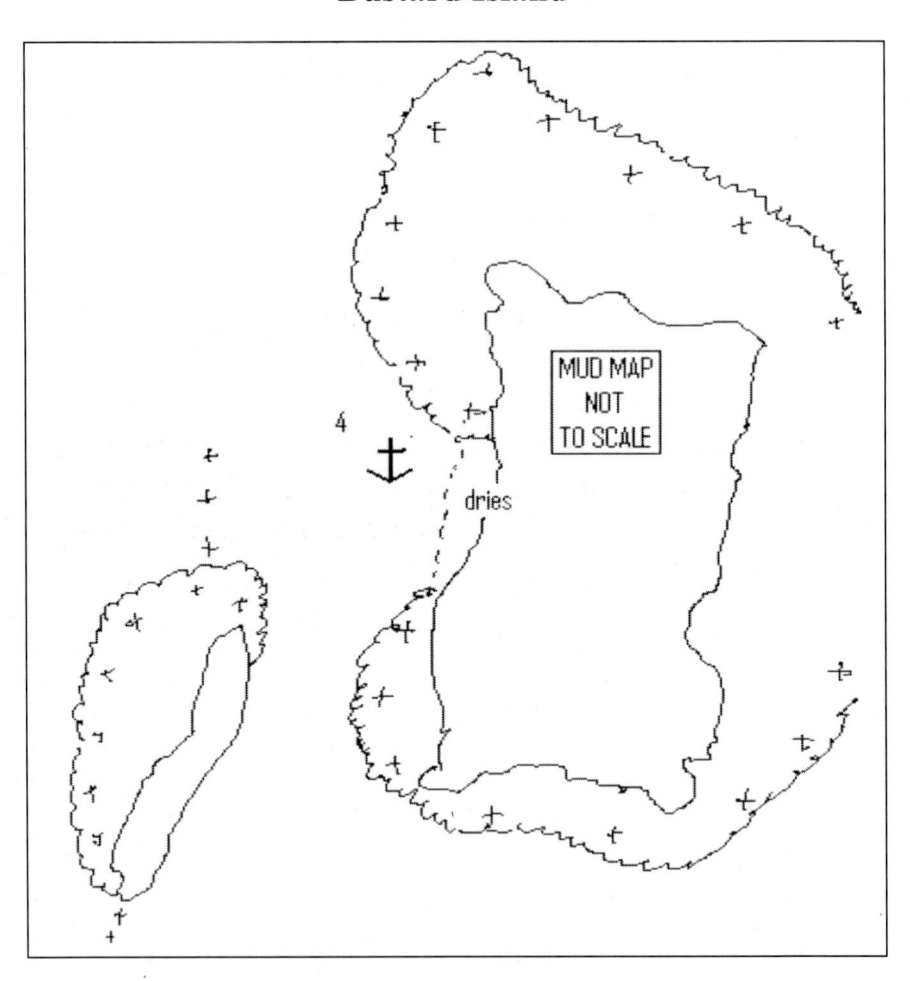

MUD MAP NOT TO SCALE

dries

HAWKNEST ISLAND – (New)

13°37.60′S – 136°24′E

CHARTS AUS 305, 14
LIGHTS Nil
TIDES   Milner Bay ANTT
CAUTION Inadequately surveyed

This is a northerly anchorage and can be approached without any problems. It is well protected from winds from the north and the east. The north-easterly winds will most likely be blowing by the time you get here. However, it may be possible to anchor on the northern side if the south-easterly winds are still blowing. I have not tried.

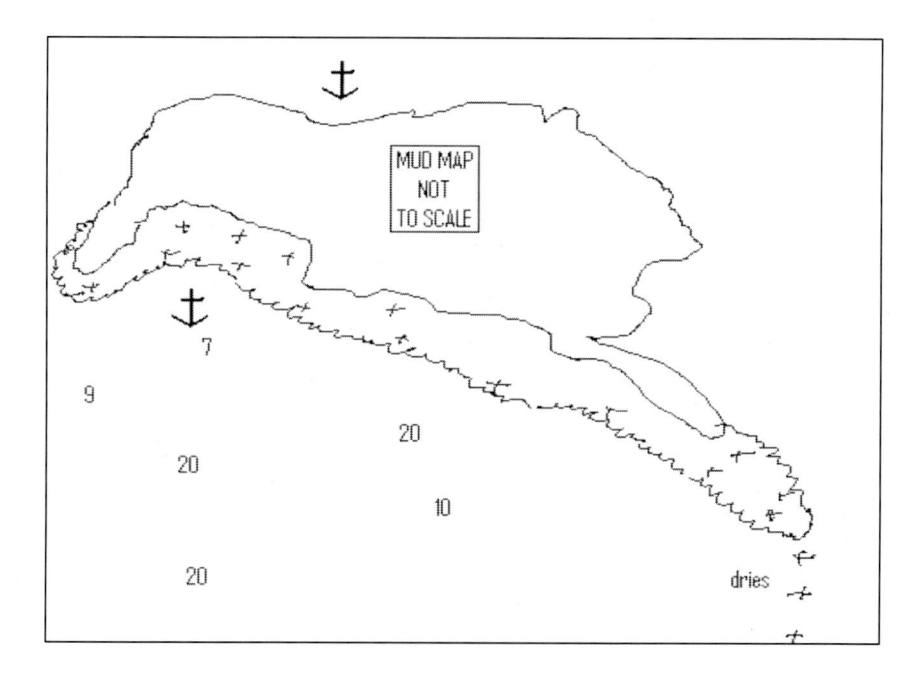

MUD MAP NOT TO SCALE

NICOLE ISLAND – (New)

13°27'S – 136°15.10'E

CHARTS	AUS 305, 14
LIGHTS	Nil
TIDES	Milner Bay ANTT
CAUTION	Unsurveyed

When approaching this island from the south, be sure to give a wide clearance to avoid the extensive reef areas to the south of the island. Both anchorages are well protected from all winds except westerly. The first anchorage is the best. I rode out a strong wind warning here in complete comfort and safety. When leaving, give the satellite island to the north a wide berth.

Nicole Island

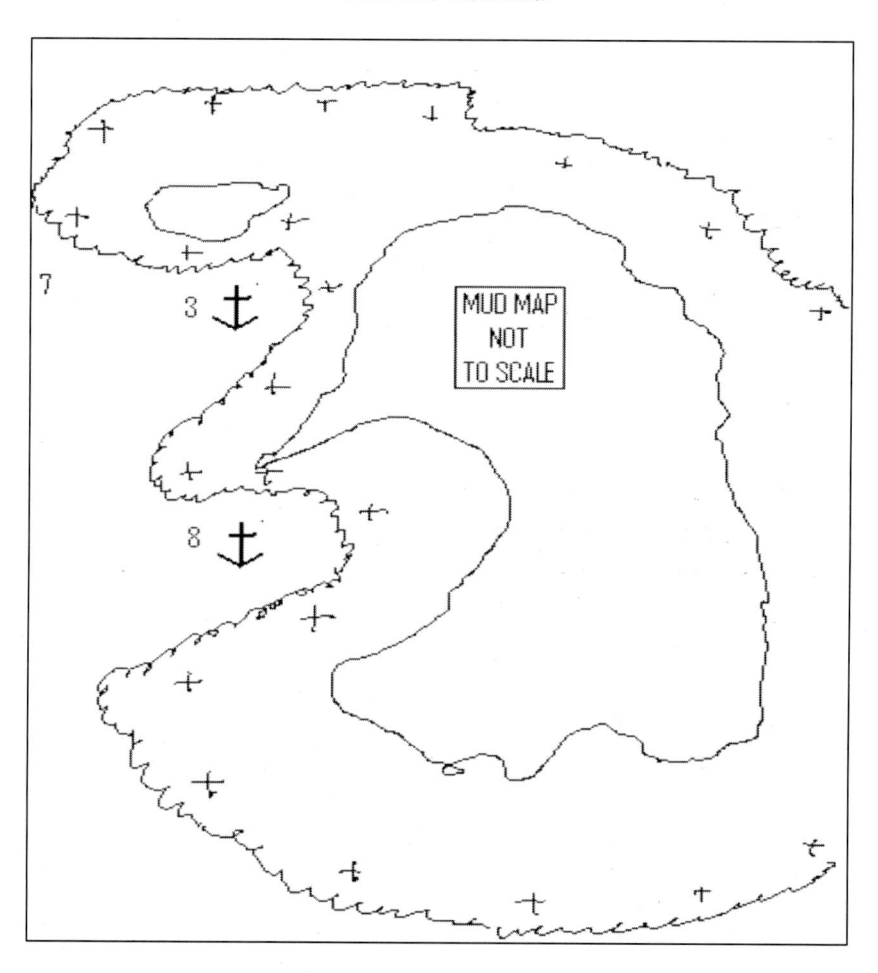

MUD MAP NOT TO SCALE

MYAOOLA BAY

13°08'S 136°20'E

CHARTS AUS 305, 306
LIGHTS Nil
TIDES Milner Bay ANTT

Myaoola Bay lies to the west of Cape Shields, at the northern end of Blue Mud Bay. Entry was found clear of dangers in 7 metres in the entrance. However, careful navigation is essential, as a large part of this area has not been surveyed. The anchorages shown were all found to have 3–4 metres. The same depth appeared to be throughout the bay.

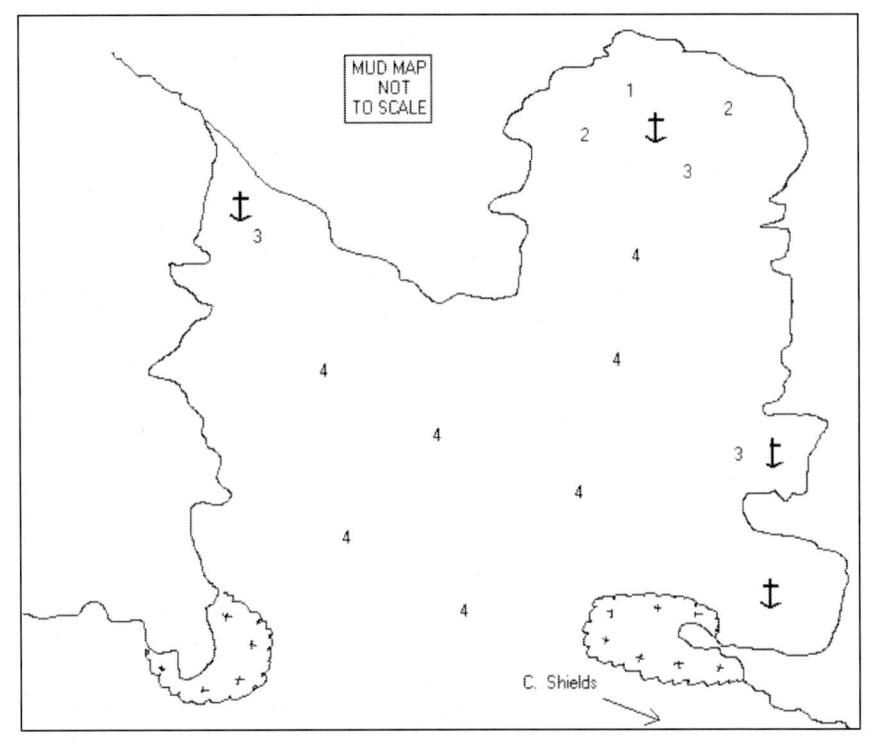

POINT ARROWSMITH

13°15.25′S – 135°27′E

CHART	AUS 305
LIGHTS	Nil
TIDES	Milner Bay (Cape Grey) ANTT

When coming from Myaoola Bay, give Cape Shields and the satellite island a clearance of at least 1.5 miles. Steer for the outside of Point Arrowsmith, as there is a large and shoal reef area to the south of the point which is not marked on the chart. You will clearly see the reef around the point as you close it, and anchor in the lee of the point out from the reef in 3 metres.

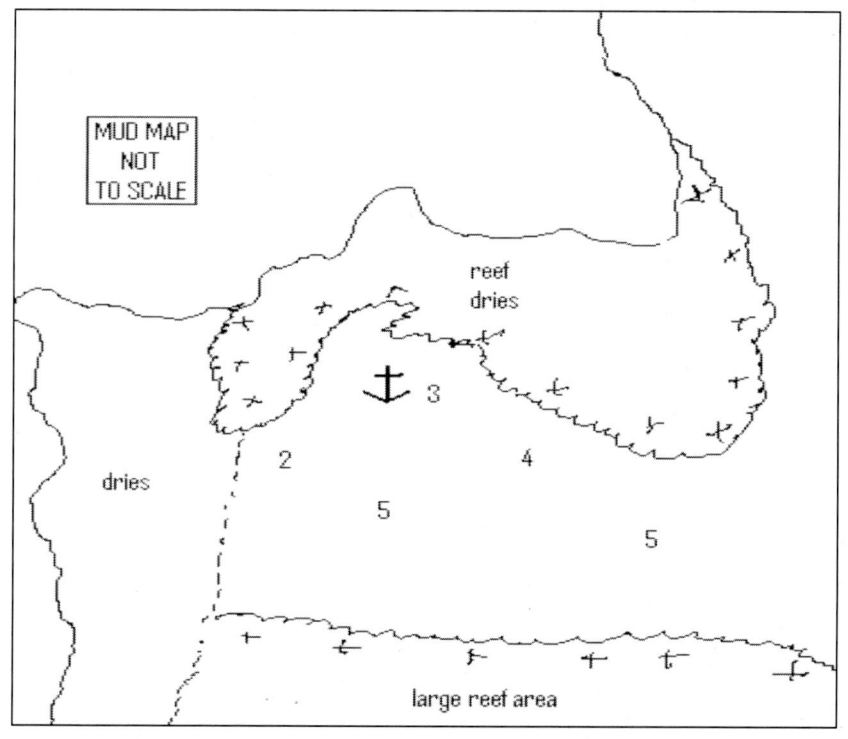

TRIAL BAY

13°02'S – 136°34'E

CHART   AUS 306
LIGHTS   Nil
TIDES   Milner Bay (Cape Grey) ANTT

Trial Bay is 22 miles northeast of Cape Shields. There are two anchorages in this bay, St Davids Bay and Wonga Bay. Trawlers use the anchorage in Wonga Bay, as this was the most convenient – it was the one I used. Entry is to clear Bald Point by at least 1.5 miles. Then enter Wonga Bay by steering a course for the centre of the bay to the west of Cape Grey. Proceed into the bay and hold this course until clear of the reef and rocks extending southwest from the point. Then anchor in the small bay behind the reef in the southeast corner. Swell may invade at the top of the tide, but anchorage is secure in mud.

Trial Bay

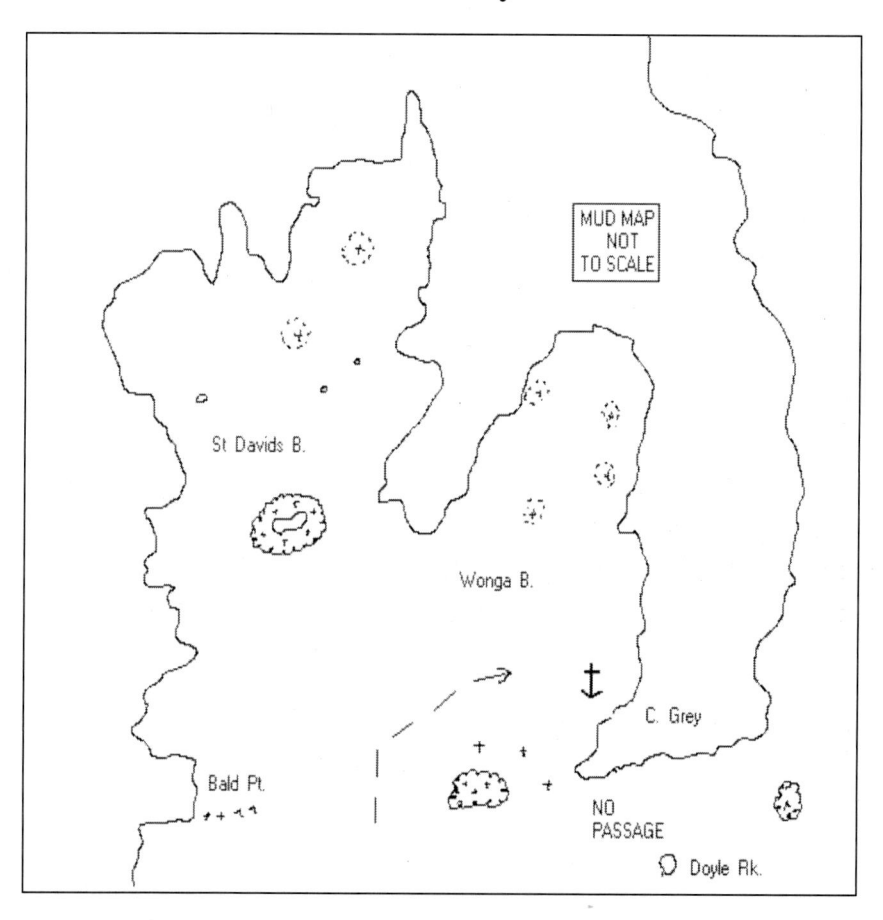

MUD MAP
NOT
TO SCALE

St Davids B.

Wonga B.

C. Grey

Bald Pt.

NO PASSAGE

Doyle Rk.

CALEDON BAY

12°51′S – 136°35′E

CHART	AUS 306
LIGHTS	Nil
TIDES	Milner Bay (Cape Grey) ANTT

On leaving Trial Bay, stay to the south of Doyle Rock. A clearance of 2 miles from Cape Grey will keep vessels clear of dangers. Entry to Caledon Bay is as shown on the chart. The bay extends northwest for 14 miles to Middle Point, where it divides into two smaller bays. The bay to the west of Middle Point was found unusable for yachts, as it is very shallow. Grey Bay to the north is a very secure anchorage, in varying depths in grey mud. Depths were generally from 5–12 metres. I used three anchorages. The first was outside the small islet, north of Middle Point in 7 metres. The next was in the small bay at the rear of the same islet in 4 metres. The third one I used was out from the small inlet over on the eastern shore of the bay in 5 metres.

Caledon Bay

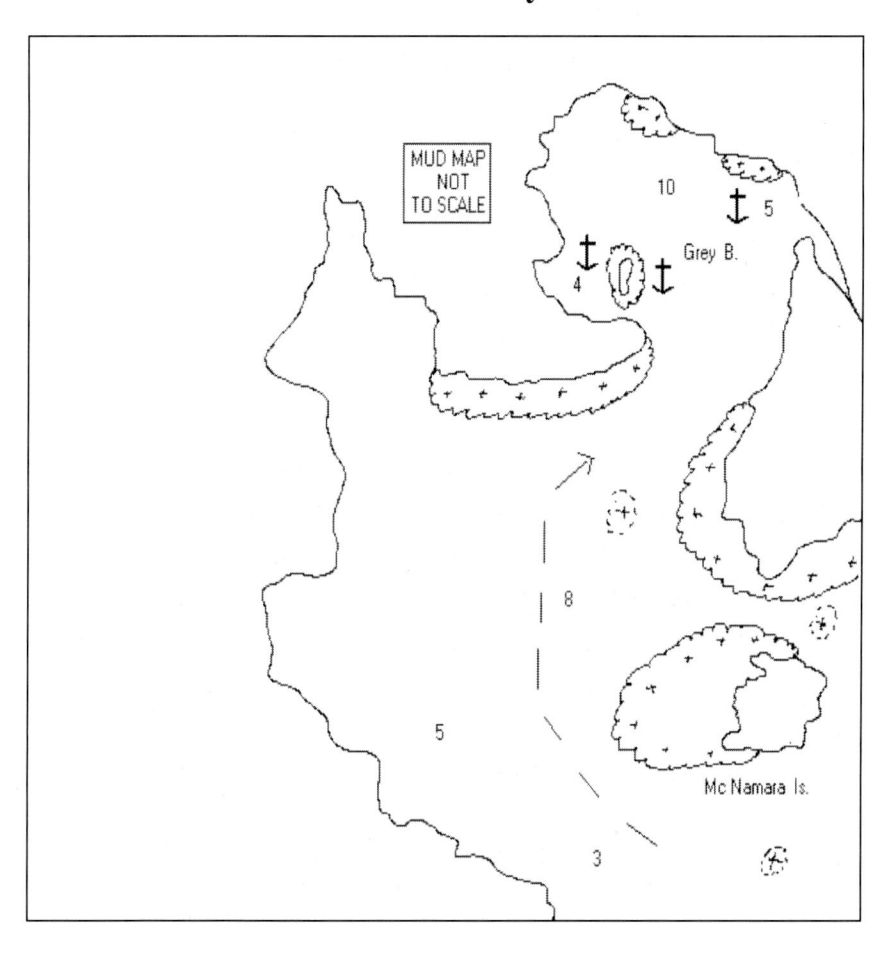

MUD MAP NOT TO SCALE

Grey B.

Mc Namara Is.

PORT BRADSHAW

12°33′S – 136°43′E

CHART   AUS 306
LIGHTS Nil
TIDES   Milner Bay (Cape Grey) ANTT

Port Bradshaw lies approximately 10 miles north of Point Wanyammera. Entry is between Point Binanangoi and Gwapilina Point to the north. The entrance is full of islets and rocks, however by staying towards Gwapilina Point, safe entry can be found. Once inside, there is good protection from the winds. After clearing Gwapilina Point, good anchorage can be found under the cliffs in the small bay to the north. The holding is good in 4 metres over sandy mud, or as close to the small beach as draft and tide allow. The local Aboriginals will come and tell you to leave. Ignore them, as they don't own the water. Their land finishes 20 metres above high tide. I generally have a weapon clearly visible when I go in there and have had no further trouble. Call their bluff.

Port Bradshaw

CAPE ARNHEM

12°21′S – 136°59′E

CHART AUS 306,715
LIGHTS Nil
TIDES Gove Harbour ANTT

Approaching Cape Arnhem from the south, stay at least 1.5 miles offshore to avoid strong rips and overfalls around the cape. In addition, Arnhem Rock, which is 2 metres high, lies 1 mile south of Cape Arnhem. After rounding Cape Arnhem, Dalywoi Bay is found to the west. The bay has a depth of 4 metres throughout and anchorage can be had anywhere draft allows. Take care of the rock in the centre of the bay. The best anchorage was found under the cliff of Cape Arnhem in 2 metres, but watch the reef in close. This is the last secure anchorage before the run up to Gove.

Cape Arnhem

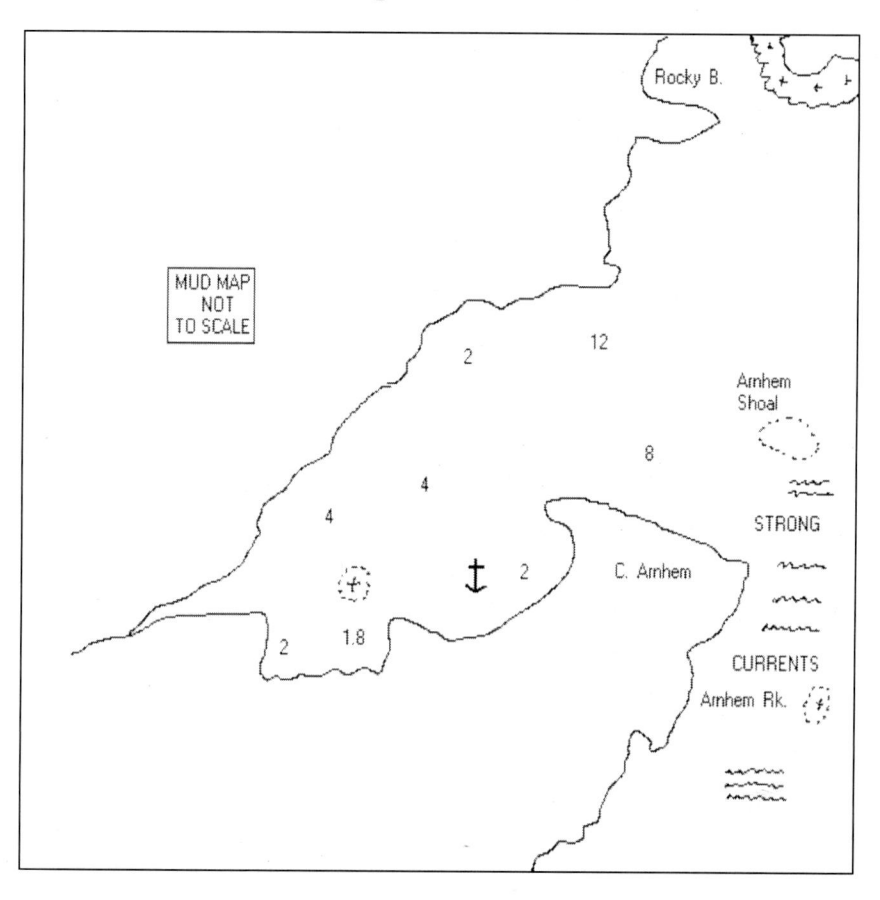

GOVE HARBOUR

FAIRWAY BUOY 12°10.8′S – 136°37.7′E

CHARTS	AUS 306, 715, 15
LIGHTS	Fairway Buoy flashes iso 10 seconds red/white. Next, a red flashes 2 every 5 seconds, then a quick red. Off Dundas Point is a quick red buoy then another red buoy. Out from the general cargo wharf is a red flashing 4 seconds. The light on Half Tide Rocks flashes 2 every 6 seconds; the last is a quick flash red on the rocks in Inverell Bay. Keep this to port when anchoring.
TIDES	Gove (Standard Port) ANTT

After leaving Dalywoi Bay, clear water is had to Miles Islet, then stay 1.25 miles offshore. This will clear Lone Rock. Clear passage between Bremer Island and Cape Wirawawoi is had. After clearing this passage, stay 1 mile offshore until the Fairway Buoy is sighted. There is no passage between Wargarpunda Point and the area 1 mile west, and northwest of West Woody Island.

After clearing the Fairway Buoy, it is by natural progress along the channel, keeping red-to-red, green to green. The first wharf is west of Dundas Point and is the bulk cargo wharf, approximately 300 metres long with a T end. There is a tanker wharf to the south. Around Dundas Point is the general cargo wharf, which extends out for 450 metres. Between here and Rocky Point is the main shipping harbour.

At the northern end of the harbour is the fuel wharf. If taking fuel, take care of the spit extending southwest of Rocky Point towards Harbour Islet. If going direct to the yacht club, stay well clear of Rocky Point.

The yacht club is located in the northeast corner of Inverell Bay. Visitors are welcome. The town of Nhulunbuy is some distance away. Locals will give you a lift to town, where everything is available but very expensive. It is worthwhile to ask about work, as there is usually some around. Woolworths also has a noticeboard. For fuel, call Perkins Shipping on Ch. 16, however fuel is probably the dearest in Australia.

Unleaded petrol has to be purchased from the servo in town. To get to town, come ashore at the yacht club and find your way out to the road. Turn left and follow this to the T-junction. Turn right. You are now on the road to town. Water is available from the hose on the beach at the yacht club.

Gove Harbour

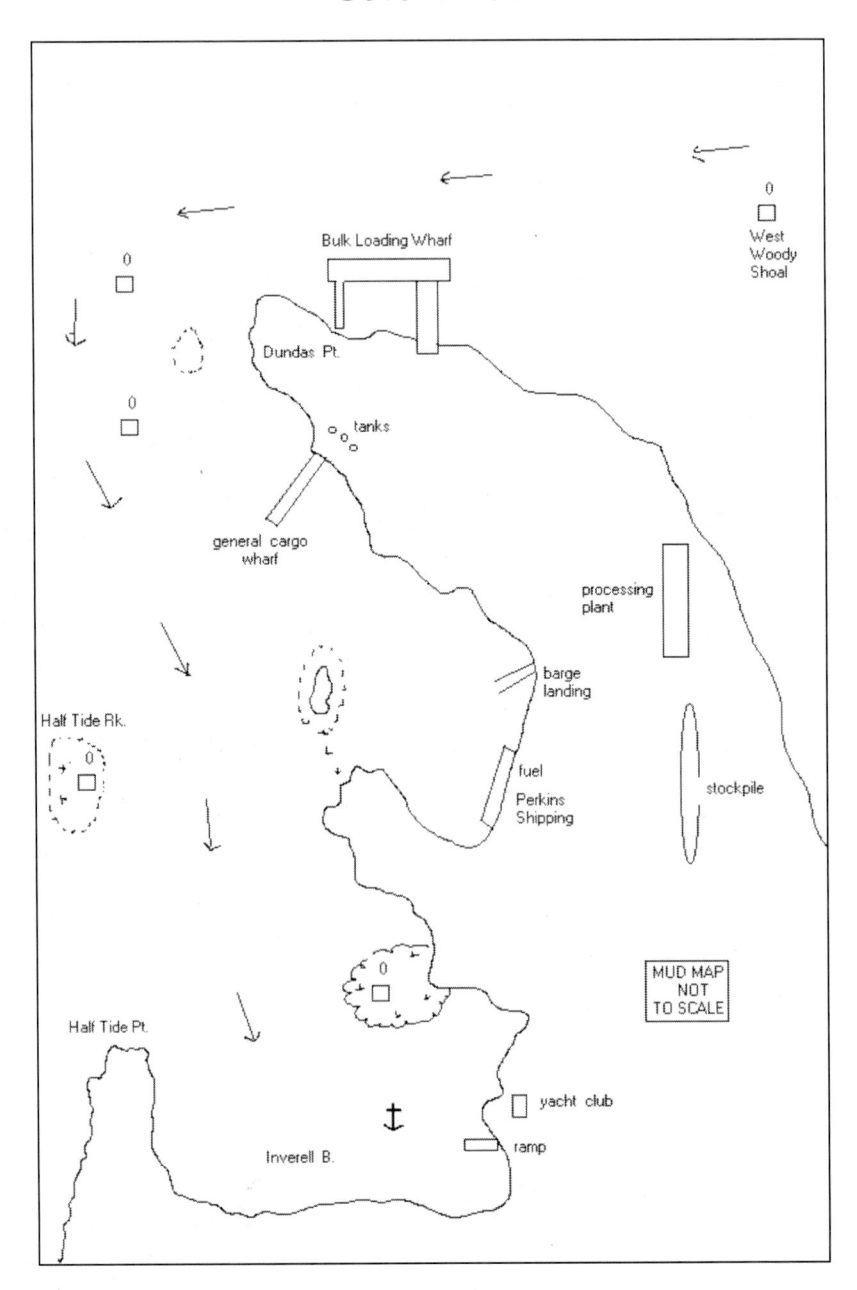

SECTION 3

Gove to Darwin

> **CAUTION**
> Crocodiles are prolific throughout
> the entire area from Gove to Darwin.

PASSAGE NOTES

Well, you got to Gove. Feeling pretty pleased with yourself having completed your trip through the gulf safely. Congratulations, I hope you had as much fun as I did.

After leaving Gove, I laid course for Cape Wilberforce, then through between Bromby Island and Point William. I then anchored in Elizabeth Bay. From here, I travelled between Wigram Island and Cotton Island, intending to pass through Hole in the Wall, but changed my mind and used the hole on my way back.

I went north to Truant Island, then around Cape Wessel and explored the western side of Marchinbar Island, where the fish and crayfish fight to be caught.

Fresh water can be found in many places. I did not need water, but what I tasted was quite all right. The hardest thing to do was to leave this paradise, but other anchorages were calling.

I carried on south and travelled through the Cadell Straits, then on to Darwin with quite a few detours. However, by this time I was mindful of the weather, as I wanted to make Darwin by late November. If intending to use Cadell Straits, it is best to do so on the return trip back east.

There are vast areas yet to explore between Cape York and Darwin, which will be done later and included in the next book.

Around Cape Wilberforce, the tide floods west at 5 knots. Floods east through Hole in the Wall and Cumberland Straits at around 10 knots, also east towards Cape Wessel at 3 knots, while in Brown Strait it floods south at 4 knots. The west flooding tide changes on the western side of Croker Island.

ELIZABETH BAY

11°54.2′S – 136°33.6′E

CHARTS   AUS 306,715
LIGHTS   Nil
TIDES   Gove (approx) ANTT

Elizabeth Bay lies to the west of Cape Wilberforce. There is passage between Point William and the unnamed island to port, but it is unsurveyed. Proceed into the bay and anchor where draft allows. I anchored where shown, out of the current, in 5 metres over sandy mud; the holding is good. There is a pearl farm on the southern side of the bay with extensive pearl rafts along the entire southern shore.

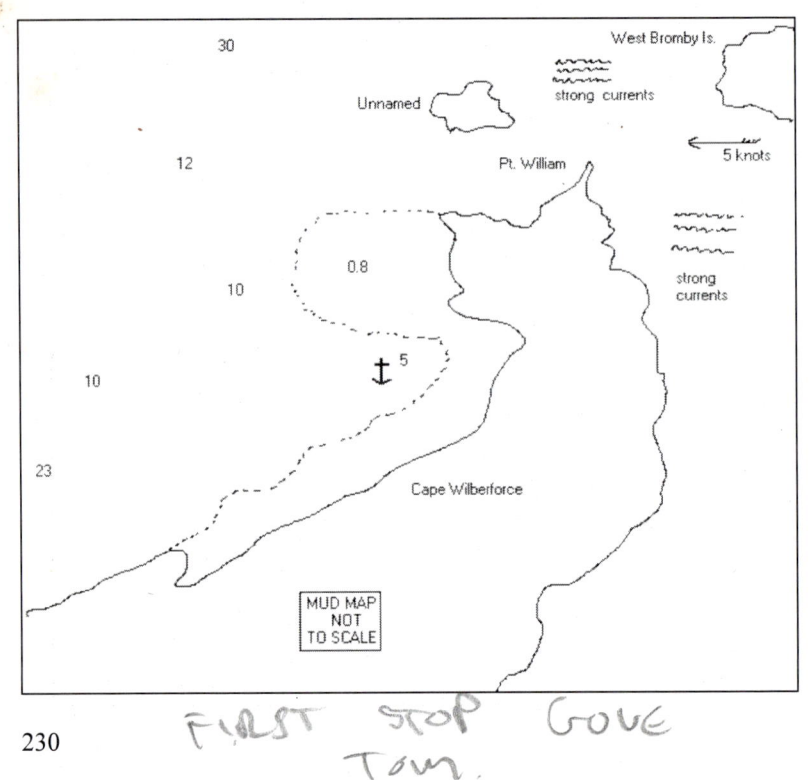

BOSANQUET ISLAND – (New)

11°58′S – 136°19.60′E

CHARTS   AUS 716, 442
LIGHTS   Nil
TIDES   Gove ANTT

This anchorage is surprisingly comfortable and is found at the northern end of the Nalwarung Strait. It is reasonably well protected from most winds. Anchor in 5 metres over sandy mud. Donington Sound is clearly visible between the two islands, enabling sight of conditions. From here, it is an easy run across to Brown Strait or the Raragala Island anchorage.

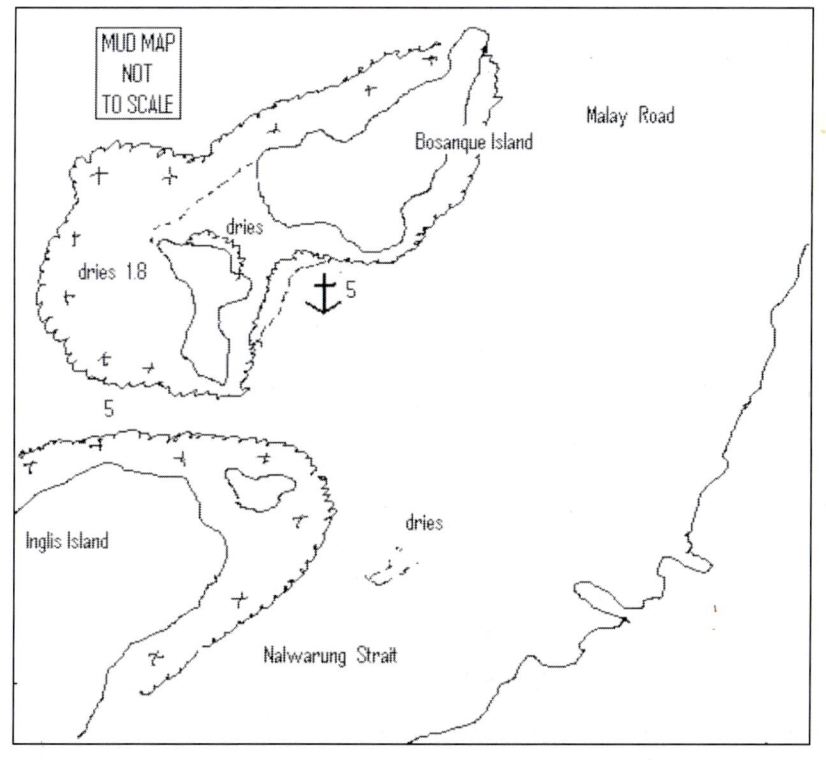

RARAGALA ISLAND – (New)

11°58.60S – 136°17.25′E

CHARTS AUS 716, 442
LIGHTS Nil
TIDES   Gove (Guluwuru Island) ANTT

This is a very secure anchorage, and is easy to enter. It is shaped like an upside-down boot. After the wet season there are three waterfalls. There is also a large crocodile. Anchorage is in the toe of the boot in 3–4 metres. There are a few beaches and over the other side in the heel is a large sandy area with a creek. I spent four weeks here during strong wind warnings of 30–35 knots in complete comfort and safety.

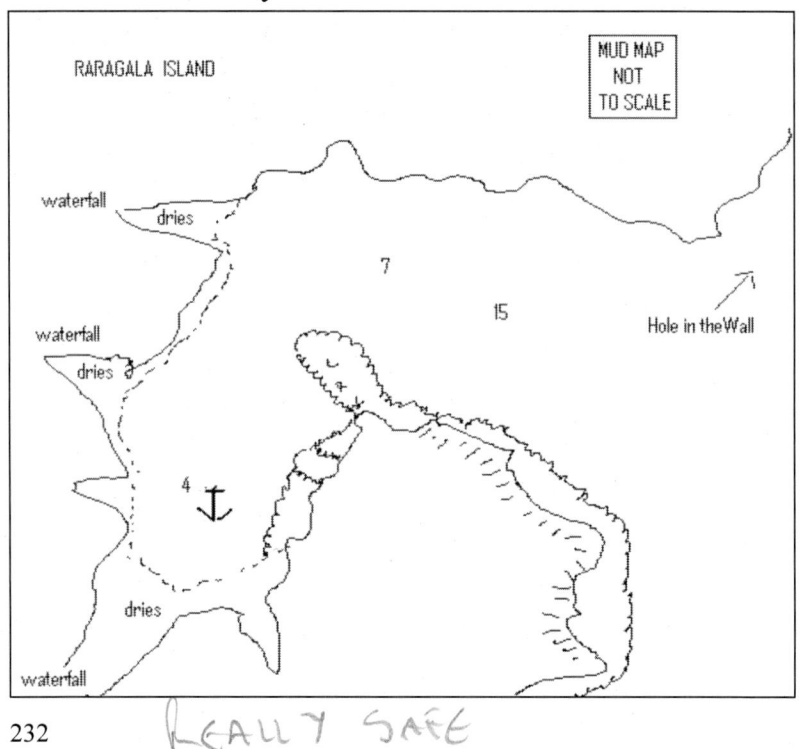

WIGRAM ISLAND

11°45.60′S – 136°34.50′E

CHARTS	AUS 306, 715, 442
LIGHTS	Nil
TIDES	Gove (Truant Island) ANTT
CAUTION	Unsurveyed area

This anchorage is on the western side of Wigram Island and is unnamed. It is a well-protected bay, and is an ideal place to anchor before going through Hole in the Wall or Cumberland Straits. Anchorage is in 3 metres well out from the fringing reef. The bottom is sand and the holding is good. No underwater dangers were found. More than a couple of days can be spent exploring. When coming in to anchor I used the saddle in the sand-hills as a guide. Other bays to the south have pearl rafts in them, while bays from here north don't.

Wigram Island

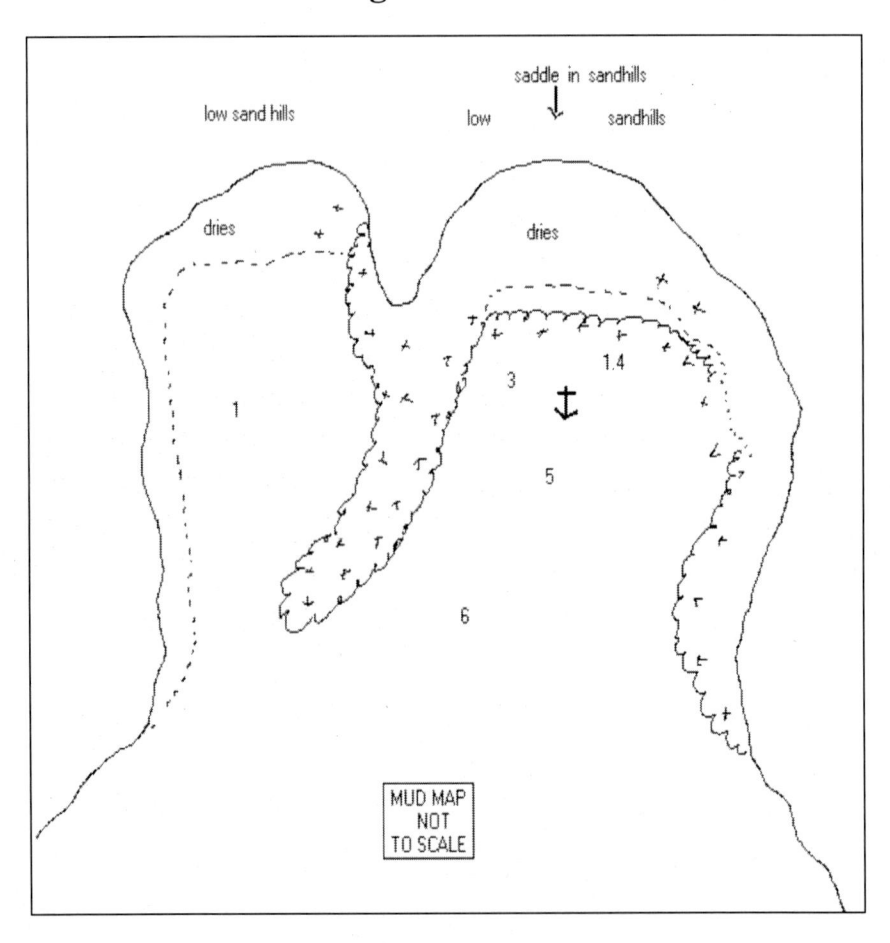

TRUANT ISLAND

11°40′S – 136°50′E

CHARTS	AUS 306, 715
LIGHTS	Truant Island flashes 15 seconds and is visible 15 miles.
TIDES	Gove (Truant Island) ANTT

The only anchorages here are in the two bays on the northwest side, where depth allows out from the fringing reef. The best one I found was in the large bay at the north-northwest corner in 5 metres. The holding is good and gives protection from winds from the east and south.

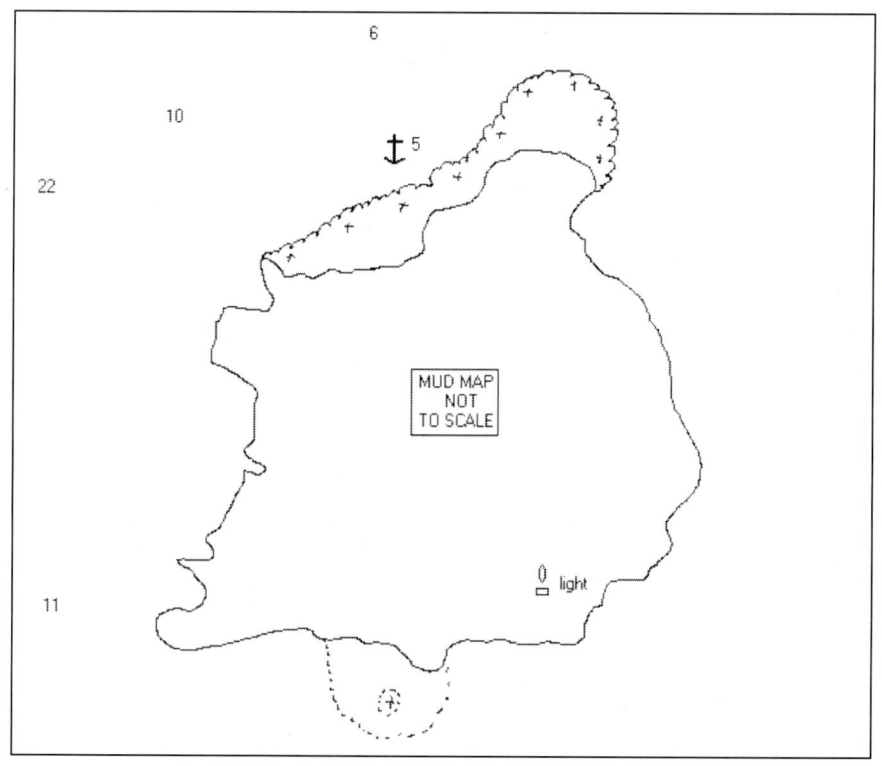

TWO ISLAND BAY

11°04′S – 136°42′E

CHARTS	AUS 306, 715
LIGHTS	Cape Wessel flashes 5 seconds, visible 15 miles. It is Racon equipped.
TIDES	Gove (Two Island Bay) ANTT

Two Island Bay is 5 miles southwest of Cape Wessel. To enter, stand well out from North Point to clear the reef and shoal ground. Both bays are protected from all winds except westerlies. The first bay to the north of North Island has good holding in 2 metres. Vessels can go close in but a lookout is necessary. DO NOT attempt to go between North Island and the main island; there is no passage. Between North and South islands is good shelter in close in 2.5 metres. There is no passage between South Island and the mainland. When moving between the two bays, stand well out from South Island; at least 0.75 miles is recommended. There is also anchorage in the bay to the south of South Island in 2.5 metres.

Two Island Bay

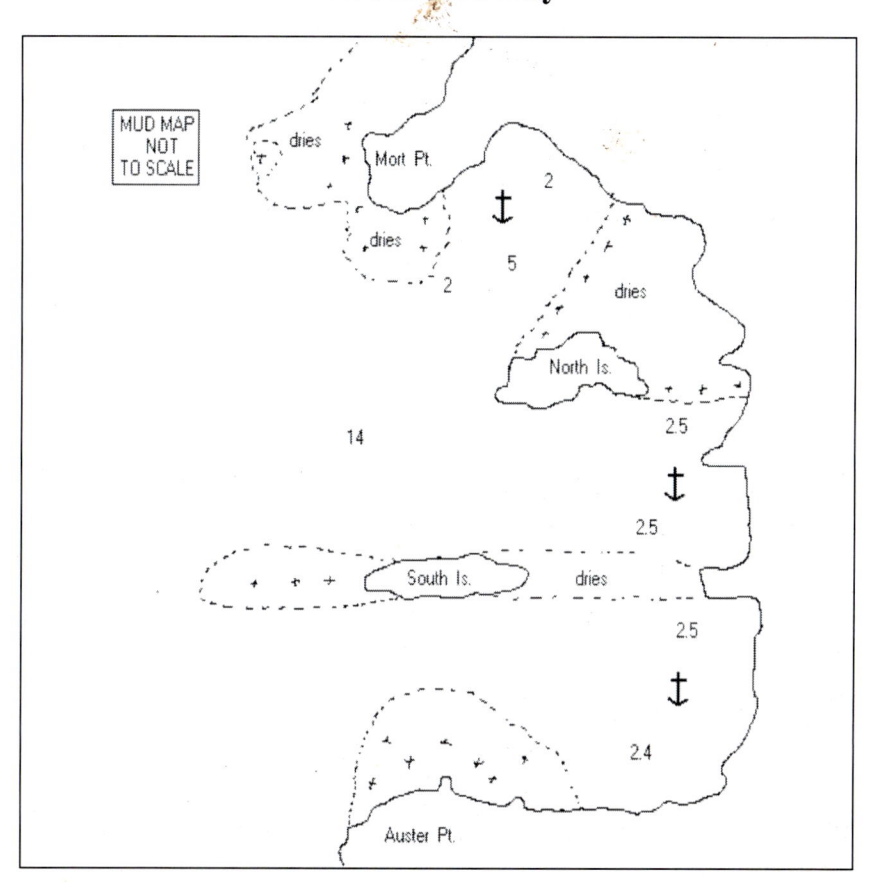

TRAFALGAR BAY

11°07'S – 136°42'E

CHARTS   AUS 306, 715, 442
LIGHTS   Nil
TIDES   Gove (Auster Point) ANTT

Trafalgar Bay is the next bay south of Two Island Bay. It is entered between Auster Point and Thumb Point. The shores are foul close in. Anchor in the bay east of Auster Point in 7 metres. Anchorage can also be found in the area to the north of the two small islets in 3 metres. There is no place to anchor to the south of these.

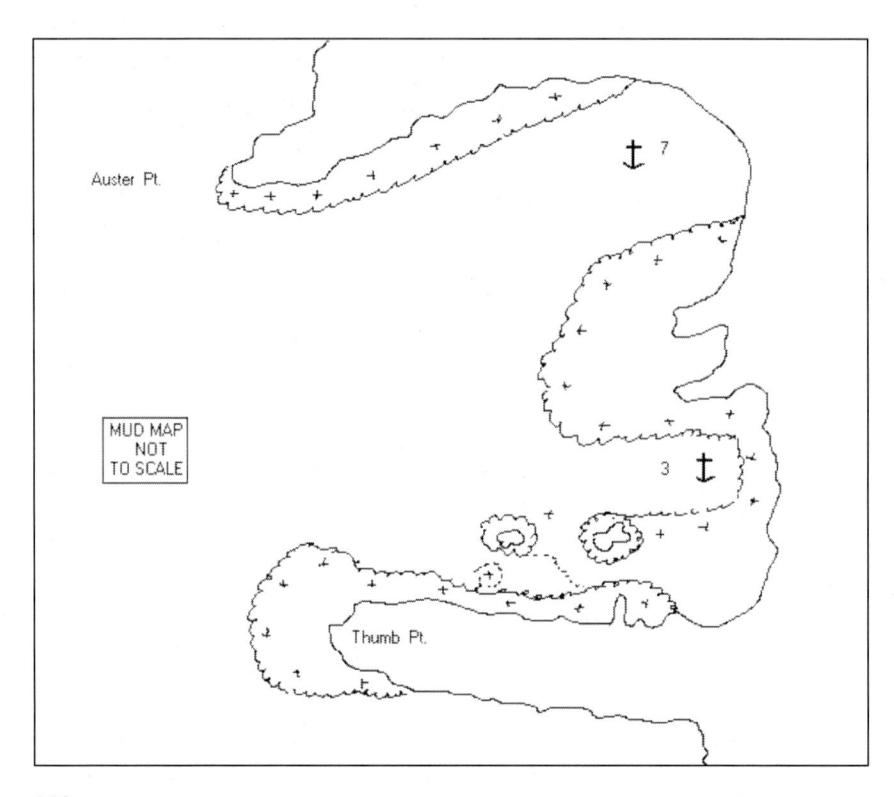

JENSEN BAY

11°08′S – 136°42′ E

CHARTS AUS 306, 715, 442, 15
LIGHTS NIL
TIDES   Gove (Auster Point) ANTT

Jensen Bay is approximately 4 miles in length and is entered south of Thumb Point and north of Shark Point. Anchorage can be found as close in as depth allows. I anchored in the bay between Thumb Point and Jensen Island in 3 metres. **Do not** attempt passage between Jensen Island and Marchinbar Island, as there are rocks and reef over the entire area. To get to the southern side, give Jensen Island at least 1 mile clearance. I used two anchorages in this area. The northern one was in 4 metres over sandy mud and the southern one was in 3 metres, again over sandy mud. Protection from winds can be had by moving around according to wind direction.

Jensen Bay

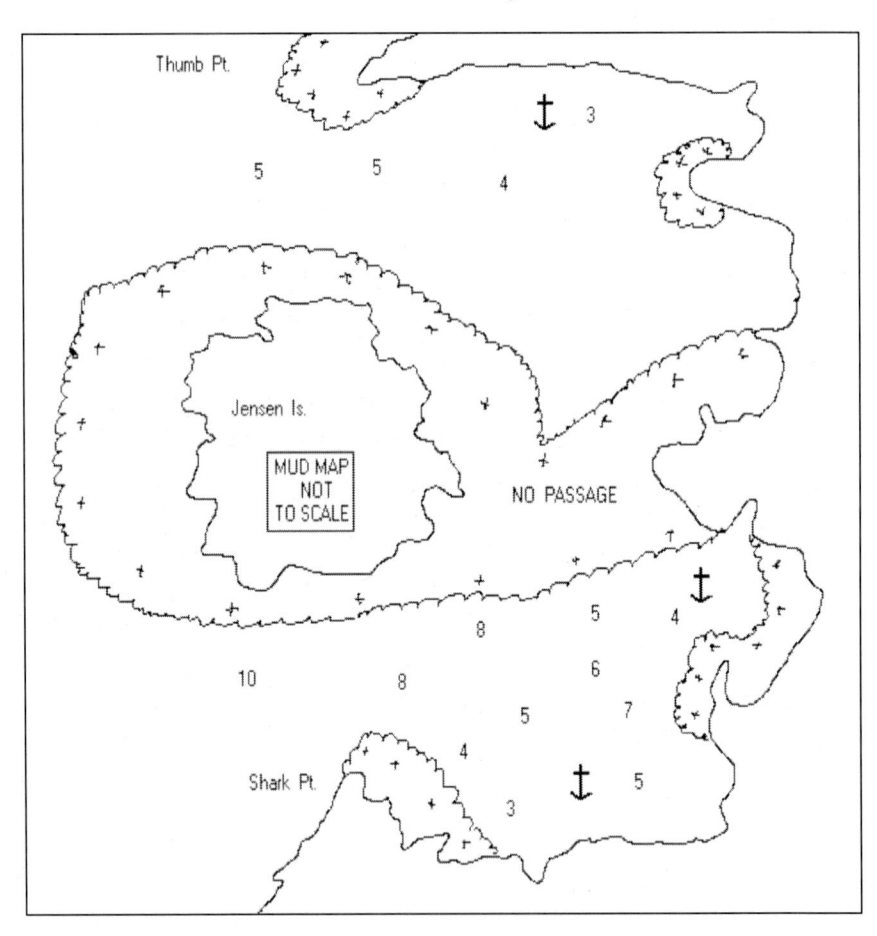

GEDGE POINT, TEMPLE BAY

11°12′S – 136°38′E

CHARTS　　AUS 306, 715, 442
LIGHTS　　Nil
TIDES　　Gove (Hopeful Bay) ANTT

Temple Bay is exposed to winds from the north and west, but is secure in all others. The conspicuous casuarina trees easily identify the bay on the western shore, towards the middle of the island. A nice sandy beach is found in the southern end of the bay. Anchorage is in 5 metres over sandy mud.

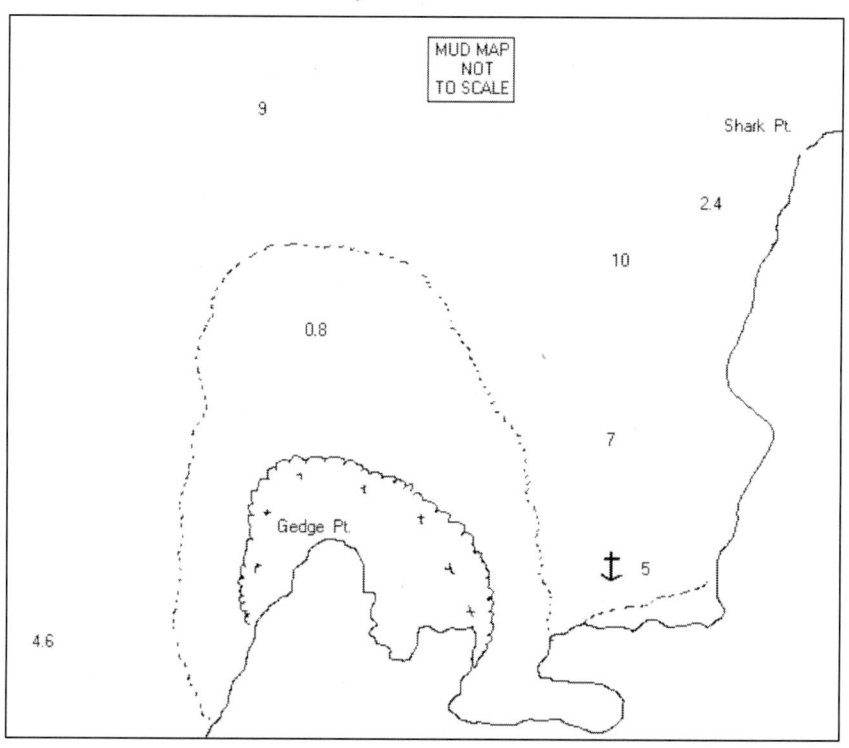

HAMMER POINT

11°20′S – 136°34′E

CHARTS AUS 306, 715, 442
LIGHTS Nil
TIDES Gove (Hopeful Bay) ANTT

There are two bays north and south of the point. Lagoon Bay is the northern bay and the southern bay is unnamed. Both are secure in all winds except westerlies. Fresh water may be found in the creek in Lagoon Bay. Anchorage in both bays is secure over sandy mud in 2–5 metres.

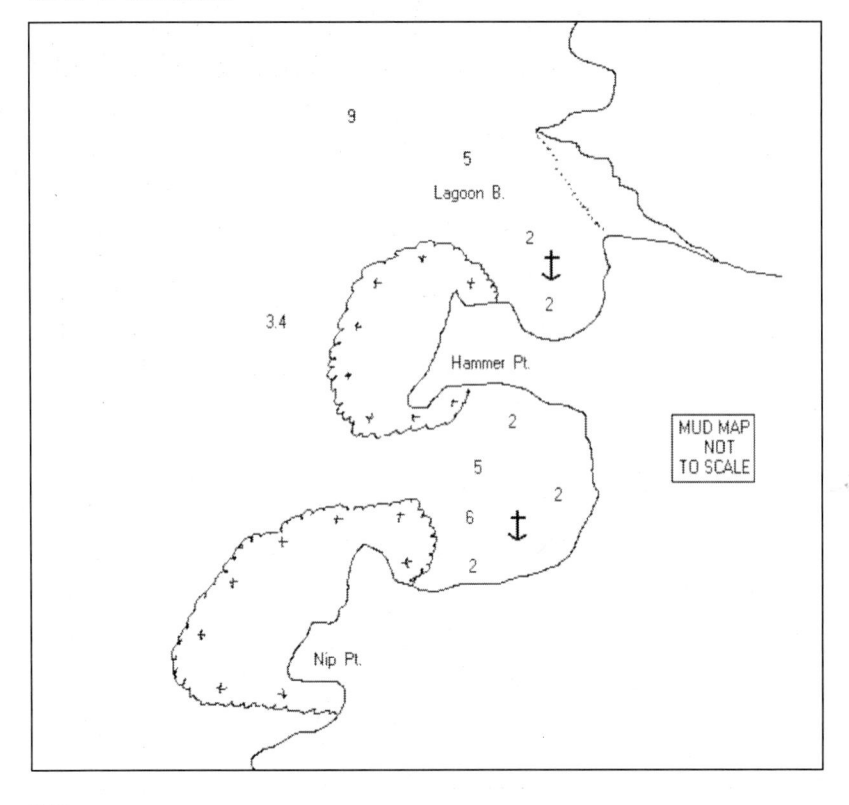

MUD MAP NOT TO SCALE

HOPEFUL BAY

11°25.6'S – 136°29.2'E

CHARTS AUS 306, 715, 442
LIGHTS Nil
TIDES   Gove (Hopeful Bay) ANTT

Hopeful Bay is a good anchorage after clearing the Cumberland Straits. It is clear of the currents and is well protected in all winds except southwest. Anchorage is in the northeast corner in 3 metres over mud. There were no offshore dangers found, but keep a good lookout. There is also an interesting bay on the northern side of Breakwater Point. I found anchorage in 4 metres, but vessels may be able to go further in. I did not check out the creek, but it looked good for crabs.

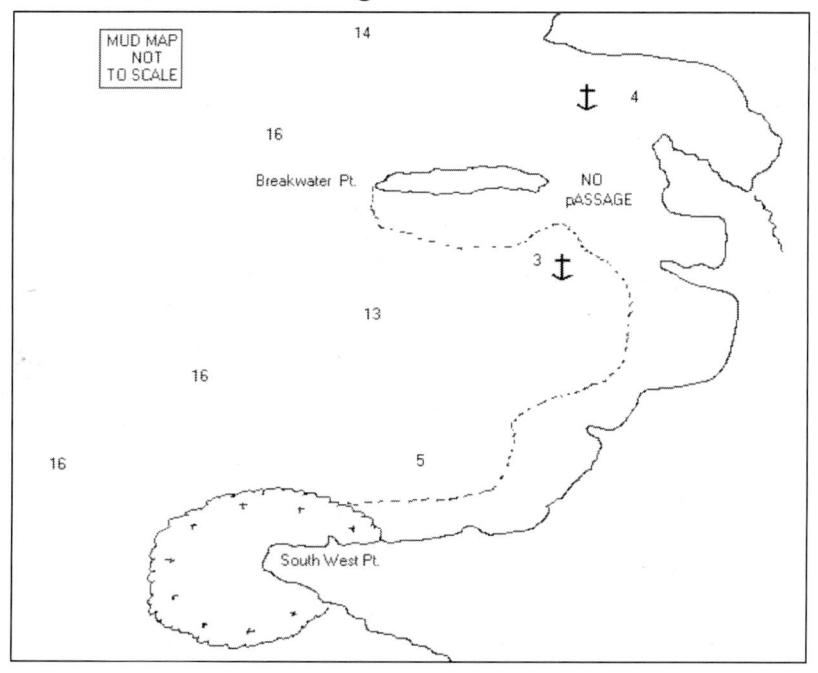

GULUWURU ISLAND

11°27.2′S – 136°26.6′E

UNNAMED BAY SOUTHERN SIDE OF CUMBERLAND STRAITS

CHARTS   AUS 306, 715, 442
LIGHTS   Nil
TIDES   Gove (Guluwuru Island) ANTT

After clearing Cumberland Straits at the western end, a good anchorage can be found 1.5 miles to the south, which is out of the current. Anchor in 4 metres in the southwest corner of the bay. At the western side of the bay is an unnamed island joined to the main island by a rock ledge. By holding course to favour this island, no offshore dangers were encountered.

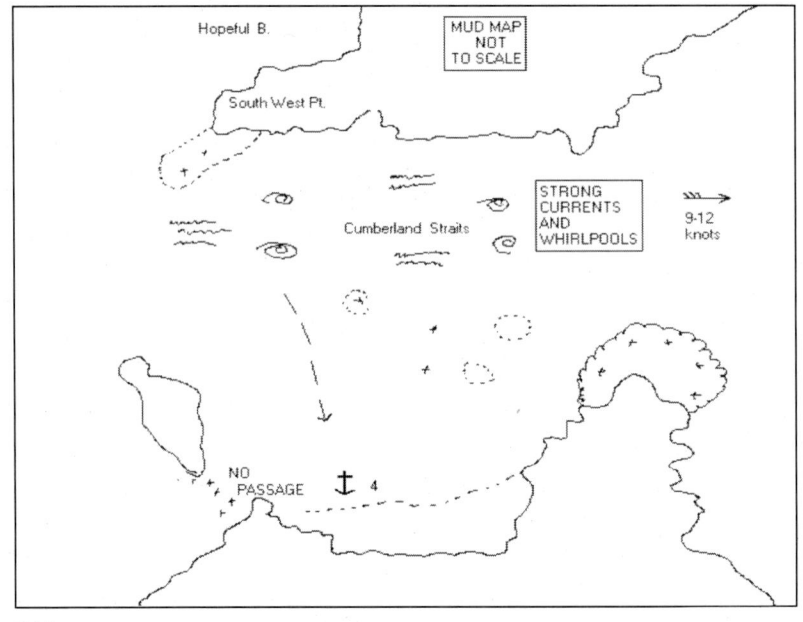

GURULIYA BAY

11°34.8′S – 136°37.2′E

CHARTS AUS 715, 716, 306, 442
LIGHTS Stevens Island flashes 2 every 10 seconds, visible 11 miles
TIDES Gove (Guluwuru Island) ANTT

Guruliya Bay is 11 miles south of the anchorage on Guluwuru Island. It is a boot-shaped bay on the western side of Raragala Island. Anchorage in the heel of the bay is in 5 metres over sand. Further, in the toe of the bay, I anchored in 2.5 metres. Rocks, especially in the toe bound the shores in this bay, so a forward lookout is necessary. The area in the toe could possibly be used as a cyclone anchorage.

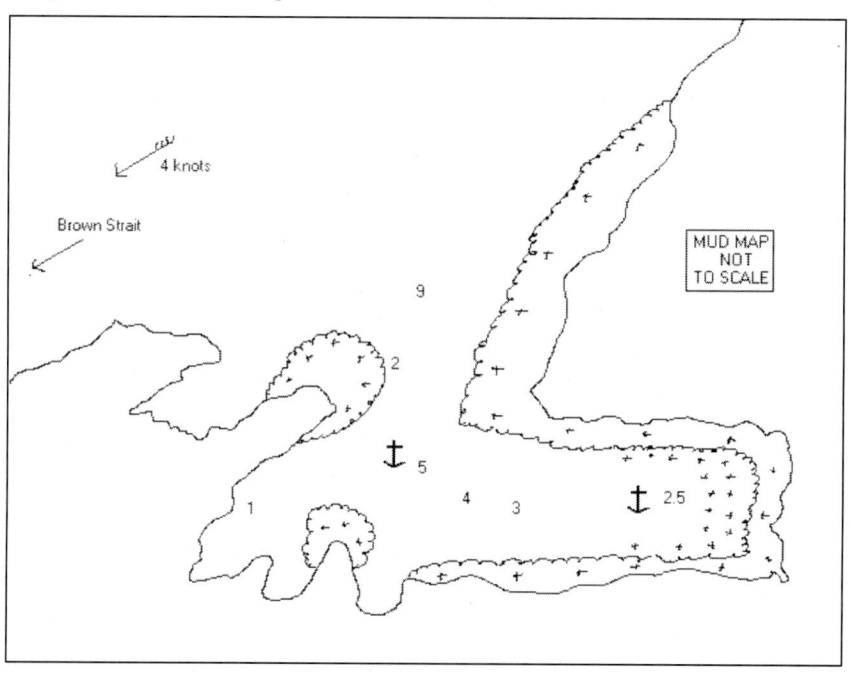

ALGER ISLAND

11°53.5′S – 135°56.2′E

CHART AUS 716
LIGHTS Warnawi Island flashes 3 every 15 seconds, visible 10 miles.
TIDES: Gove (Cadell Straits) ANTT

There is no useful anchorage in this group of islands, except in the bay on the southwest corner of Alger Island, 30 miles south of the Raragala Island anchorage. However, to anchor in close, you must cross the 5 metre flats or stay out wide in 9 metres. An early start is necessary to cross the entrance bar of the Cadell Straits. This is 6 miles south and requires high tide to cross.

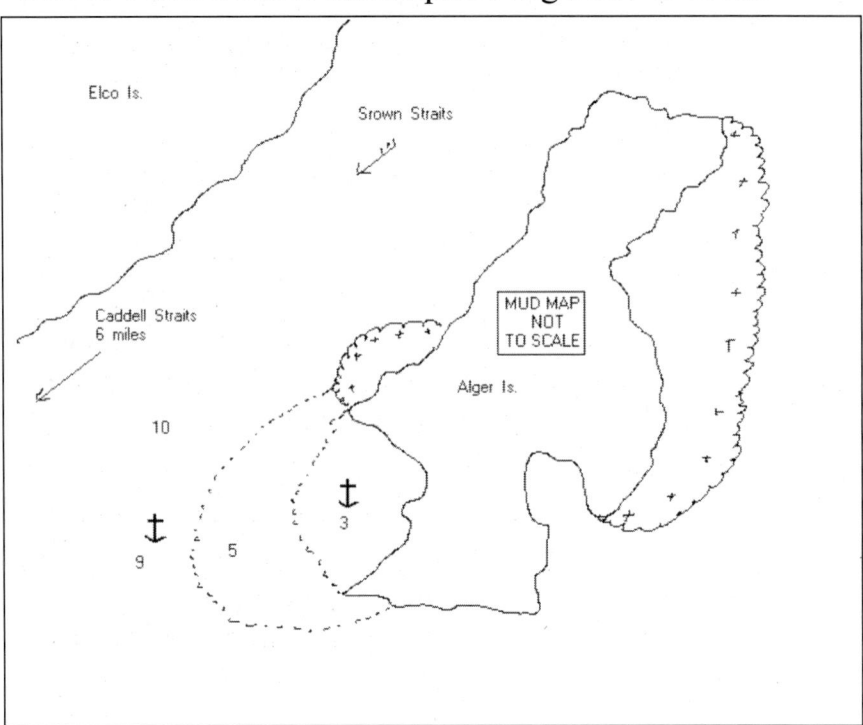

CADELL STRAITS

Entrance Beacon East End 11°56.4′S – 135°51.8′E

CHARTS   AUS 716, 15
LIGHTS   Red, green and black channel markers
TIDES   Gove (Cadell Straits) ANTT

Cadell Strait carries a 0.5 metre drying bar at its eastern end, and requires a minimum of this plus ship's draft, plus a bit for safety. Only attempt to cross on a rising tide, which floods east. The first beacon is a green; keep this to port. The next is a black; this can be passed on either side. At this point, you are over the bar. Follow the beacons, keeping red to starboard, green to port, and black to either side. The narrowest part is 8 miles in from the eastern end of Djunytjunur Point (pronounce that if you can!), and despite the disturbed waters caused by the tidal race is quite deep. After exiting the narrows, the next beacon is red. Approximately 2 miles past the barge landing on Elcho Island, is Warrandhanur Rock, out from Matjaganur Point. There is a channel between the two, but the safest channel is around the outside of the two. Do not turn north too soon, as shoal water and rocks extend west for 0.6 miles. Two miles north is the Galiwinku Mission; this is to the south of the conspicuous tank. There is a small hospital, supermarket etc. and an air service to Darwin. Anchor out from the mission in 2–7 metres. Watch your petrol. Petrol sniffing teenagers may try to board in the middle of the night looking for unleaded petrol. Recommend anchoring well out.

Cadell Straits

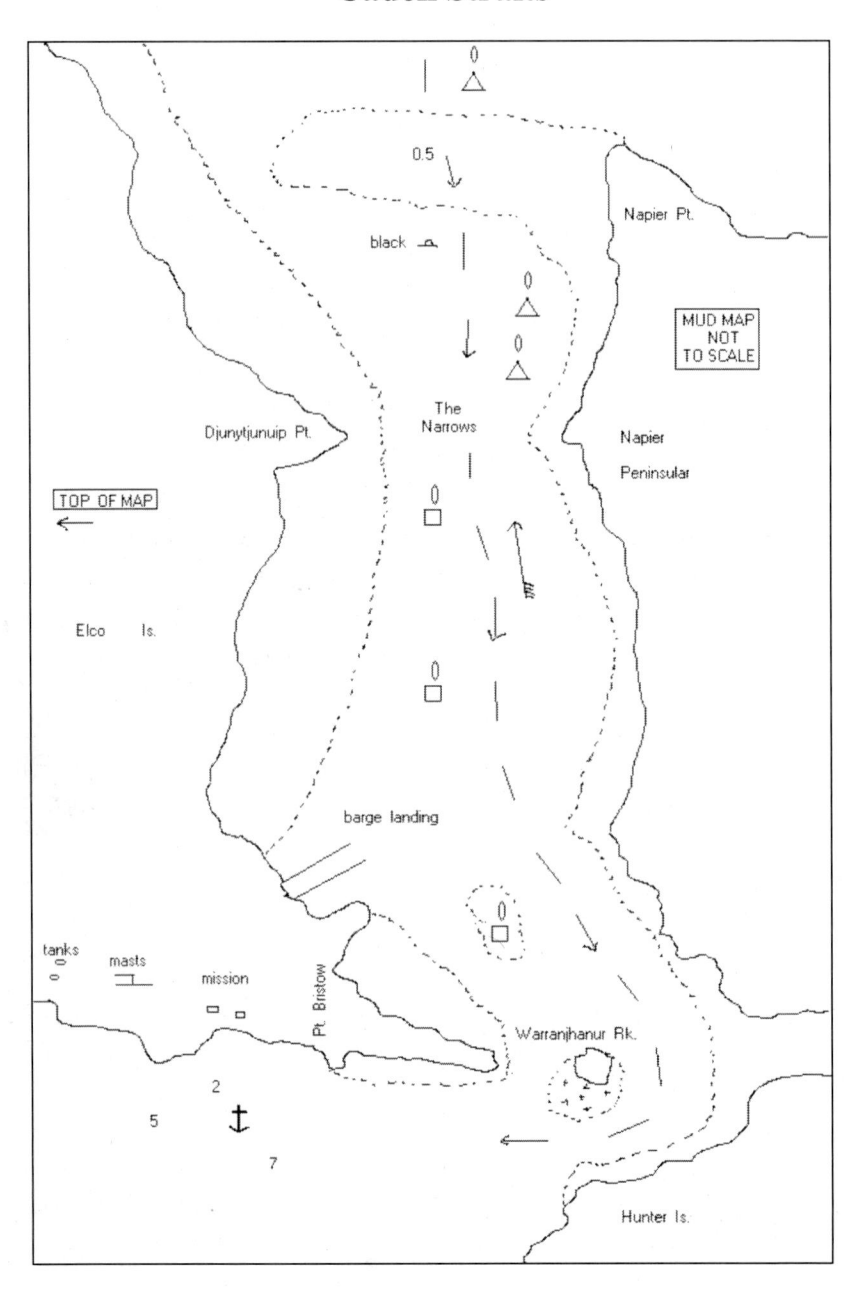

REFUGE BAY, ELCHO ISLAND

11°48.90′S – 135°50.30′E

CHARTS   AUS 716, 442
LIGHTS   Nil
TIDES   Gove (Guluwuru Island) ANTT

This is a very large bay situated at the northwestern side of Elcho Island. Anchorage is in 3 metres over sandy mud. This depth holds over most of the bay, making it possible to anchor anywhere. The best sheltered area I found was in the northern end out from the small drying creek. Give the northern entry a wide berth until the bay proper is identified, as there are rocky areas extending seawards and to the south for a short distance. No hazards were found.

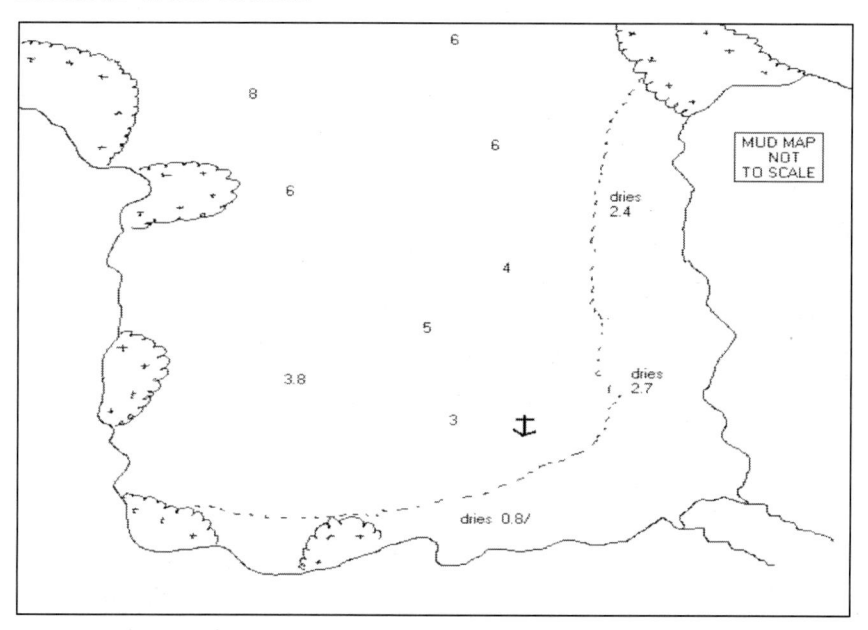

ELCHO ISLAND, UNNAMED BAY EAST OF WARRNGA POINT

11°56.20′S – 135°37.90′E

CHARTS AUS 716, 442
LIGHTS Nil
TIDES Gove (N.W. Crocodile Island) ANTT

This unnamed bay is a useful anchorage. It shortens the distance through the Crocodile Islands to either Cape Stewart or Boucat Bay. It is entered between Ganawa Point and Warrnga Point. Anchor in 2 metres over sandy mud in the head of the bay. When leaving it is necessary to give Warrnga Point a wide clearance, as the area around the point dries for some distance out to sea. I found no underwater dangers, but keep an eye out.

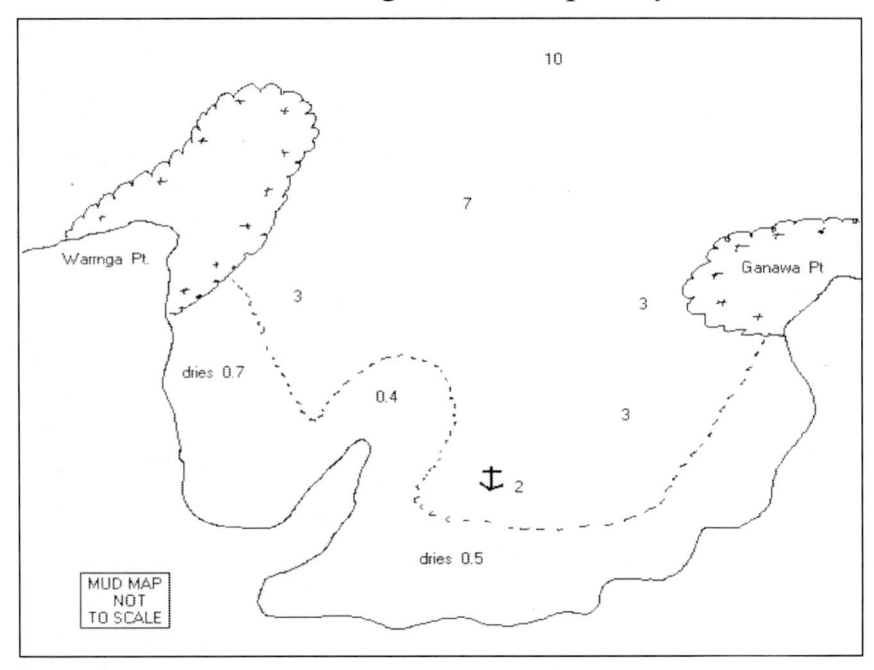

HOWARD ISLAND – (New)

12°05' – 135°20.60' E

CHART	AUS 442
LIGHTS	Nil
TIDES	Gove (Hutchinson River) ANTT

This anchorage is the first worthwhile anchorage after Elcho Island. It is a large bay with a sandy bottom, and is easily identified by the windsock, which is seen first, and then some houses on the eastern end of the bay. Give the eastern point a reasonable clearance when entering. No other dangers were noted. A secure anchorage.

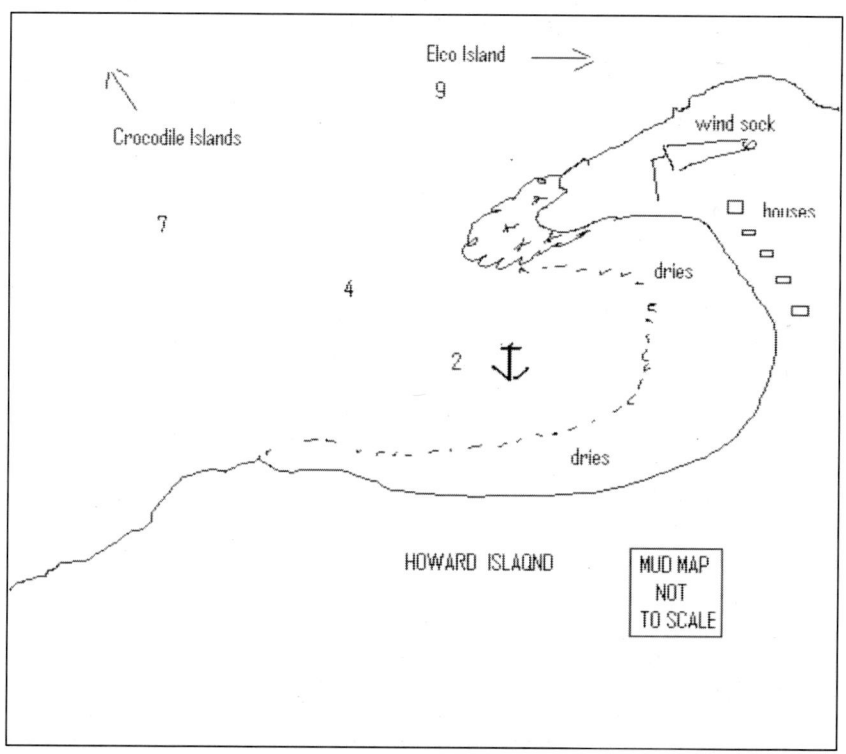

CAPE STEWART

11°56.00′S – 143°45.00′E
(34)

CHART   AUS 442
LIGHTS   Nil
TIDES   Gove (N.W. Crocodile Island) ANTT

This is a rather exposed anchorage. However, you pitch more than roll, making it quite tenable up to around 15 knots. The bottom is good-holding, sticky grey mud, very similar to Gove. Anchorage is in 2–3 metres towards the sand blow in the centre of the bay. Make sure to clear Sand Island to the west when leaving, as it is surrounded by reef and there is definitely no passage between the island and the mainland. This is the only anchorage at the end of the day, if you cannot make it around into Boucat Bay before dark.

Cape Stewart

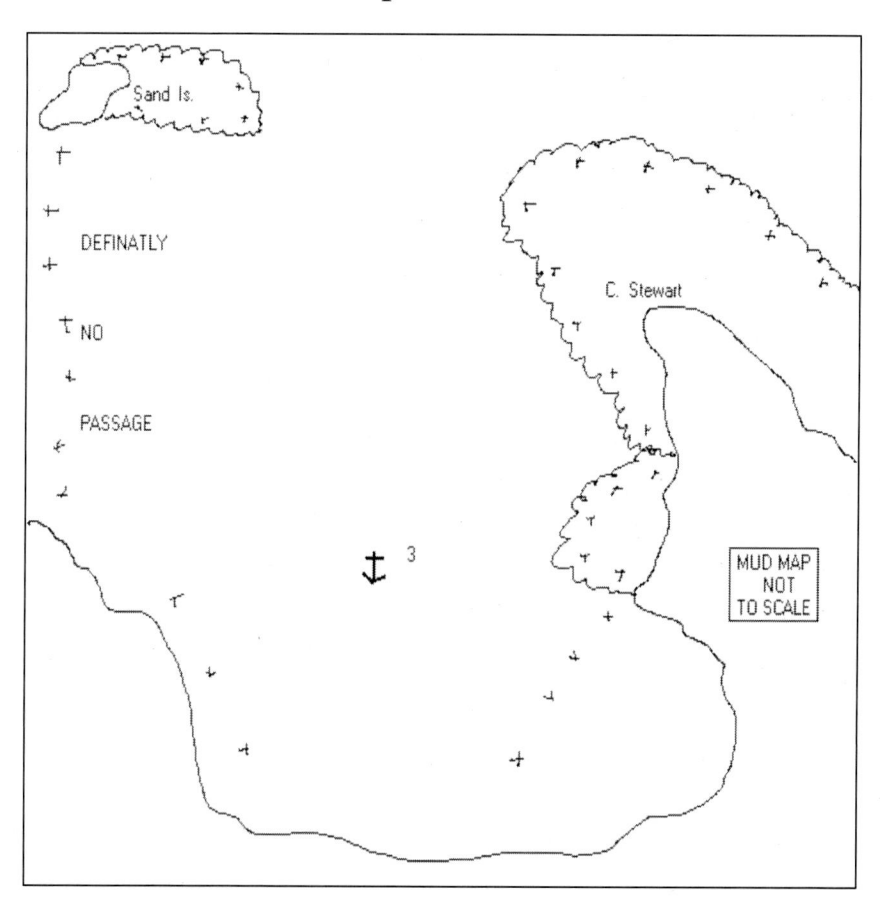

Sand Is.

DEFINATLY

NO

PASSAGE

C. Stewart

⚓ 3

MUD MAP
NOT
TO SCALE

253

BLYTH RIVER

$12°03'S - 134°35'E$

CHART   AUS 442
LIGHTS Nil
TIDES   Gove (Yambooma) ANTT

The Blyth River is about 70 miles west of Elcho Island. If unable to do this leg in daylight, or too late to catch the tide to enter, anchorage can be found just to the west of Cape Stewart. The top half of a rising tide is needed to enter the river. Approach the very conspicuous casuarina trees on the eastern bank on a course of about 176° T. When about 1–1.25 miles offshore, turn towards the centre of the river entrance. There is an outstation of the Kopinga Mission located around 1 mile upstream on the western bank.

Blyth River

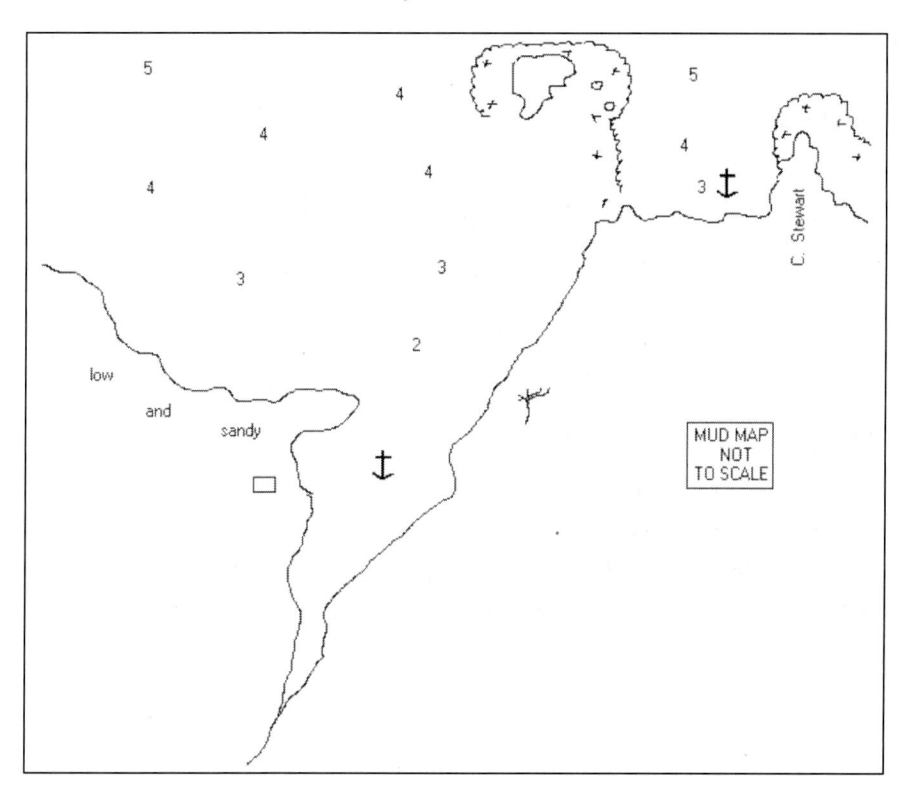

LIVERPOOL RIVER

12°00'S – 134°12'E

CHART AUS 442
LIGHTS Nil
TIDES Darwin (Entrance Island) ANTT

From Blyth River, keep at least 5 miles offshore from Skirmish Point to avoid the shoals in this area. The Liverpool River can be entered by either going around Haul Around Island, or going between Haul Around Island and Entrance Island. If using this option, stay north, then change course to clear the western side of Entrance Island. Anchorage can be found on the southern side in 4 metres. Anchorage can also be found to the northeast of South West Point in 4 metres of mud. On the east bank of the river, the settlement of Maningrida is located. Below the few buildings is a barge landing. There is an all-weather airstrip and an aircraft radio beacon. The river is navigable for some distance with care. It is not really worth going past Mangrove Bluff. There are no channel marks, so enter on sounder. Once again, watch your petrol with petrol sniffing kids.

Liverpool River

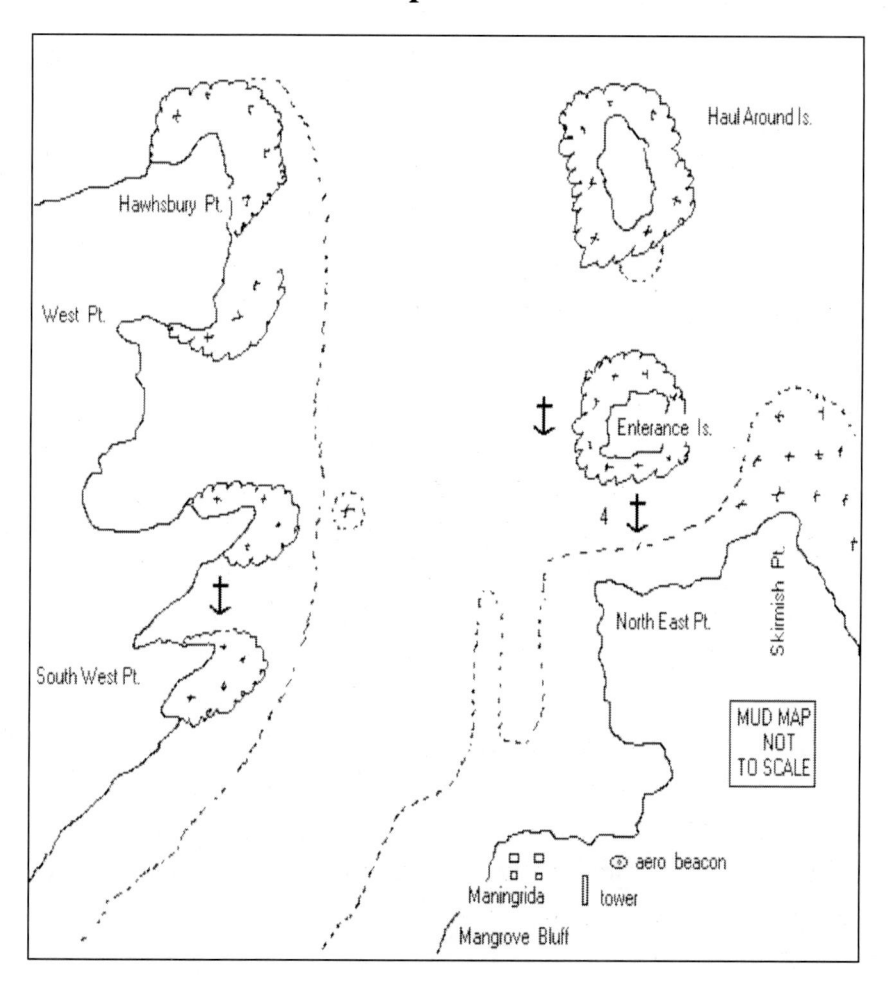

HAUL AROUND ISLAND

11°54.00′S – 134°12.50′E

CHART   AUS 442
LIGHTS   Nil
TIDES   Darwin (Entrance Island) ANTT

Haul Around Island is the outer of the two islands out from the mouth of the Liverpool River. The island is a sand cay about 1.2 metres high and is surrounded by reef and rocks. Anchorage is out from the light remains on the western side of the island. This is a useful anchorage if not wishing to enter the Liverpool River. I found it quite comfortable in 25 knots of wind. Anchorage is in 6 metres over sand, but you will need to check out where to drop the anchor, as there are quite a few rocky patches. You may be able to get closer. I did not check this out, as it was late in the afternoon. There is a cleared area where the light maintenance boat lands, giving access to the beach.

Haul Around Island

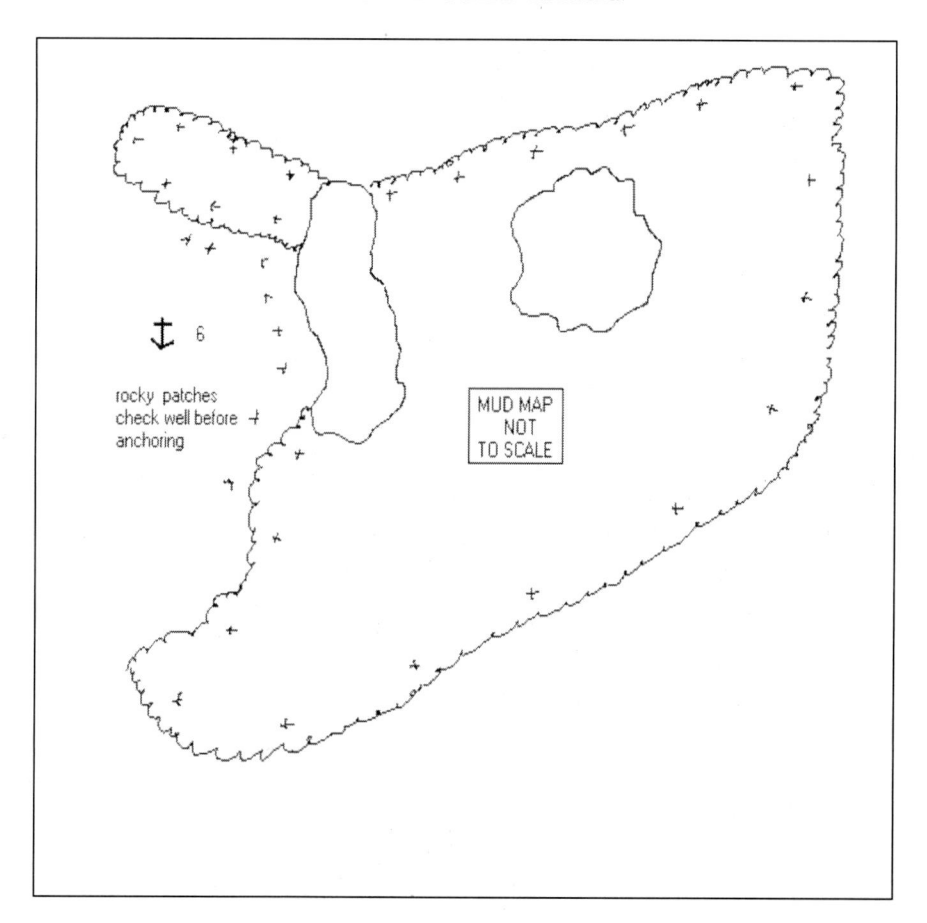

CUTHBERT POINT – (New)

11°44′S – 133°47′E

CHART AUS 442
LIGHTS Nil
TIDES Darwin (North Goulburn Island) ANTT

This is secure and comfortable in strong winds. To get to the anchorage, it is possible to cross the marked shoal area, but keep an eye on the sounder, especially at the western end. Don't turn in too soon, as there are rock areas along the east bank. The remains of a wrecked dinghy are on the beach. Don't try to anchor here, as there are two rock arms with scattered rocks between. Anchor past here in 4 metres. The water is generally clear and the rocks can be seen.

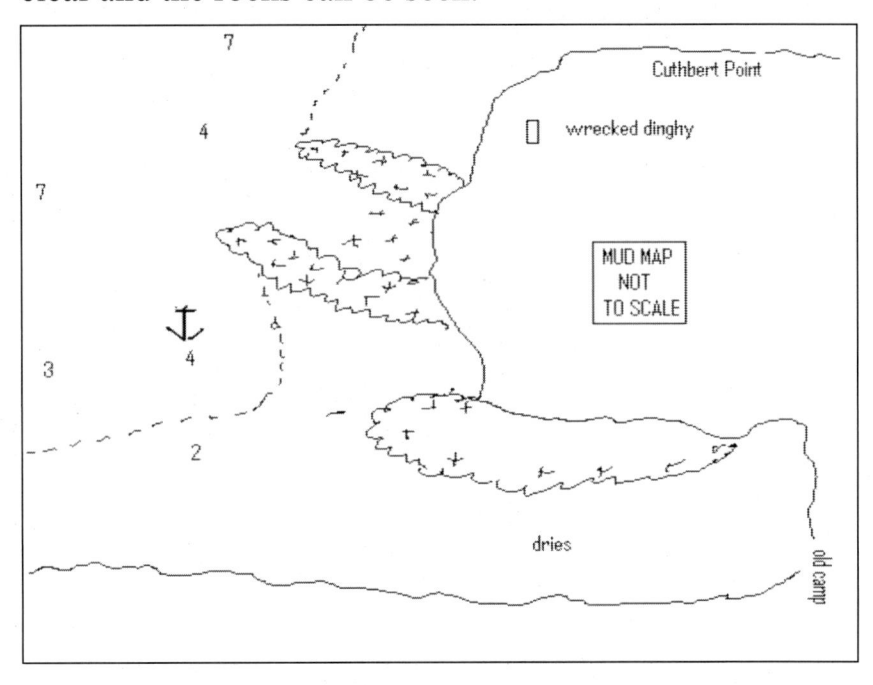

GUION POINT

11°46'S – 133°40'E

CHART AUS 442
LIGHTS Nil
TIDES Darwin (North Goulburn Island) ANTT

If intending to use these bays, be sure to clear Cuthbert Point by at least 6.5 miles minimum, to clear the shoal water around it. Guion Point extends 1 mile west from the mainland and has bays to the east and west. The best one is the bay to the west; it is deeper and has a constant depth of 3–5 metres. It is reported to have a shoal entrance, but I did not encounter it. However, there is a rocky area extending about 2 miles to the north of the western point. Give this a good clearance if intending to enter the King River.

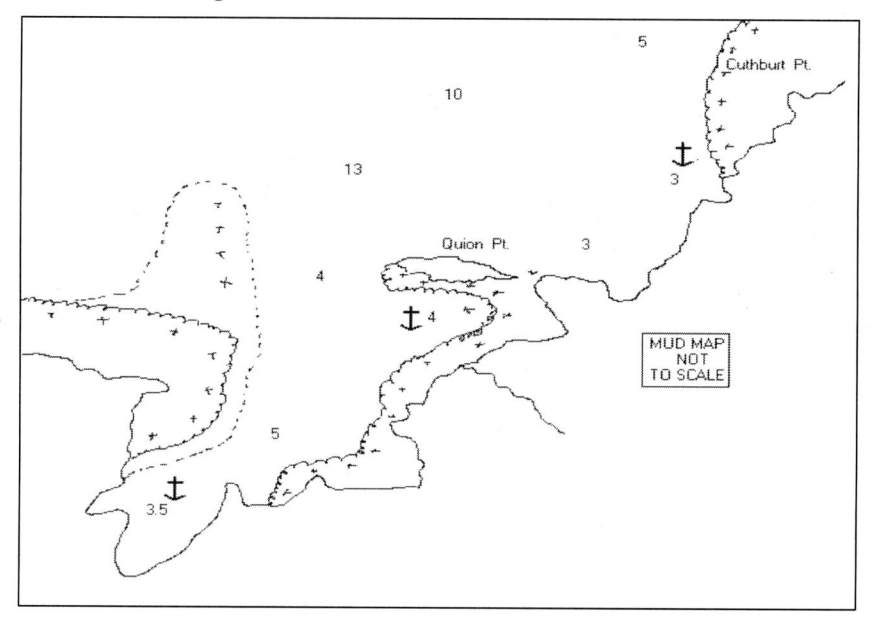

KING RIVER

11°47.5′S – 133°33′E

CHART AUS 442
LIGHTS Nil
TIDES Darwin (North Goulburn Island) ANTT

The King River is entered east of Turner Point. The entrance has no bar and the mouth has depths of 5–8 metres, which makes it a suitable shelter in strong winds. The river can be safely travelled for about 3 miles, with depths of 5 metres. At the island, an anchorage will be found in 3 metres. There is a huge colony of flying foxes. When they come or go, the noise is unbelievable.

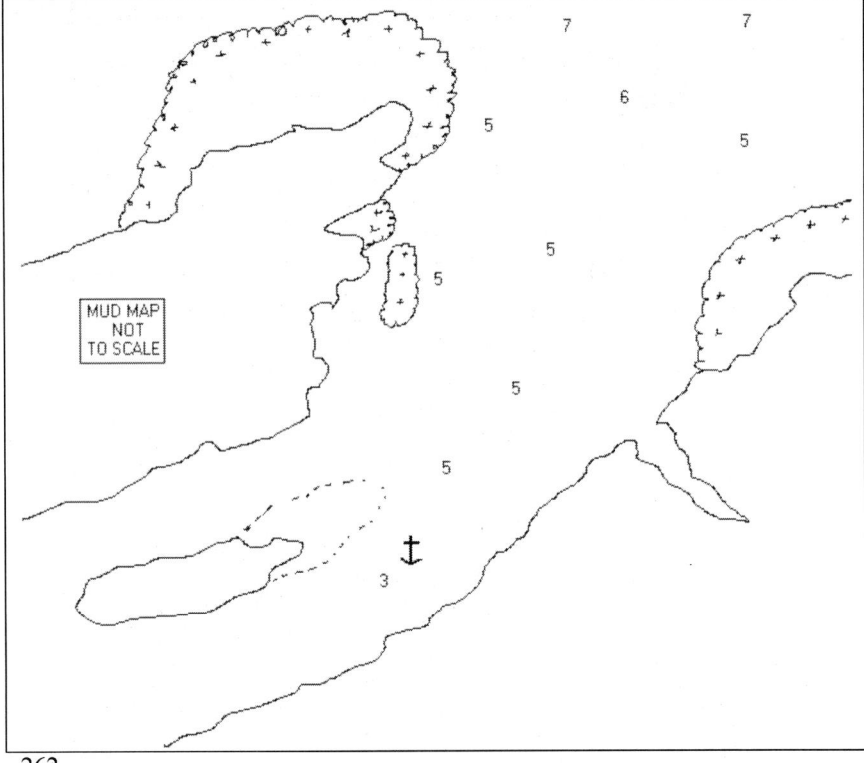

NORTH GOULBURN ISLAND, MULLET BAY

11°31'S – 133°24'E

CHARTS	AUS 308, 442
LIGHTS	Nil
TIDES	Darwin (North Goulburn Island) ANTT

From King River, I travelled, direct to North Goulburn Island, as I felt it was safer than the shoal and foul ground in Macquarie Strait. In addition, a 2–3 knot current floods southeast. Mullet Bay lies on the western side of North Goulburn Island, and is entered between Cone Point in the north and Sand Point in the south. The best anchorage was found to be at the northern end of the bay in 3 metres over mud, but stay well out, as the shores are rocky. If coming from the south, be careful not to enter too soon, as there is a below-water rock to the north of Sand Point which has 1.8 metres of water. It is not recommended that vessels try to travel between this rock and the island, as a survey by dinghy showed foul water and varying depths to 1 metres.

Mullet Bay

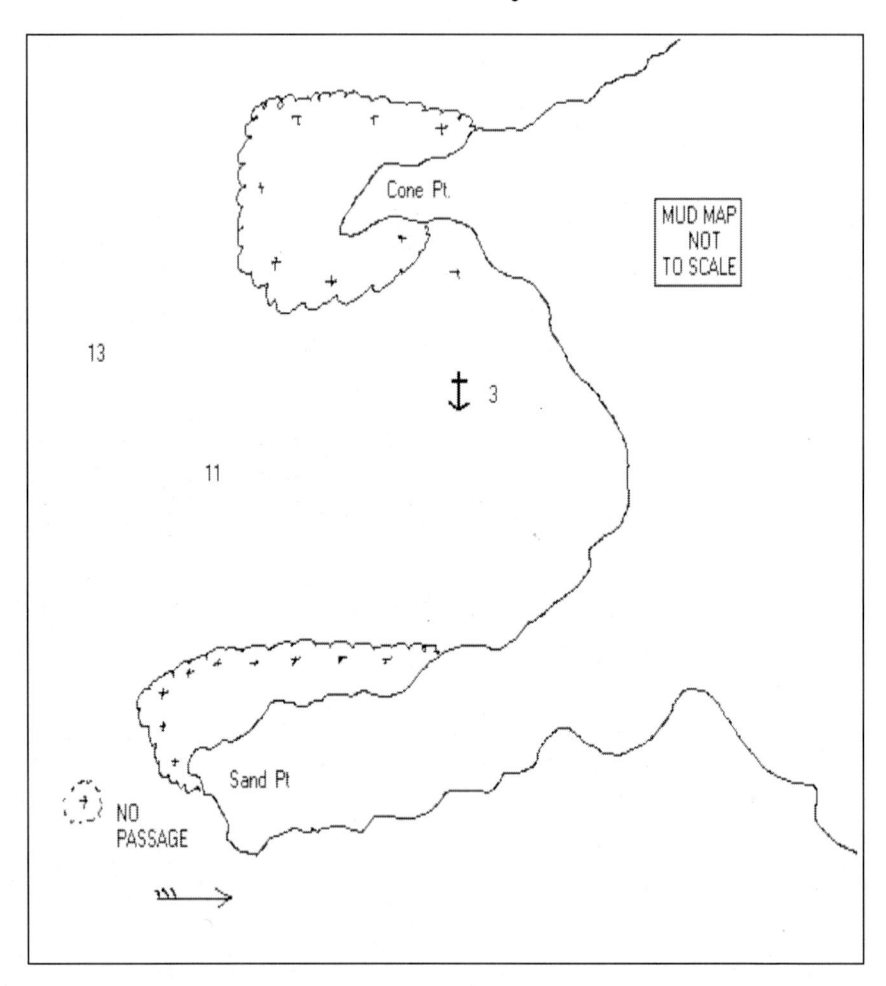

Cone Pt.

MUD MAP
NOT
TO SCALE

13

⚓ 3

11

Sand Pt

NO PASSAGE

WHITE POINT – (New)

11°42.50′S – 133°17′E

CHART	AUS 308, 442
LGHTS	Nil
TIDES	Darwin (North Goulburn Island) ANTT

This anchorage is southwest of Simms Island. After clearing Macquarie Strait, continue towards Simms Island until deep water is found. Ross Point has reef and shoals extending out for some distance. Stay out wide in 5 metres until White Point is identified. This is easy, as the rocks are white, being covered in bird droppings. Anchor south of here in 3–4 metres.

White Point

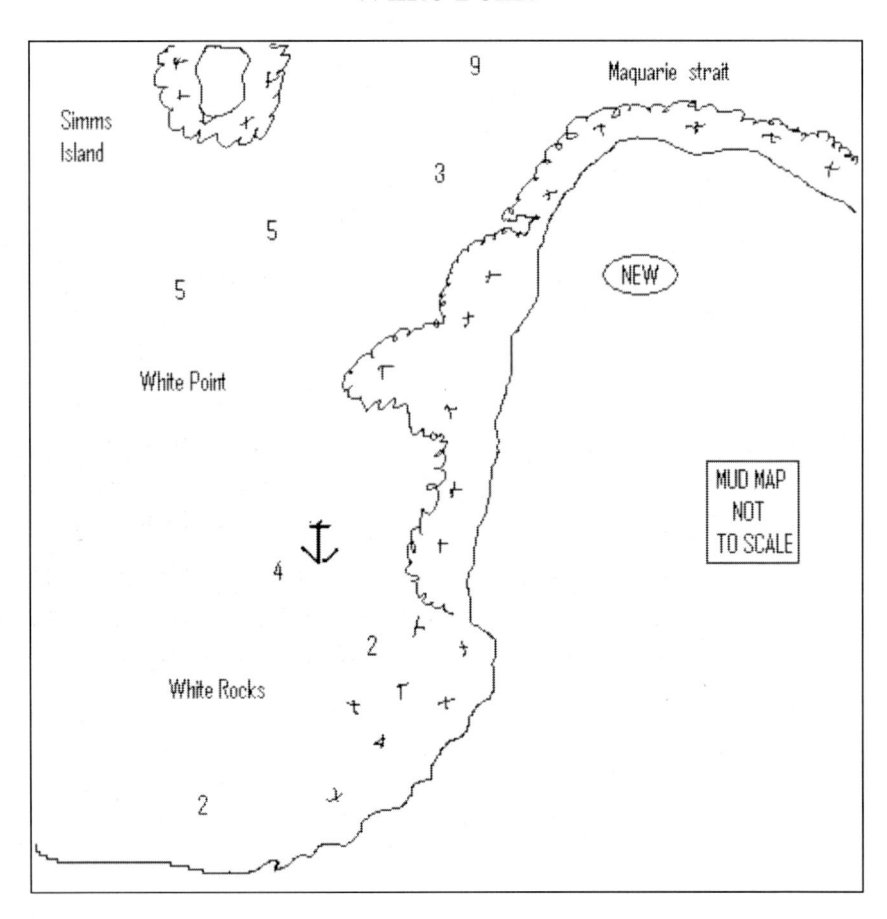

Mud map not to scale

Labels on map: Simms Island, Maquarie strait, White Point, White Rocks, NEW

MALAY BAY

11°23′S – 132°53′E

CHARTS AUS 308, 442
LIGHTS Nil
TIDES Darwin (Cape Croker) ANTT

Approaching Decourcy Point from the Goulburn Islands, a distance of 2 miles offshore between this point and Cape Cockburn is recommended, to clear the foul ground north of the cape. Before turning to enter Malay Bay, have Cape Cockburn well clear astern; this will clear the foul ground. Malay Bay is entered between Cape Cockburn in the north and Annesley Point to the south. Entry is in deep water and appeared to be clear of underwater obstructions. However, take care to avoid the reef, which runs north of Annesley Point for 1 mile; favour Cape Cockburn. Anchorage is in 4 metres over mud off the northern beach and is well protected.

Malay Bay

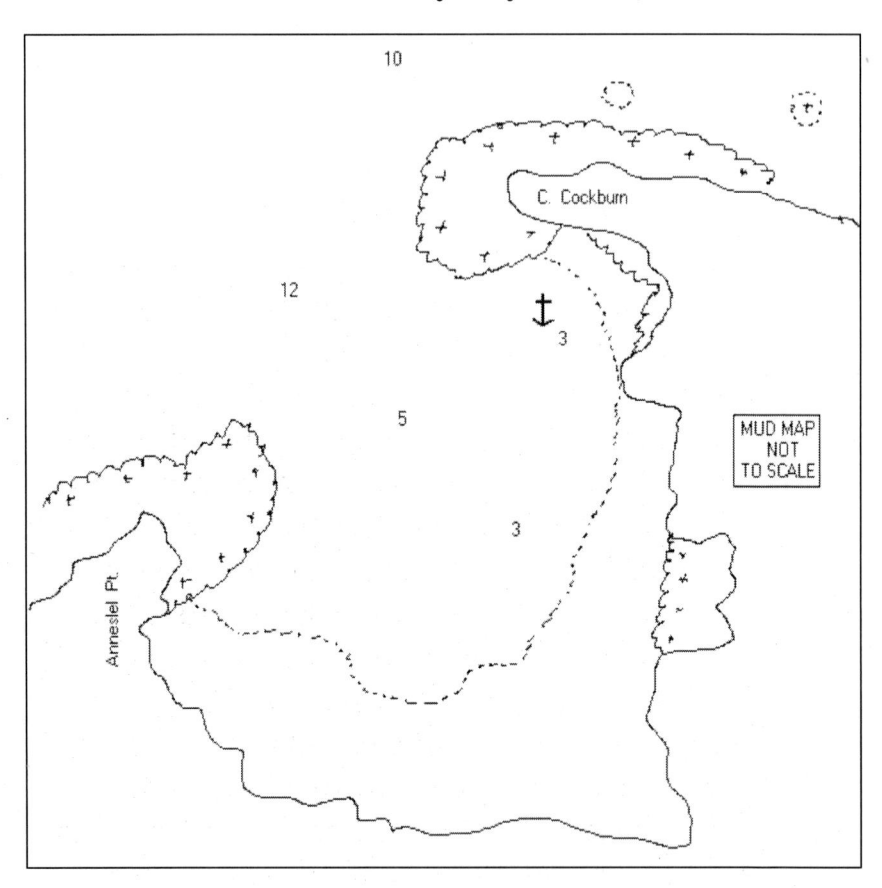

VALENTIA ISLAND

11°23.00′S – 132°48.00′E

CHARTS   AUS 308, 442
LIGHTS   Nil
TIDES   Darwin (Cape Croker) ANTT

Valentia Island is found to the southwest of Malay Bay, and 2.5 miles west of Annesley Point. Both the pilot book and chart say there is no passage between Annesley Point and Valentia Island, but this is not correct. There is 6.5 metres of water at low tide in the centre of the channel. The waypoints are Annesley Point 11°22.00′S – 132°50.25′E and Valentia Island 11°24.50′S – 132°48.60′E. On the southern side is a beautiful anchorage, in a large bay where days can be spent. The bottom is sandy and there is deep water close in, although the shore has some rocky patches. The eastern end of the bay is well sheltered and clear of rocks. In fact, you can put the bow on the beach if inclined. Depths are from 47–6 metres. From here, it is an easy 12 miles across to Bowen Strait. In suitable conditions, it is possible to anchor in the bay on the western side of the island.

Valentia Island

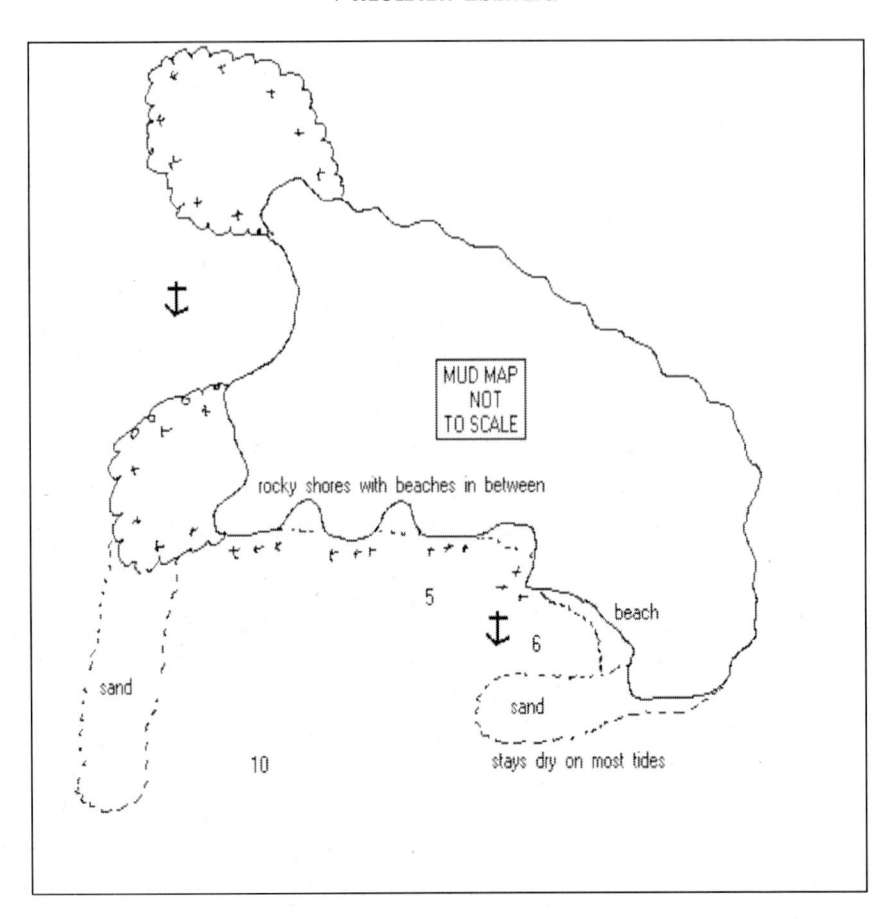

MUD MAP NOT TO SCALE

rocky shores with beaches in between

5

beach

6

sand

sand
stays dry on most tides

10

OXLEY ISLAND

10°59.3S – 132°48.9′E

CHARTS AUS 308, 442
LIGHTS Cape Croker flashes 5 seconds, visible 10 miles.
TIDES Darwin (Cape Croker) ANTT

Oxley Island is 13 miles east of Cape Croker and is a great spot. I rode out a strong wind warning here in comfort, with no problems. Anchor outside the fringing reef, but be aware of the scattered coral heads. A forward lookout is recommended when closing the anchorage. To anchor, come in towards the red cliff on the western side of the northern island, until close enough to anchor in 7–8 metres. The reef exposes all around the island at low water, and provides good fishing and plentiful oysters, but watch the time and tide, or you may have difficulty getting back home.

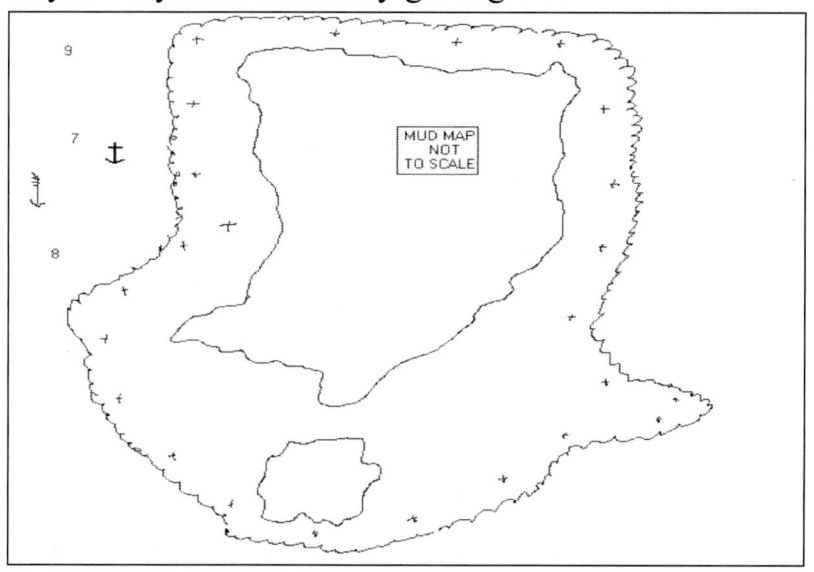

SOMERVILLE BAY

11°01′S – 132°30′E

CHARTS AUS 308; 442
LIGHTS Cape Croker flashes 5 seconds, visible 10 miles
TIDES Darwin (Cape Croker) ANTT

Take care rounding Cape Croker, as the reef extends seaward for about 1 mile, and extends around into Somerville Bay. The only place I found to anchor was off the eastern shore in 5 metres. Landing is difficult. Average depth in the bay was found to be between 7–11 metres, but the shoreline is rocky and surrounded by reef. Protection is good.

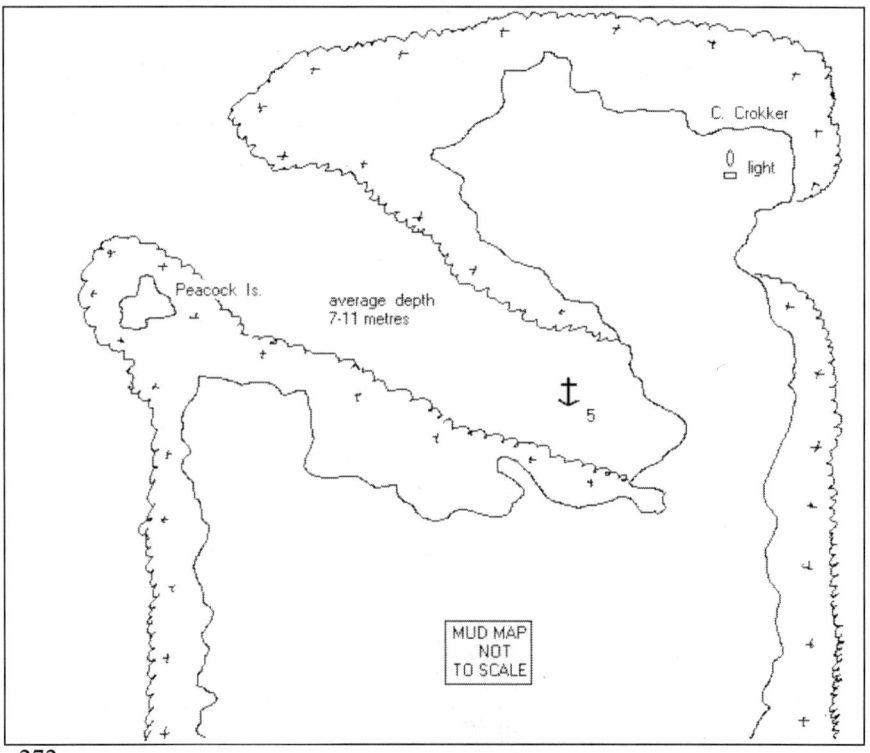

PALM BAY

11°08′S – 132°29′E

CHARTS AUS 308, 442
LIGHTS Nil
TIDES Darwin (Cape Croker) ANTT

Palm Bay lies to the south of Somerville Bay. After clearing Peacock Island, the run is in clear water, but stay well out to avoid the reefs along Croker Island. The only anchorage is off the beach in the southeast corner where it appears that a barge lands occasionally. The rest of the bay is foul, and protection is not good owing to the low nature of the island in this area. Average depth appears to be between 5–8 metres.

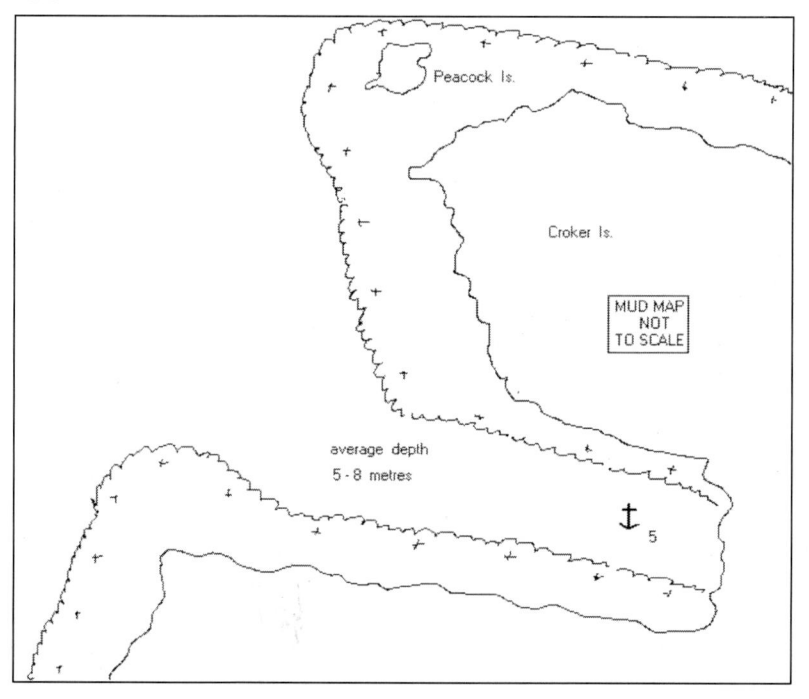

Peacock Is.
Croker Is.
MUD MAP NOT TO SCALE
average depth 5 - 8 metres

RAFFLES BAY

11°10′S – 132°23′E

CHARTS	AUS 308, 442
LIGHTS	Nil
TIDES	Darwin (Port Essington) ANTT
CAUTION	Pearl rafts

Raffles Bay is on the mainland to the southwest of Palm Bay. The bay is entered between High Point and D'Urville Point, 3 miles to the west, and offers safe anchorage in 3–5 metres. Both entry points as well as the shores of the inner bay are fronted by rocks and ledges, which only leaves an area about 1 mile wide, and this has numerous pearl rafts. About 2 miles south of High Point is a cliff with a small island out from it. The best anchorage is to the south of this island in 2 metres. Reef runs south of this island for about 400 metres. This bay gives good shelter from all winds except north. South of the pearl farm are the remains of Fort Campbell (1827 to 1829). There is a faint track in from the cleared patch. When leaving the bay, give D'Urville Point a wide clearance to clear the reefs. Once clear, it is safe to go to the west of Campbell Reef which caries 1.5 metres, lies 3.5 miles northwest of High Point, and is in the approach to Raffles Bay. The pearl farm can be contacted on VHF Ch 72.

Raffles Bay

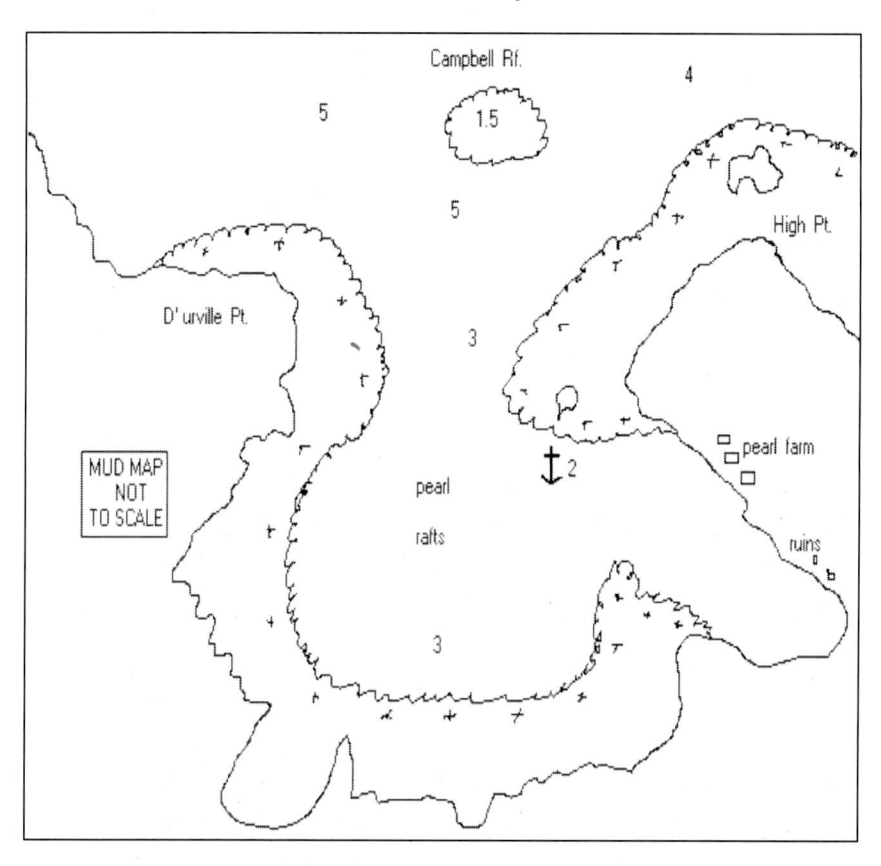

PORT BREMER

11°08′S – 132°15′E

CHARTS	AUS 308, 442
LIGHTS	Nil
TIDES	Darwin (Port Essington) ANTT
CAUTION	Pearl rafts

From Palm Bay, stay well out to sea to clear Danger Point. Entry is between Sandy Islet No 1 in the west, and Sandy Islet No 2 to the east; both these islets are surrounded by reef. The outer part of Port Bremer is fringed by reef, rocks and sandbars, extending around 2–3 miles offshore in places. Do not alter course until the entrance is open to the south. As you approach Steward Point, favour the eastern shore to clear the reef off Steward Point, but not too far over as there are reefs below Edwards Point. Port Bremer has numerous pearl rafts in its southern half. Be sure to anchor well clear. The pearl farm is to the south of East Station Point. Anchorage was found in the bay to the south of Edwards Point in 4 metres just north of the pearl rafts. There is a vast area to explore in the dinghy. There are a large number of sea eagle nests, but I did not see any young birds.

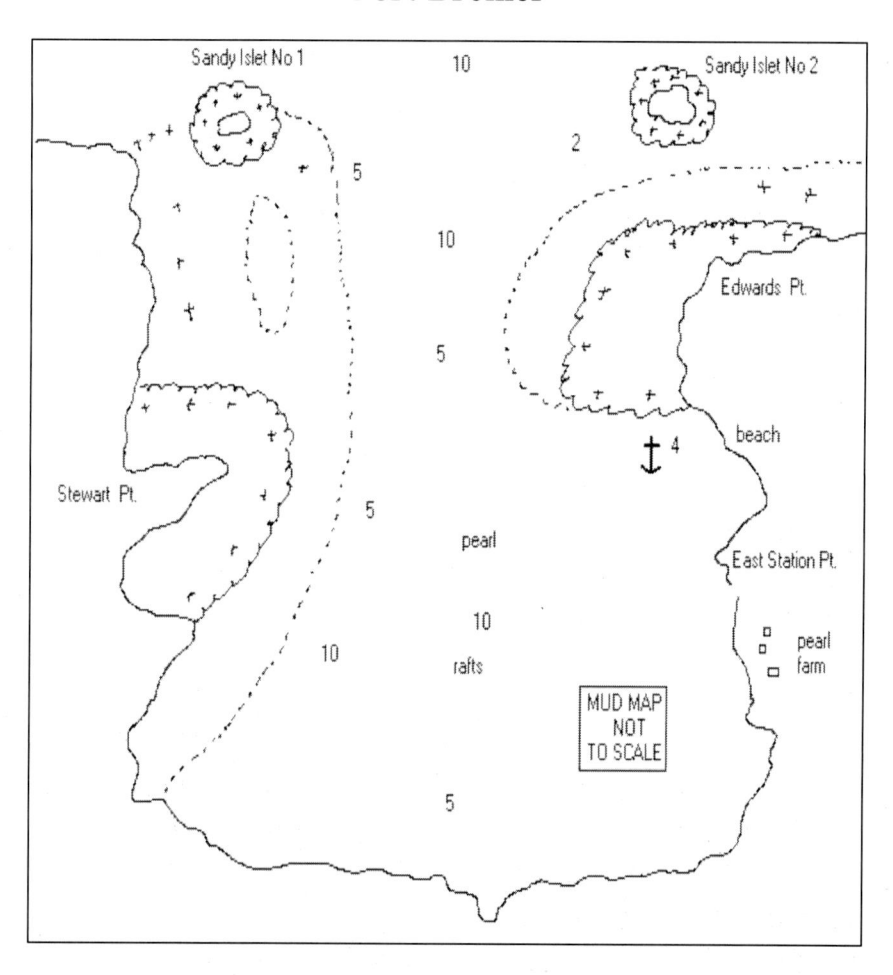

Port Bremer

PORT ESSINGTON

CHARTS AUS 18, 308, 442
LIGHTS Orontes Reef Light Buoys
TIDES Darwin (Port Essington) ANTT
FACILITIES Coral Bay has a small resort with restaurant, fuel, ice, guided walks and fishing. Moorings are available, but call VHF 16 first. There is a jetty at the Victoria Settlement ruins. Contact the ranger at Black Point for permits before proceeding.

Port Essington is a very scenic inlet, 18 miles long, with many secure anchorages. The port is divided into two harbours by a shoal patch that runs northwest from Record Point towards Oyster Point. This is about two-thirds of the way south from the entrance. The ruin of the settlement of Victoria lies on the western shores of the inner harbour, south of Minto Head. It was a British garrison from 1838 until 1849. I thoroughly enjoyed myself in this area. It is vast, with many secure, secluded anchorages. I will show the ones I used, but many others are available. Pearl farms exist in Knocker Bay on the western side, south of a line from Curlew Point to Oyster Point. Keep well clear when anchoring. Port Essington is entered between Smiths Point and Vashon Head. The entrance is approx 8 miles wide. Take care to clear Orontes Reef (11°04′S – 132°05′E) about 5 miles northwest of Smiths Point. On the south side of the reef are a number of underwater rocks. These and the reef are difficult to see, as the water is discoloured and the sea does not always break over them.

Port Essington

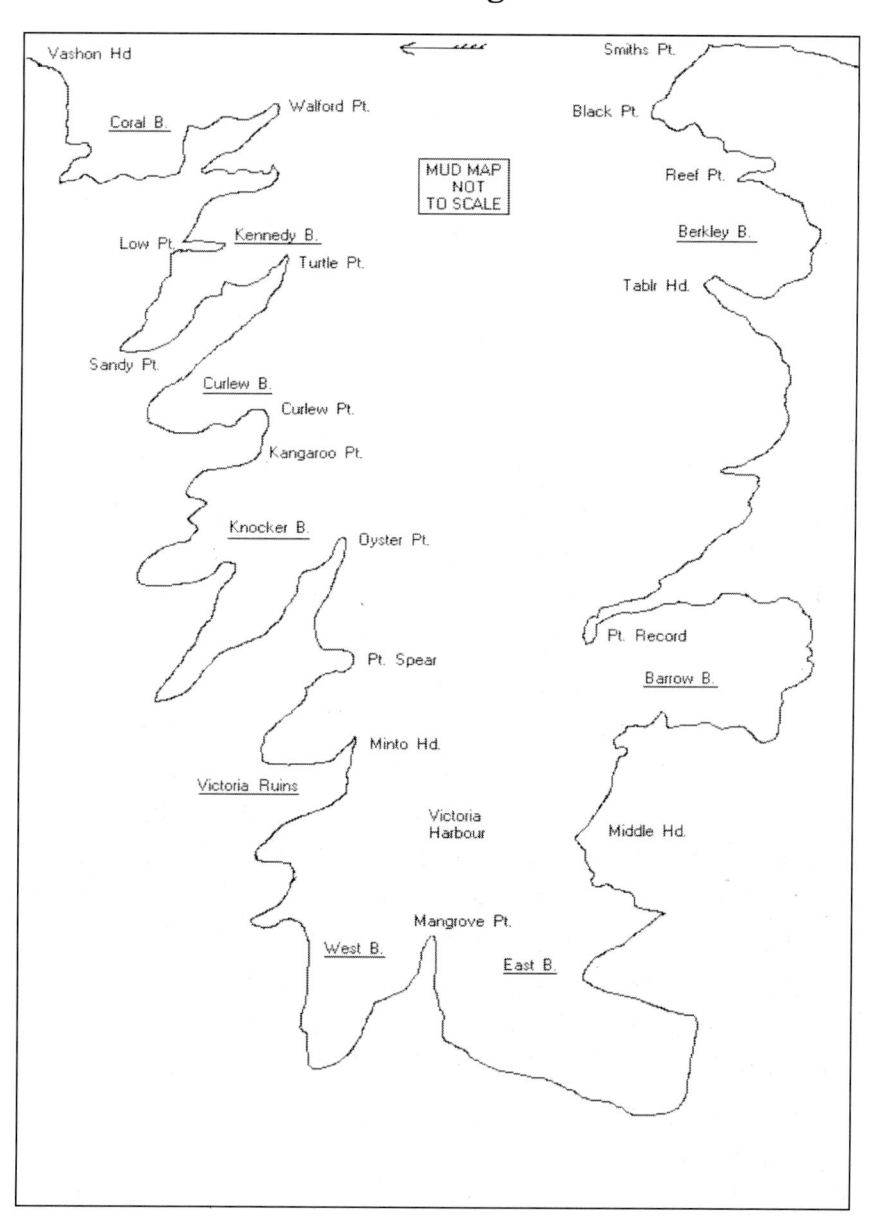

MUD MAP NOT TO SCALE

- Vashon Hd
- Coral B.
- Walford Pt.
- Low Pt
- Kennedy B.
- Turtle Pt.
- Sandy Pt.
- Curlew B.
- Curlew Pt.
- Kangaroo Pt.
- Knocker B.
- Oyster Pt.
- Pt. Spear
- Minto Hd.
- Victoria Ruins
- Victoria Harbour
- Mangrove Pt.
- West B.
- East B.
- Smiths Pt.
- Black Pt.
- Reef Pt.
- Berkley B.
- Tablr Hd.
- Pt. Record
- Barrow B.
- Middle Hd.

PORT ESSINGTON

SMITHS POINT 11°07'S – 132°08'E

Smiths Point is the eastern entrance to Port Essington and is easily identified by the monument on the point, which stands 8 metres high. South of this, towards Black Point will be seen a radio mast anchor out from this in 2 metres over sand. A reef extends halfway to Black Point, so give a clearance of 1.25 miles for safety. The flood tide runs west across the entrance.

BLACK POINT 11°09'S – 132°09'E

Black Point is located two miles south of Smiths Point. This is where the ranger station is located. Anchorage is west of the jetty at the end of the sandy beach outside the shore reef. The tall trees above the cliff are around the conspicuous buildings of the ranger station. To go ashore, dinghy to the boat ramp, on the other side of the jetty. Anchor in 3 metres. Trawlers often anchor around this area. All vessels should visit the ranger station to obtain a permit to go ashore in the port area. The cost is $15 per person. Fuel and water are available, but depth may be a problem. There is a small store with limited supplies opening daily from 3–4 PM, but check the hours. There is a cultural centre that is worth a look. A walk out to Smiths Point is also rewarding. Both fuel and stores are extremely overpriced. Check the use-by dates on all purchases from the store.

Smiths Point and Black Point

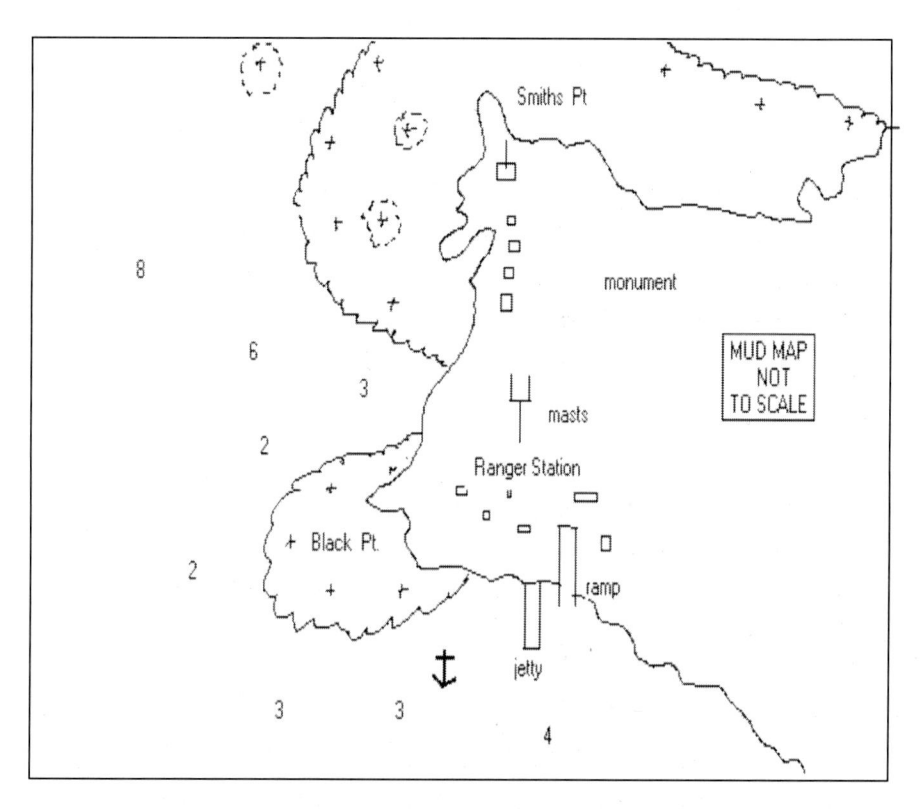

PORT ESSINGTON

BERKELEY BAY 11°13.5'S – 132°11.5'E

Berkeley Bay anchorage lies to the north of Table Head, out from Caiman Creek in 3 metres over mud. The creek can be travelled by dinghy at high tide. When coming south from Black Point be sure to give Reef Point a wide clearance, as the reef area extends out from the point for a bit over half a mile.

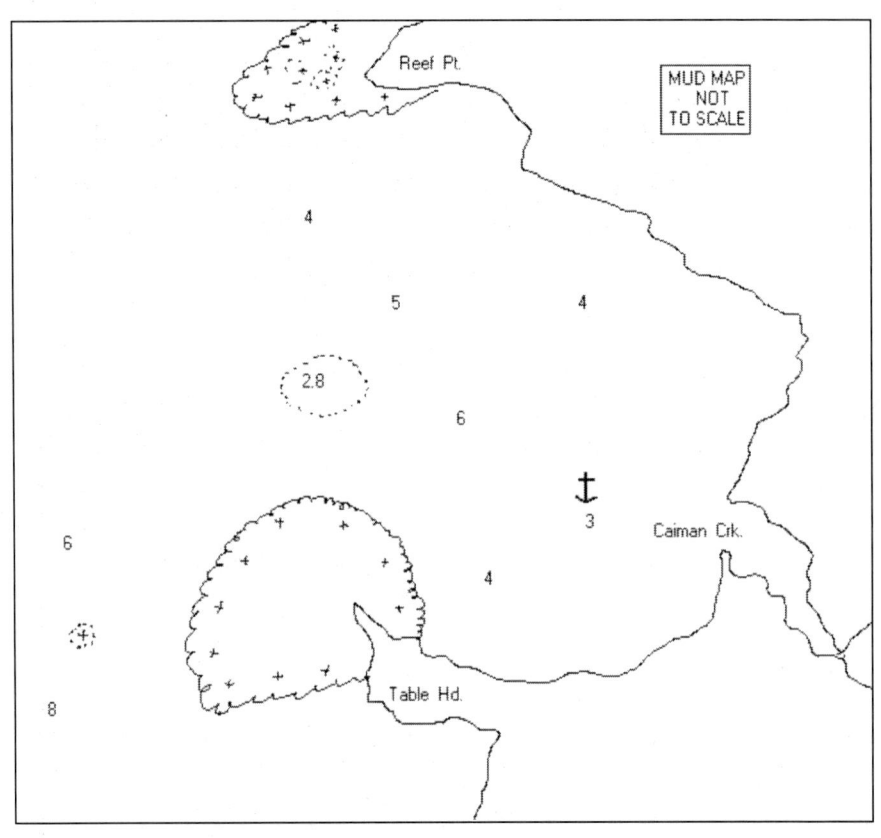

PORT ESSINGTON

BARROW BAY 11°20'S – 132°12.7'E

Barrow Bay is in the inner harbour, and is entered to the south of Record Point. Do not turn in too soon, as the mud flats extend south for around 0.25 mile. Anchorage can be taken anywhere depth allows, but do not anchor too far in, as the mud flats extend out from the mangroves for about 0.50 mile and in the southeast corner for nearly 1 mile. There is also a shoal patch in the southeast corner out from the end of the mud flats. In the centre of the bay there is also a patch of 1.7 metres with surrounding waters of 2–3 metres. When coming from Berkeley Bay, give Table Head a wide berth, as there is reef running northwest from the point, and a drying rock 0.5 mile west of Table Head.

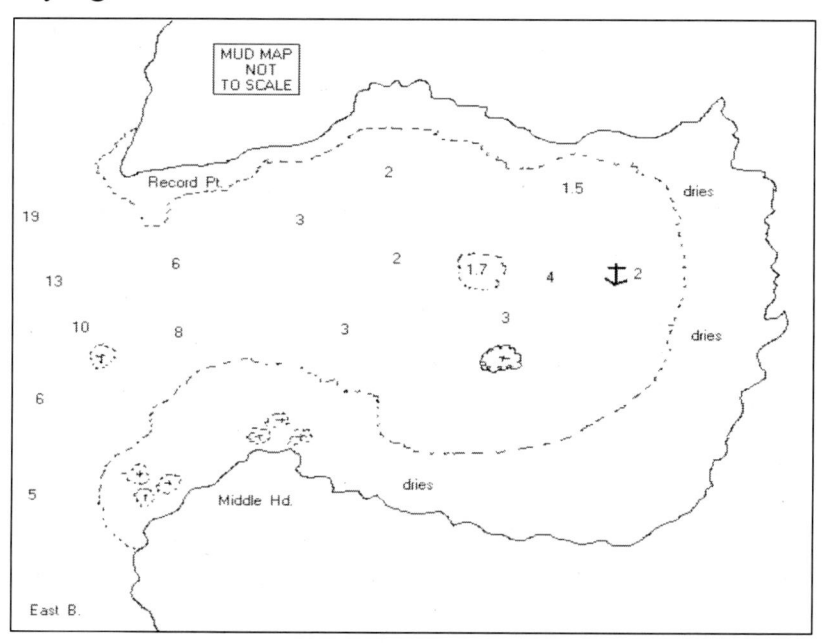

PORT ESSINGTON

MANGROVE POINT 11°23.9'S – 132°10.7'E

South of Middle Head is Mangrove Point, which has two bays, one on either side. East Bay cannot be penetrated too far, as it is shoal and dries. Anchorage was found best in the middle of the entry in 2 metres over mud. Do not go much further in than the two entry points. West Bay can be entered for about 0.75 miles south of Mangrove Point. Anchor in mid channel in 2 metres over mud. Mangrove Point has a drying spit that extends a bit over 1 mile to the north and northwest.

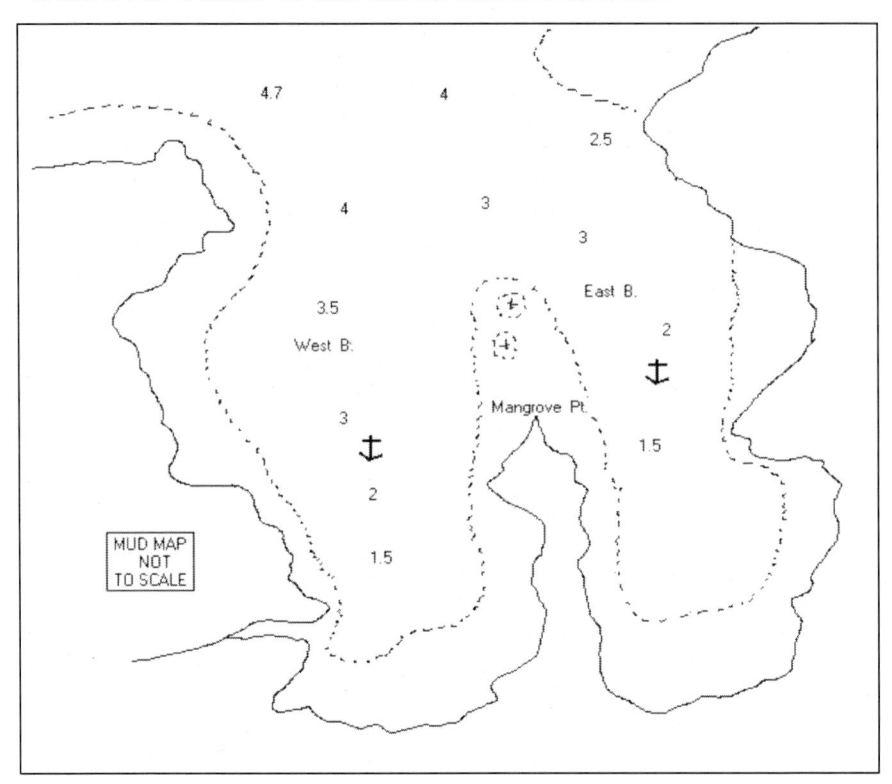

PORT ESSINGTON

VICTORIA RUINS 11°21.6'S – 132°09.4'E

The old settlement of Victoria lies on the western shore of the Inner Harbour to the south of Minto Head, on top of the red cliffs extending south to Adam Head. I anchored in 3 metres out from Adam Head, south of the jetty. It is an interesting place to visit, and is hard to imagine how anyone could survive here for eleven years last century, from 1838 to 1849 with very little contact with the outside world.

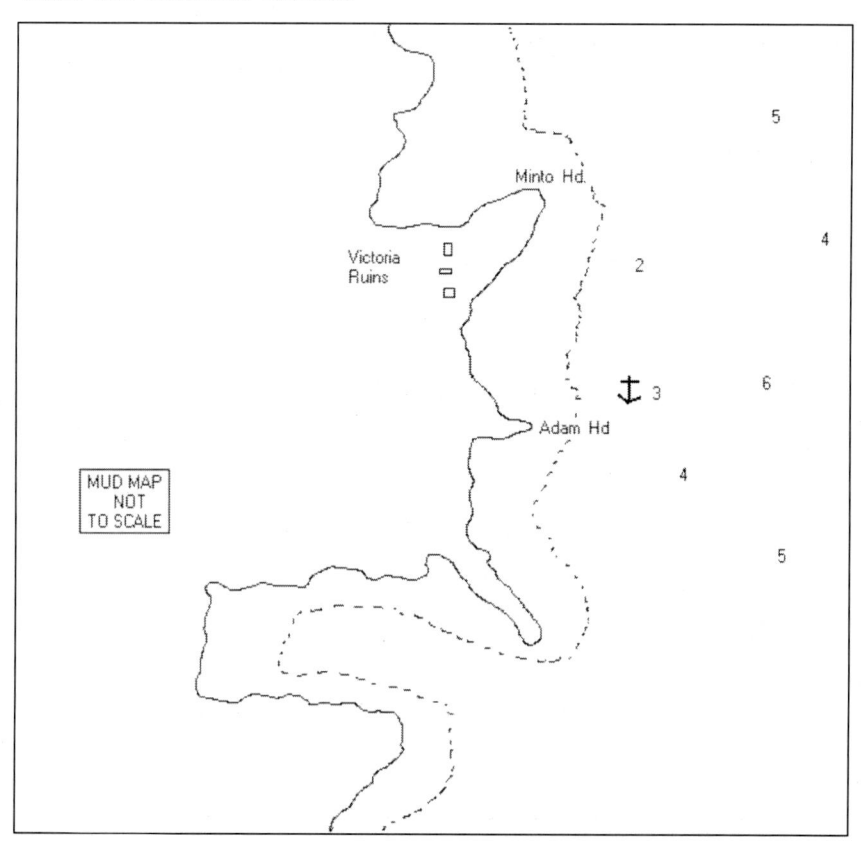

PORT ESSINGTON

KNOCKER BAY 11°18'S – 132°0.7'E

CAUTION Pearl rafts

Knocker Bay is found to the south of Oyster Point and Kangaroo Point. The shores are bordered by shoal water with patches of reef. Entry is not difficult, but be aware that the bay is used for pearl farming, so there are numerous rafts and moorings. Take care not to interfere with them in any way. With care, it was possible to anchor to the south of the rafts in 3 metres just to the south of Point Sleeman, but this may change if more rafts are added. It may be best to anchor to the north of the farm first and decide from there.

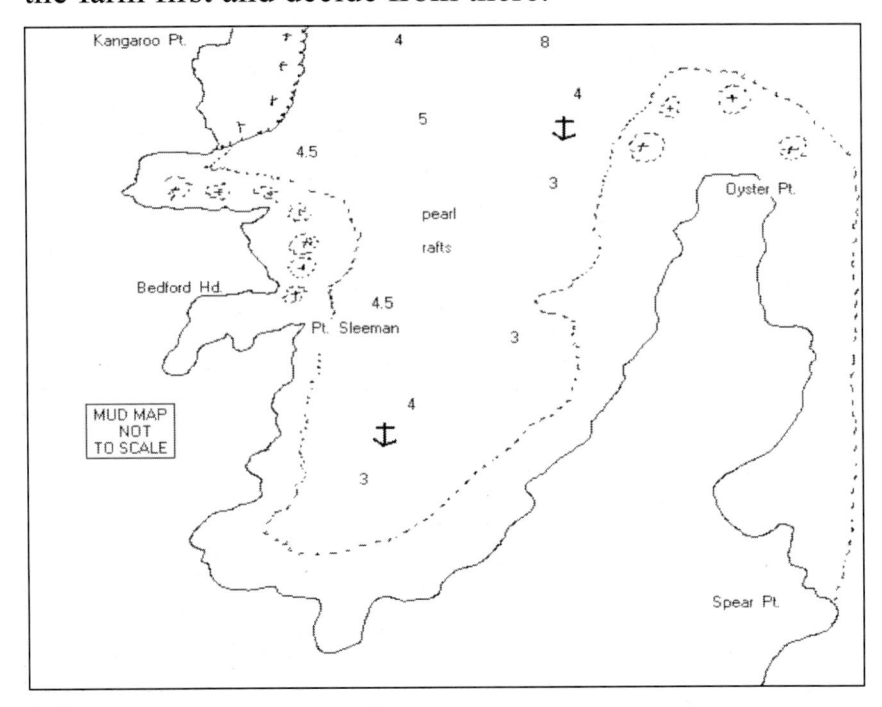

PORT ESSINGTON

CURLEW BAY 11°15.7'S – 132°05.8'E

This bay is found to the west of Curlew Point. It is a calm weather anchorage only and cannot be penetrated far, and it is exposed to winds from the north through to south. Anchorage is in the centre of the bay in 2.5 metres. The shores extend out into the bay and are shoal and drying with patches of reef. Do not go any further in than Curlew Point on your beam.

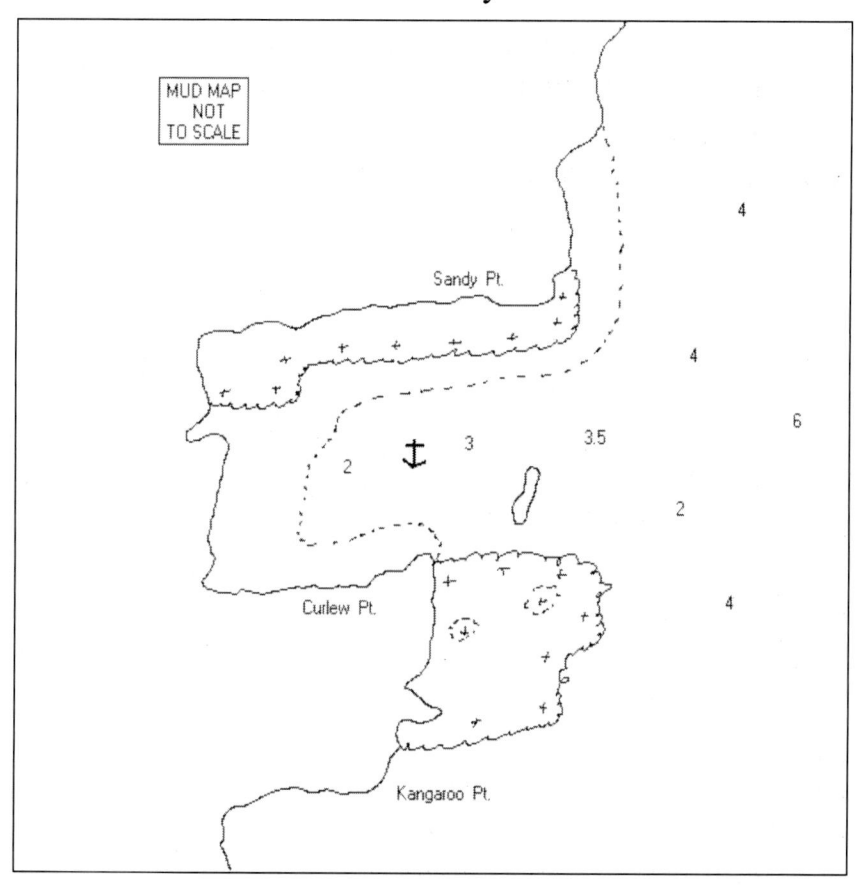

MUD MAP NOT TO SCALE

Sandy Pt.
Curlew Pt.
Kangaroo Pt.

PORT ESSINGTON

KENNEDY BAY 11°12.5′S – 132°06′E

Kennedy Bay offers good protection and is found to the west of Turtle Point. The best anchorage I found was out from the centre of the second bay south from Turtle Point, in 3 metres of good holding mud. When coming from the south, be sure to give False Turtle Head a wide berth, as reef extends east for around 0.7 mile. Also, give Turtle Point a good clearance, as the reef runs nearly 1 mile to the east and the northwest.

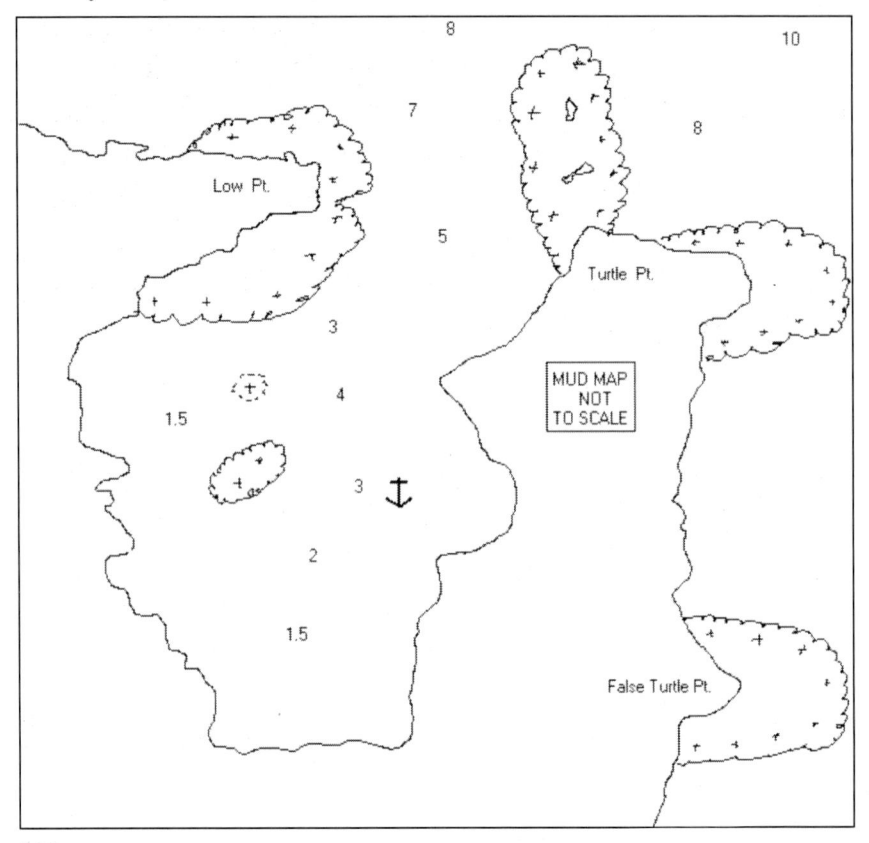

PORT ESSINGTON

CORAL BAY 11°10.7'S – 132°03.2'E

When coming from Kennedy Bay, give Low Point a clearance of at least 0.7 miles, to clear the reef. Also, give Balford Point a clearance of at least 1.25 miles, especially in the northwest, as the reef extends out for nearly 1 mile. The eastern shores of Coral Bay also have reef extending for some distance. It is suggested that the western shore be favoured, but not too far over, as there are more reefs. There are a number of anchorages in this area, including Seven Spirit Bay, where there is a small resort where fuel, ice and moorings are available, but call first on VHF16, as permission must first be obtained before entering the resort area. This may entail having to buy a meal at $25, but it is worth it. Also, after clearing the reef around Balford Point, anchorage can be found in 3 metres, out from the fringing reef in the first bay along the eastern shore.

Coral Bay

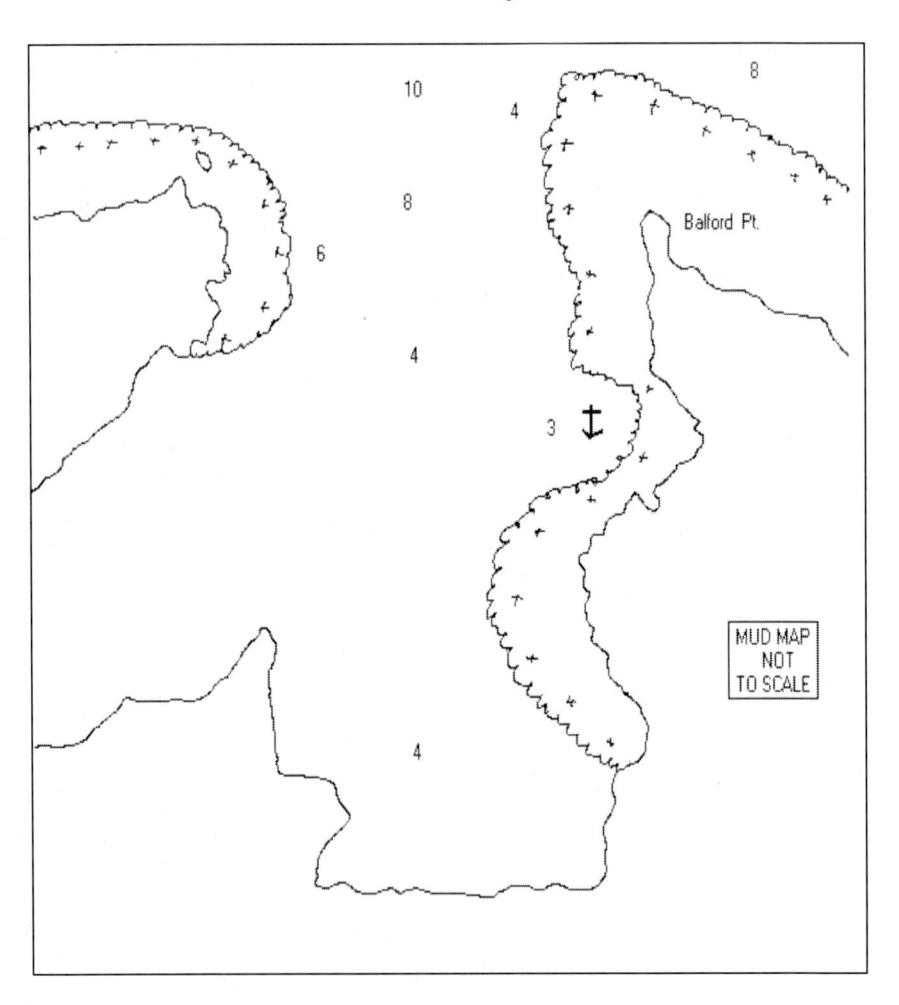

Balford Pt.

MUD MAP
NOT
TO SCALE

PORT ESSINGTON

GUNNERS QUOIN 11°11.3′S – 132°02.5′E

Gunners Quoin lies on the western shore of Coral Bay, and gives a good anchorage out from the fringing reef in 4 metres. Do not go any further in than with the small island to the east on your beam. The fishing is quite good throughout Coral Bay.

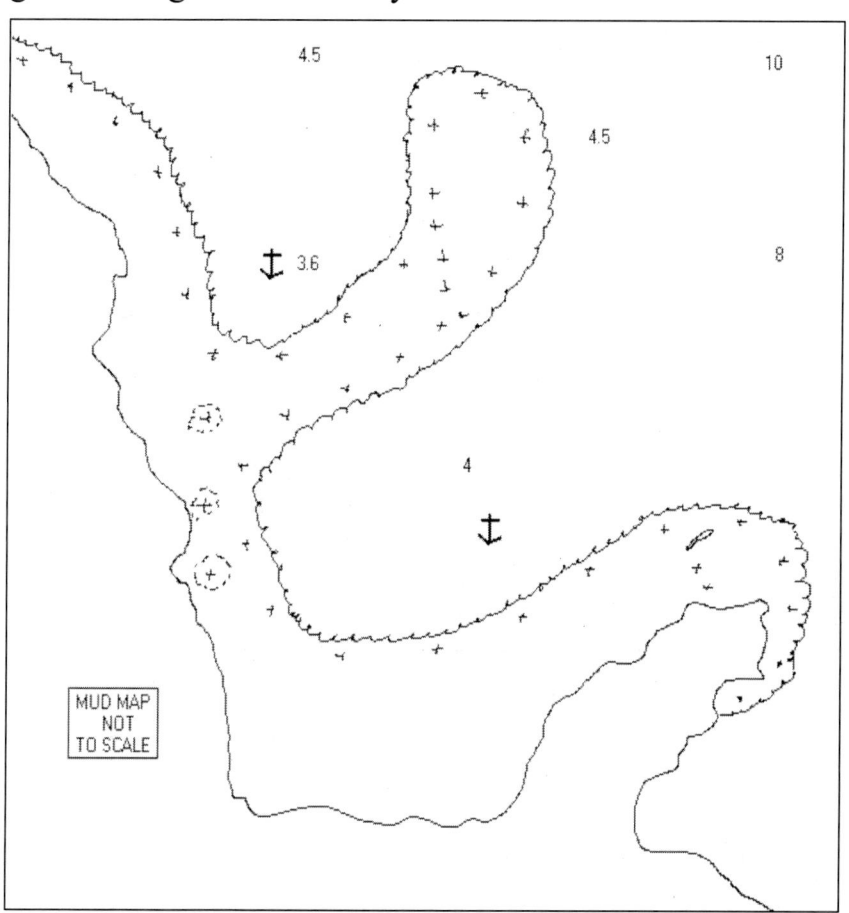

MUD MAP NOT TO SCALE

TREPANG BAY

11°11'S – 131°56'E

CHARTS AUS 308, 442
LIGHTS Nil
TIDES Darwin (Port Essington) ANTT

When leaving Port Essington, an offshore distance of 3.5 miles should be kept to clear the shoals of Vashon Head. This should be maintained until entry to Trepang Bay. The entry has a depth of 10 metres, which shoals gradually as vessels go further in. Take care to avoid the extensive reef areas out from Madjari Point to the north, and Aruru Point to the west. The best anchorage was found in the eastern corner of the bay, with Aruru Point bearing approximately 290° T. The bay affords good shelter in most winds, except those from the north and west. There are shore reefs in the area of the anchorage, which expose at low tide, and along the western shore. The creek can be travelled by dinghy on a rising tide. At the end is a track that connects with the resort in Seven Spirits Bay, but be aware of the tide and time to be able to get back to the boat.

Trepang Bay

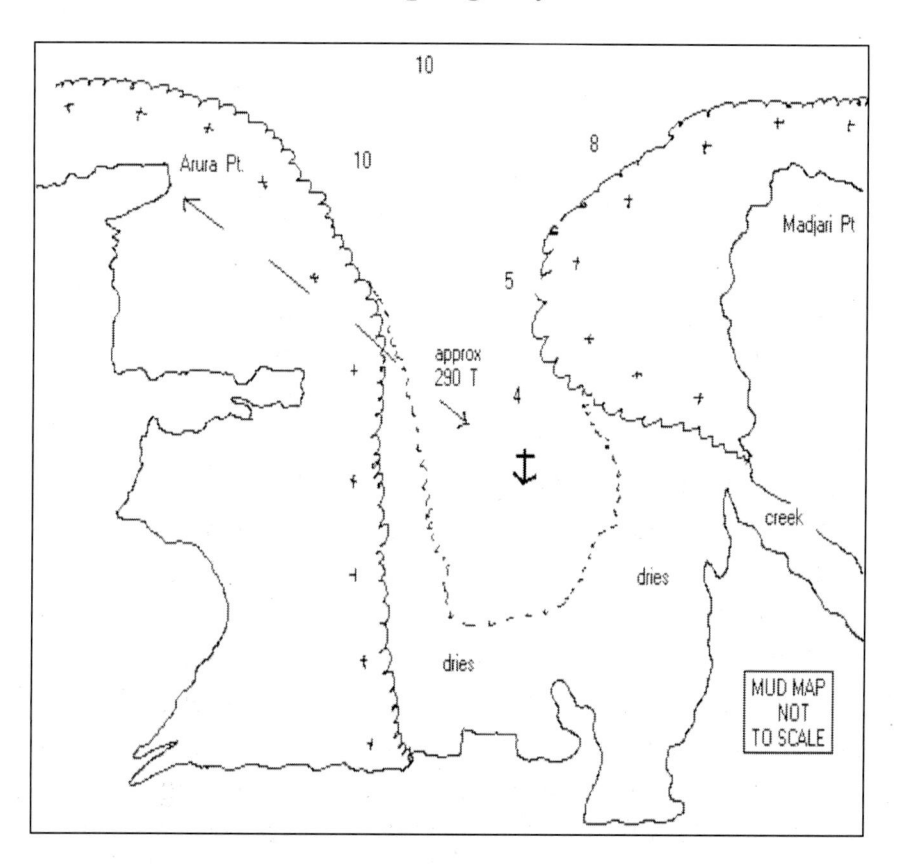

BLUE MUD BAY

11°12′S – 131°51′E

CHARTS AUS 308, 442
LIGHTS Nil
TIDES Darwin (Cape Don) ANTT

Blue Mud Bay is 4 miles wide at its entrance. It is almost enclosed by reef, but there is a deep channel about 0.75 miles wide. There are two bays; one runs to the southwest, the other southeast. This is the better one to anchor in. It is best to anchor out wide or towards the bottom of the tide, when the reefs can be seen. I anchored in 4 metres over mud. The water is always discoloured and the tide floods southwest at 2.5 knots.

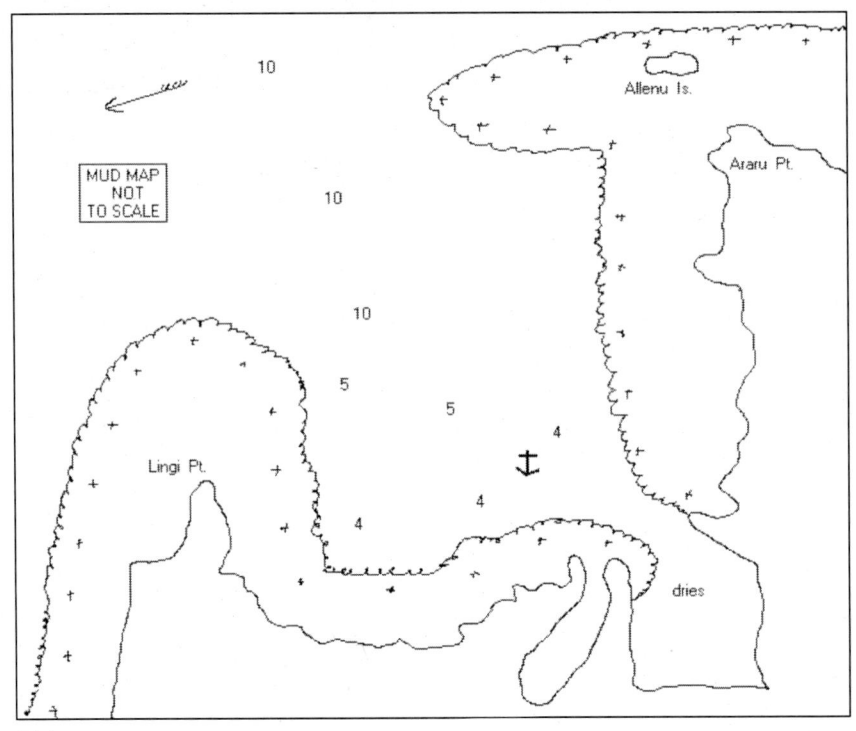

POPHAM BAY

11°15′S – 131°48′E

CHARTS	AUS 308, 442
LIGHTS	Cape Don flashes 10 seconds, visible 22 miles.
TIDES	Darwin (Cape Don) ANTT
CAUTION	4–6 knot current in this area that floods southwest

Popham Bay is found to the southeast of Lingi Point. There are extensive reef systems on both shores. The navigable channel is reduced to about one third of the entrance width. Anchorage will be found towards the creek at the southeast corner of the bay. A beach marks the southern side of the creek, and there is a red cliff on the northern side. Anchorage is in 3 metres over sand. At high tide, I dinghied into the creek and it took me all the way into Van Diemen Gulf. I sighted many crocodiles, but had no problems.

Popham Bay

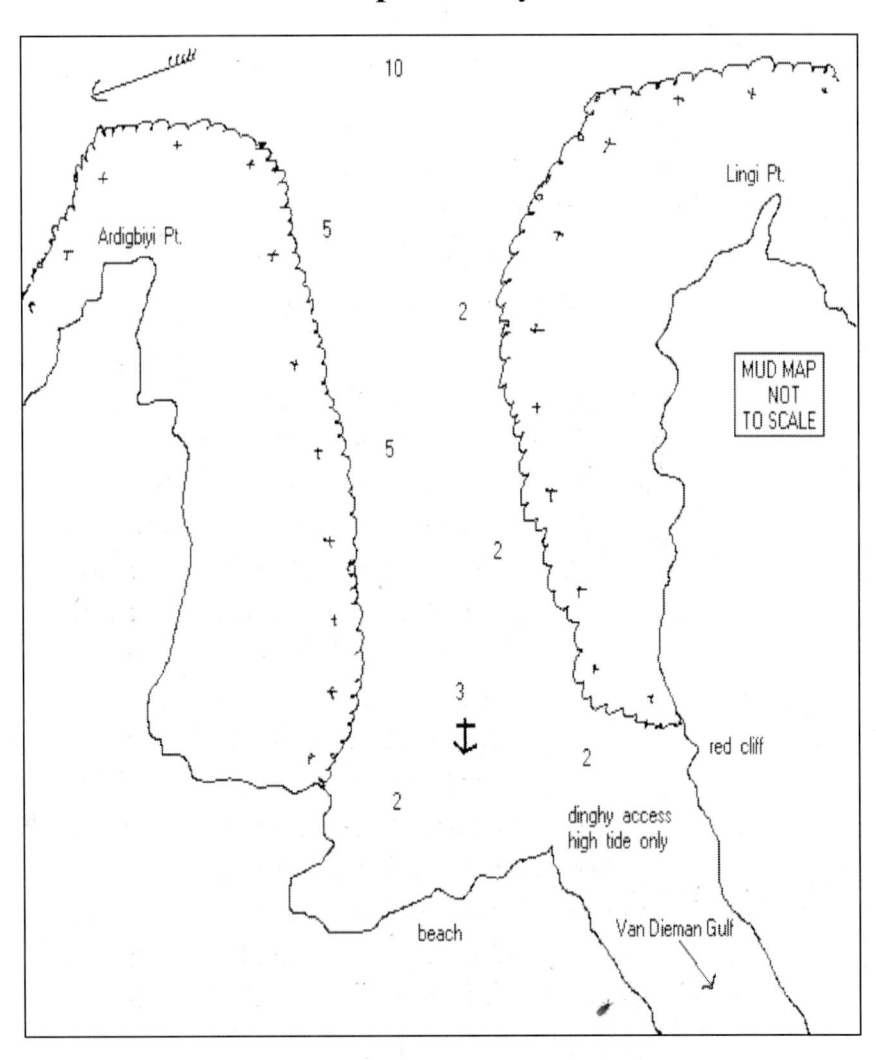

ALCORA BAY

11°17'S – 131°49'E

CHARTS	AUS 308, 442
LIGHTS	Cape Don flashes 10 seconds, visible 22 miles.
TIDES	Darwin (Cape Don) ANTT
CAUTION	6 knot current floods southwest

Alcora Bay is entered to the south of Ardigbiyi Point, which should be given a wide berth, as the reef extends some distance out. Allow for the strong current across the entrance. Anchor out from the red cliff at the southern side of the bay, but to the west of the creek in the corner. Anchorage is in 2 metres. The bay is used to service the Cape Don Lighthouse. A landing and road to the lighthouse is located in the creek entrance. The lighthouse is about a 5 km walk. If this is too far, anchorage can be found in Christies Bay close in under the lighthouse. The entrance, however, is hard to find amongst the mangroves and is hazardous owing to the tide race. Anchorage can be had in the entrance in 5 metres of sticky mud. The dinghy can be taken up to the jetty ruins at the head of the bay where there is 0.8 metres alongside a high tide. It is hardly worth the trouble.

Alcora Bay

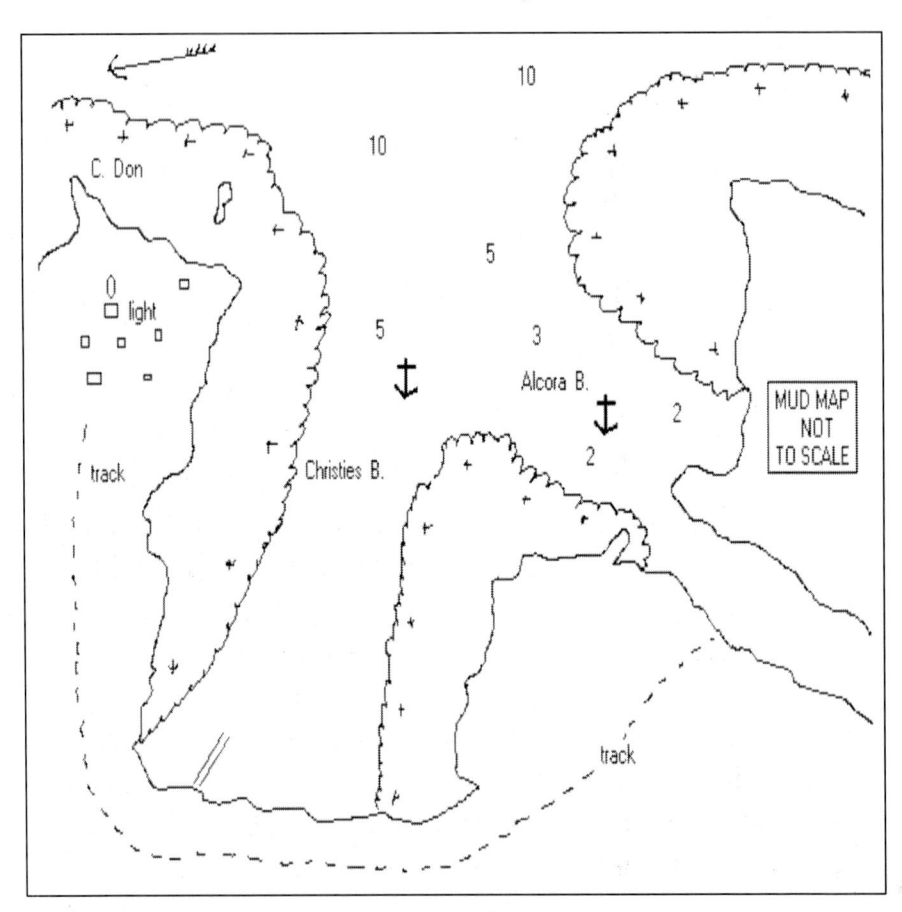

ADAM BAY AND ADELAIDE RIVER

12°09′S – 131°12′E

CHARTS   AUS 308, 722
LIGHTS   Cape Hotham shows a white/red sector light (see chart for sectors). The light flashes 3 every 9 seconds, visible 12 miles white, 9 miles red.
TIDES   Darwin (Cape Hotham) ANTT
CAUTION   Be very aware of crocodiles in this river. Charter boats have taught them to jump high for tourists, a stupid practice.

Adam Bay is found west-southwest of Cape Hotham and is entered between Escape Cliff and Point Stephens. In the southeast corner of Adam Bay, the mouth of the Adelaide River will be found. The best entry I found through the shoals was to steer a course for the red cliffs on Point Stephens, then to the west of Middle Bank, which dries at low tide. The channel is slightly east of Hart Point. Once inside Ayres Point and Hart Point you are in Port Daly and you should have a depth of 5–8 metres. From Hart Point turn to the northern bank where anchorage will be found in 3 metres. From here, follow the southern shore past Andrews Point, and then cross to the northern side at the narrows to avoid a drying rock in mid-channel. Hold this side for a bit over a mile, until clear of Beatrice Rock. You are now in the river proper.

There is good water from here to the Road Bridge, but look out for logs and changes after the wet season floods, as conditions may change. I travelled 41 miles upstream and had no difficulty. If unsure, follow the outside of the bends. I found no reason that vessels with a 2.5-metre draft could not navigate this river. Anchor anywhere that depth allows.

Adam Bay and Adelaide River

PORT OF DARWIN

12°28′S – 130°51′E

CHARTS	AUS 722, 26, 28
LIGHTS	Fairway Buoy 12°20.2′S – 130°40.8′E Flashes green 2.5 sec. Then various lights in main channel. Lights and buoys in main harbour area.
TIDES	Darwin (Standard Port) ANTT

Darwin is the capital of the Northern Territory. It is a thriving city with a vast number of cultures. The cost of living is a bit high, and humidity in the wet season will drive you crazy.

Pile berths are available in Francis Bay, but you need to get there well before the cyclone season as the port fills up very quickly (local fishing boats get first preference), so make mooring arrangements well in advance. Anchorage can also be found at the top end of Fannie Bay, well out from the yacht club. At the other end of Fannie Bay is a marina, which is entered through a series of locks. The cost is rather high, $100 per week 2000, and you cannot live on board, as an Asian company owns it and they have built condominiums around it and made the whole lot into body corporate. I have been told that the local council is making moves to stop this. I also understand that there are plans for two more marinas, but I do not know when this will happen.

If doing the trip down through the gulf, it may be better to lay over in Gove, where there is plenty of work available. Then carry on to Darwin after the wet, and use Darwin as a short stopover for supplies and fuel before travelling on to the Kimberleys or overseas.

Darwin is a port of entry, with yachts from all over the world coming and going. All facilities associated with a busy shipping port will be found here, though a bit expensive. Unfortunately, since being rebuilt after Cyclone Tracey, Darwin has really spread out and has lost its laid back and informal attitude, but it is still a pretty place. There are also a lot of harbour and shipping facilities being constructed and demolished and a lot of land reclamation.

There is a Travellift and dry storage in Ludmilla Creek, also known as Racecourse Creek. It is found around the headland north of Fannie Bay and is operated by Gordon Onn. Contact Spot On Marine on 8921 7244. For swing moorings in Francis Bay or possibly a berth in the Trawler Marina, contact the Harbour Master on 8999 3900 or Ch 16. The Dinah Beach Cruising Yacht Association is located in Sandgroves Creek and has dinghy access. Top meals and facilities are available. Contact them on 8981 7816. The town centre is only a short walk away. Tipperary Waters Marina is the only marina that allows live aboard. Contact Peter on VHF Ch 8 or telephone 0407 075 077.

Port of Darwin

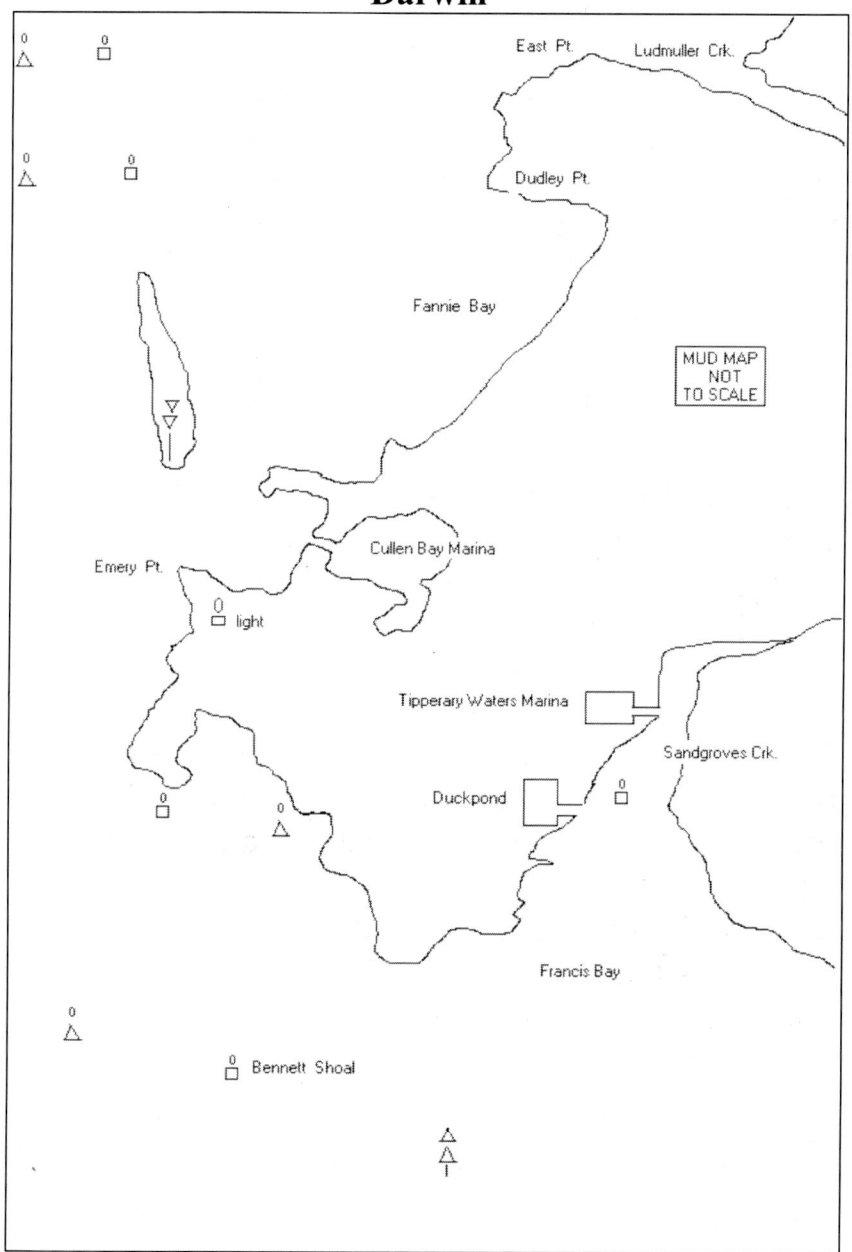

East Pt. Ludmuller Crk.
Dudley Pt.
Fannie Bay

MUD MAP
NOT
TO SCALE

Emery Pt.
Cullen Bay Marina
light
Tipperary Waters Marina
Sandgroves Crk.
Duckpond
Francis Bay

Bennett Shoal

303

USEFUL INFORMATION

Toilet maintenance

Add 2 tablespoons of vinegar to the toilet weekly and leave overnight or as long as possible. This will help stop the salt build up in the system.

Salt water bathing

Use any shampoo – the cheap ones work just as well. Apply shampoo to a wet cloth and wash yourself thoroughly. To wash your hair, you will need to wash and rinse twice, as the first time will not lather and clean the hair properly. When you have finished, wet yourself again and dry yourself with a towel or chamois. You must be wet before drying yourself, as this prevents the sticky feeling.

The only two things that I have found you cannot do with salt water is shave and brush your teeth.

A useful product to have on board is Cousins Morning Fresh. It has a number of uses and it works well in salt water. You can wash your greasy hands, wash the decks, do the washing and even have a salt-water bath etc.

Storing eggs

Method 1: Leave eggs in their carton and store in a cool place, but you must turn the carton over every two to three days.

Method 2: Remove eggs from the carton and cover each egg with Vaseline, then wrap each egg in newspaper and place in a shopping bag and store in a cool dry place.

Eggs can be stored in this manner for up to three months.

RECIPES

These two recipes were given to me by Val on *Mulloka 2*.

All in one bacon and egg pie

4 eggs
½ cup self-raising flour
1 cup grated cheese
1 cup chopped bacon
1 cup onion chopped
1 cup milk
lots of pepper (no salt)

Mix all ingredients together in a bowl until combined. Pour into a greased baking tin or pie dish or casserole dish. Bake in oven until cooked. Also, try in a pan with the lid on over a low heat on the stovetop or BBQ. Add slices of tomato on top if desired. You can also, delete the bacon and add salmon, chicken or tuna. If this is done add 120 grams of melted margarine and a cup of milk with a little parsley and a little salt. When cooked it automatically comes out with the pastry on the bottom and the filling on top.

A quick and easy tea cake

1 cup hot black tea
1 cup dried fruit
¾ cup sugar
2 cups self-raising flour

Soak the tea, fruit and sugar together until cool. Combine with the flour. Cook in a loaf tin in a moderate oven for 45 minutes or until cooked.

Soda bread

This recipe was given to me by Delmah on *Lowana IV* and is great with maple syrup, bacon and eggs or with anything else. It is best to use it the same day, but is still okay the next day.

2 cups plain flour
1 teaspoon baking soda
1 teaspoon salt
300 ml milk

Mix to a soft dough and place in a greased frying pan. Cook each side on a low heat for 10 minutes until golden brown. I sometimes add ground ginger or cinnamon. It is also very tasty with mixed fruit added.

ROYAL FLYING DOCTOR SERVICE

To contact the Flying Doctor if you do not have their emergency call button fitted to your HF Radio, or you cannot make contact, tune to their primary frequency and call to any listening outpost and ask them to press their emergency button. Then, when the RFDS answers, you reply.

It is also necessary to register with the RFDS, giving them all relevant details before leaving Cairns.

The St Johns Ambulance covers the RFDS in the Northern Territory and you will need to register with them before leaving Darwin.

Base locations, radio frequencies, telephone numbers etc. are shown on the accompanying map.

ROYAL FLYING DOCTOR CLINIC VENUES

These clinics are located along the east coast and west coast of Cape York and are covered from Cairns Base. Arrangements should be made through them as to times.

Venue	Location	Times
Cape Flattery	Mine First Aid Room	Four weekly
Lizard Island Resort	First Aid Room	Four weekly
Lockhart River	Community Hospital	Weekly

West Coast of Cape York

Venue	Location	Times
Aurukun Hospital	Community	Weekly
Pormpuraaw	Community Hospital	Weekly
Kowanyama	Community Hospital	Twice weekly

The Mount Isa Base covers these clinics and they should be contacted as to times.

Venue	Location	Times
Sweers Island	Island Resort	Four weekly
Burketown	Town Hospital	Weekly
Mornington Island	Community Hospital	Two weekly
Normanton	Town Hospital	Two weekly

CYCLONE ANCHORING

Cyclones are a problem for cruising boats, however if some common sense is used the problem is greatly reduced.

The first thing to do while in a cyclone area is to find a suitable place to hide if it becomes necessary. The best place is where you can get the boat amongst the mangroves or in a creek on high tide. Find this first in the dinghy well in advance.

When a cyclone warning is issued, take the boat into the place that you have found. It is best to do this before the cyclone gets too close and the wind increases.

Once in the mangroves or small creek, drop the anchor and let out excess chain. Next, take a stern anchor out and set it. Return to the boat and pull the excess chain in until the boat is about midway between the two anchors, the boat is now in position.

Next, take ropes diagonally out from each corner of the boat to a strong point in the mangroves and tie them off. Do not worry about the slack being in the water, this will be adjusted later.

The next step is the one that will ensure that the boat stays upright when it dries out, which is the best thing to do. Using halyards from the masthead, I use the main sail and spinnaker halyards, add extra rope to both of these halyards. Secure the ends of these two halyards to the mast, then take the other end out and tie them to a strong point in the mangroves; it does not matter about the slack rope being in the water. Now tie a weight to each rope where the rope and halyard join. **These must be of equal weight**.

Now that all the above has been done, go back on board and adjust all the ropes, allowing enough slack in the corner ropes to allow the boat to settle on low tide. Adjust the ropes with the weights on so that the weights are just clear of the water on high tide. You are now secure and can relax. If you have done things properly, the boat will stand up without any problems. Only minor adjustments will be required.

Over the past twenty years I have hidden from many cyclones and have used this method successfully without any problems or damage.

Tying off for a cyclone

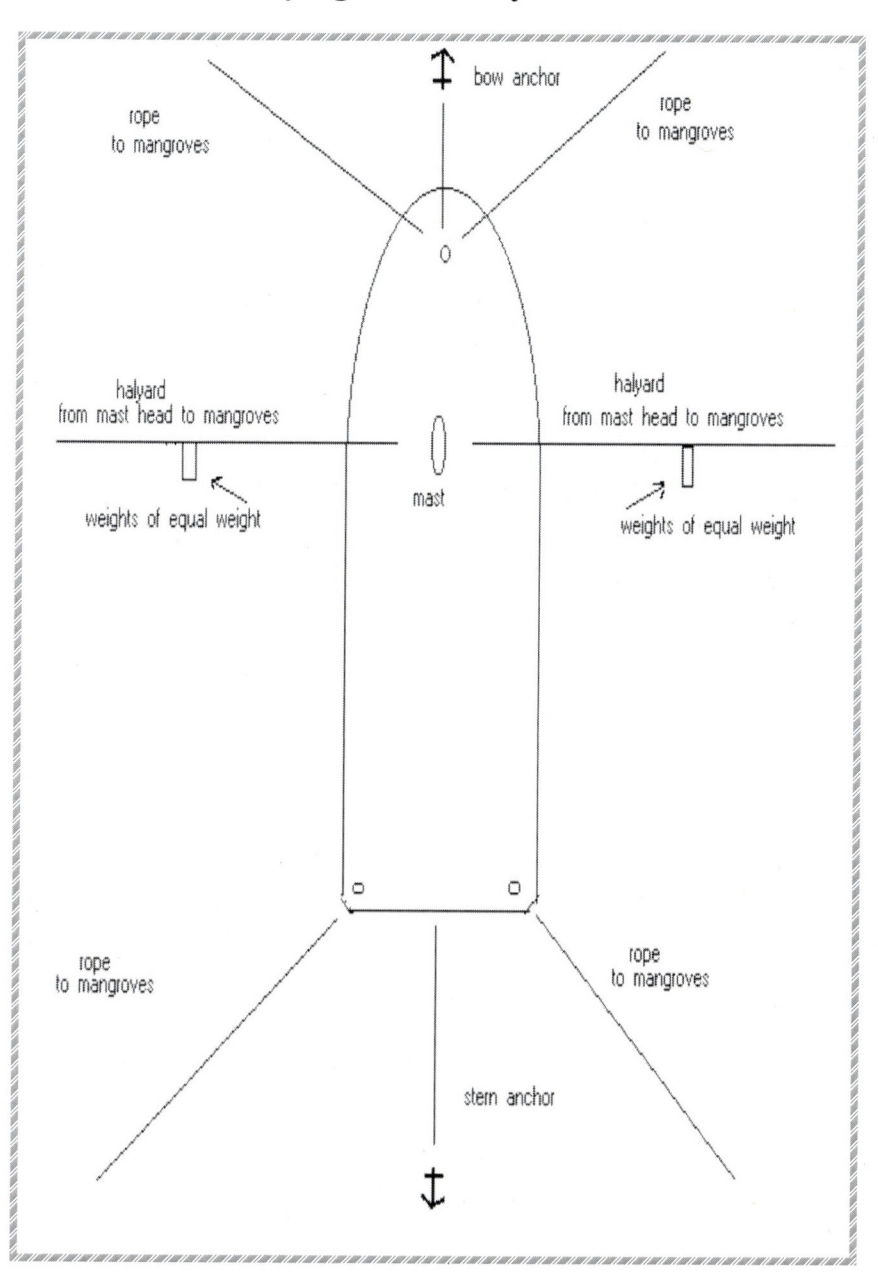

- bow anchor
- rope to mangroves
- rope to mangroves
- halyard from mast head to mangroves
- halyard from mast head to mangroves
- weights of equal weight
- weights of equal weight
- mast
- rope to mangroves
- rope to mangroves
- stern anchor

USEFUL RHYMES

Here are some easy rhymes on navigation, wind and weather. Their origins appear to have been lost in time, as I could not find the original source. I have changed the language to today's language.

Two ships meeting
When you see three lights ahead
Starboard your helm and show your red.

Two ships passing
Green to green or red to red
In perfect safety go ahead.

Two ships crossing
If to your starboard red appears
It is your duty to keep clear
To act as judgement says is proper
To port or starboard back or stop her.

But when upon your port is seen
A starboard light of green
There is not so much to do
For green to port keeps clear of you.

Both in safety and in doubt
Always keep a good look out.
In danger with no room to turn
Ease her, stop her, and go astern.

Now these four rules we all must note
Are of no use in a sailing boat
When we are dependent upon the wind
Another set of rules begins.

Sailing boats

A close hauled ship you'll never see
Give way to one that is running free
It is easier running free to steer
So that's the reason to keep clear.

With wind the same side running free
One ship to windward the other to lee
The leeward ship goes straight ahead
The other alters course instead.

Both close hauled or both quite free
On different tacks we all agree
The ship that has the wind to port
Must keep well clear is what we are taught.

At all other times the altering craft
Is that which has the wind right aft.

The weather

If the wind shifts against the sun,
Trust it not for back it will come.

If the sun goes pale to bed,
Will rain tomorrow so is said.

Long foretold, long past, short notice, soon past.

Comes the rain before the wind
Then your sheets and halyards mind
But if the winds before the rain
Soon you may make sail again.

A hollow wind begins to blow
The clouds are black the glass is low
Last night the sun went pale to bed
The moon has haloes around her head
Lookout my lads a whickered gale
With heavy rain will soon assail.

Red sky at night is a sailor's delight
Red sky in the morning is a sailor's warning.

Seabird seabird don't stay on the sand
We will not have good weather with thee on land.

Mackerel sky and mare's tails
Makes lofty ships carry low sails.

When mists take to the open sea
Fair weather shipmate it's sure to be.

At sea with low and falling glass
Soundly sleeps the careless arse
Only when it's high and rising'
Truly rests the careful wiseun'.